LIBRARY OF PHILOSOPHY

As may be seen from the original programme printed in Erdmann's *History of Philosophy* under the date 1890, the Library of Philosophy was designed as a contribution to the History of Modern Philosophy under the heads: first of different Schools of Thought—Sensationalist, Realist, Idealist, Intuitivist; secondly of different Subjects—Psychology, Ethics, Aesthetics, Political Philosophy, Theology. While much had been done in England in tracing the course of evolution in nature, history, economics, morals and religion, little had been done in tracing the development of thought on these subjects. Yet "the evolution of opinion is part of the whole evolution."

By the co-operation of different writers in carrying out this plan it was hoped that a thoroughness and completeness of treatment, otherwise unattainable, might be secured. It was believed also that from writers mainly British and American fuller consideration of English Philosophy than it had hitherto received might be looked for. In the earlier series of books containing, among others, Bosanquet's *History of Æsthetic*, Pfleiderer's *Rational Theology since Kant*, Albee's *History of English Utilitarianism*, Bonar's *Philosophy and Political Economy*, Brett's *History of Psychology*, Ritchie's *Natural Rights*, these objects were to a large extent effected.

In the meantime original work of a high order was being produced both in England and America by such writers as Bradley, Stout, Bertrand Russell, Baldwin, Urban, Montague and others, and a new interest in foreign works, German,

French and Italian, which had either become classical or were attracting public attention, had developed. The scope of the Library thus became extended into something more international, and it is entering on the fifth decade of its existence in the hope that it may contribute in this highest field of thought to that Intellectual Co-operation which is one of the most significant objects of the League of Nations and kindred organisations.

GENERAL EDITOR

LIBRARY OF PHILOSOPHY

GENERAL EDITOR

PROFESSOR J. H. MUIRHEAD, LL.D.

Library of Philosophy
GENERAL EDITOR: PROF. J. H. MUIRHEAD

CONTEMPORARY INDIAN
PHILOSOPHY

CONTEMPORARY INDIAN PHILOSOPHY

by

M. K. GANDHI

RABINDRANATH TAGORE

SWĀMI ABHEDĀNANDA

K. C. BHATTACHARYYA

G. C. CHATTERJI

ANANDA K. COOMARASWAMY

BHAGAVAN DAS

SURENDRANATH DASGUPTA

HIRALAL HALDAR

M. HIRIYANNA

S. RADHAKRISHNAN

R. D. RANADE

V. SUBRAHMANYA IYER

A. R. WADIA

Edited by

S. RADHAKRISHNAN, D.Litt. 1888 –

and

J. H. MUIRHEAD, LL.D., F.B.A.
*Professor Emeritus of the University
of Birmingham*

NEW YORK

THE MACMILLAN COMPANY

1936

FIRST PUBLISHED IN 1936

37-2311

B
131
R25
1936

CONTENTS

59155

FOREWORD

THE contribution of India to the philosopical literature of the world may by this time be said to be an open book to English readers. For the last sixty years, since Max Müller began the publication of the Sacred Books of the East in 1875, the great scroll of its story has been gradually unrolling itself before their eyes. Within the last few years comprehensive and scholarly histories of Indian philosophy in all its many schools by Professor Das Gupta and Sir S. Radhakrishnan and many monographs and handbooks by less-known writers have been published both in India and in England. Even the slightest acquaintance with these sources is sufficient to convince the reader of the justice of the claims put forward on their behalf,[1] that "there is hardly any height of spiritual insight or rational philosophy attained in the world that has not its parallel in the vast stretch that lies between the early Vedic seers and the modern Naiyāyikas," who with their analytic and critical methods may be said to stand to the Vedānta in somewhat the same relation as Kant and his followers stand to the great neo-Platonic and Patristic tradition of the West.

While we may thus well be convinced that Indian thought in the past represents a chapter in the history of the human mind that is full of vital meaning for us and well fitted by its profound sense of a Spiritual Presence brooding over the world of our ordinary experience to wean us from too exclusive occupation either with secular life or with the temporary formulations, in which Western theology has too often sought to imprison religious aspiration, it may still be asked whether in India itself all this exists to-day as a mere tradition or has formed the soil and supplied the seed for fresh developments. It was in the conviction that in present-day philosophy there is more than a tradition, and that, owing partly to the inherent genius of the race, partly to a fructifying contact with Western thought, the tree of philosophical knowledge has recently put forth fresh

[1] *Indian Philosophy*, S. Radhakrishnan, Vol. I, p. 8.

flower and fruit that the idea of this volume as a continuation
of the series on Contemporary British and Contemporary
American Philosophy, when suggested by an Indian friend, was
welcomed by the Editor of the Library of Philosophy. Coming
as it did at a moment when, on the eve of the gigantic political
experiment legislated for in the Indian Act, the need of a fuller
understanding of the mind of the leaders of thought in that
country, some of whom are certain to be called to take a prominent
part in the new administration, is above all things desirable, the
proposal seemed to be one of more than theoretic interest. What
are the ideas of these men as to the ends of human life and the
form that should be given to it through education and "the
spirit of the laws" so as to make it seem to the present and
future generations of this vast continent to be truly worth living?
It was our own Berkeley who said: "Whatever people may think,
the man who has not deeply meditated on the human mind and
on the *summum bonum* may possibly make a thriving earthworm,
but will undoubtedly make a sorry politician and statesman."
Is there ground for the faith that among the leaders of thought
in India there are men who belong to the type that Berkeley
had in view, and who possess the kind of insight which can be
trusted to guide their people through the desert of political
experimentation and controversy that lies between them to the
land which seems both to them and to most of us so full of
promise? It is because it is believed that some reassurance
on this head will be derived from the essays in this volume
that, apart from technical value in the field of philosophy, a
certain political importance and timeliness may be claimed
for it.

Going beyond any temporary political bearing its publication
may, it is further hoped, contribute to a better mutual understanding between the whole mind of East and West. It is surely
with justice that one of the contributors has pilloried the verse
"East is East and West is West and never the twain shall meet"
as "an utterance of abysmal ignorance and the deepest discouragement," and has set against it the power of that "intellectual wisdom, which is one and the same at all times and for

all men and is independent of all environmental idiosyncrasy," to provide an effective *entente* between them. It may therefore not be inappropriate in this Foreword to mention one or two of the points in which many Western thinkers will, it is believed, find themselves in profound agreement with the spirit that animates most of the writers.

Contrary to what is usually thought of the remoteness from practice of Indian philosophy, what here strikes one is the lively sense of its practical value. As one of the writers has quaintly put it, "its chief concern has not been to conceive of a philosophical scheme like a toy machine to play with, but to make of it a chariot in which man could ride."

Another equally striking feature (again contradictory to popular views) is the spirit of tolerance that breathes in their teaching—the conviction that it is one truth that is expressed in all forms of anything that can be called in a true sense religion. "If we study religions," we are told by the same writer, "with a view to discovering, not how much of error, but how much of truth, each embraces, we shall be far more impressed by their similarities than by their diversities." And again: "In Hindu philosophy a man is regarded as a true teacher who gives to any individual a better access to that individual's own scriptures, for 'the path men take from every side is Mine' . . . There is always a natural manifestation of the one Almighty God amongst all right-thinking men."

Surprising too (to mention only one further point) to many who have accused Indian philosophy of a prevailing note of pessimism is the tone of hopefulness that pervades one and all of the contributors, and for which the authority of the whole course of Indian philosophy is claimed. "No Indian seer," writes another, "has allowed himself to be overpowered by a sense of evil." We hear much indeed of philosophy as a call to transcend the narrowness of egoism and identify ourselves with something greater than ourselves as the way of salvation, but this is not in order to escape from the ineradicable evil of existence but in order to find ourselves in things that give to existence its only true value. For "in the man who transcends his narrow self and merges it in the life of the whole philosophy as truth, religion as devotion and morality as goodness meet."

The Editors had hoped that Mr. Gandhi, the leader of Indian religious reformers, might have been tempted by the questionnaire sent to him to give a fuller statement than we have as yet had of the philosophy underlying his political teaching, but perhaps we ought not to regret that he has refused to devote even a small portion of his time to anything less important than the great mission he has undertaken to redeem his country from the most deeply rooted of the evils it has inherited from the past. He has, however, sent a condensed statement of the answers he would be prepared to give to the editorial questions, and we print it with gratitude below.

Owing to the necessity to impose some easily understood limit to the range of choice, the essays which follow are all written by philosophers of or about forty-five years of age. They fall into two main groups: those in which the writer devotes himself chiefly to the exposition of the great Vedic tradition as he has apprehended it and made it the basis of his own life's work; and those in which the writer, while on the whole remaining true to the spirit of that tradition, has sought to give new interpretations of it, either by instituting comparisons of it with the Western doctrines most closely allied to it or by treating of modern problems in a way which, though suggested by what he has learned from the West, is yet stamped with the mark of his own racial sympathy. Western readers will naturally find the latter group more attractive; but this volume will have failed of its purpose if it does not give them some sense of the truth that underlies even the essays with which, owing to the presuppositions on which these are founded, they find themselves least in sympathy.

Whichever of the two groups attracts the reader, it is well that he should remind himself that, as in politics so in philosophy, India stands at the opening of a new era in her history which requires above all things, along with an abiding admiration of her past achievements, a forward-looking faith in the power of the soul of her people to rise as high as, and perhaps even to excel the greatest of them.

One conspicuous omission in the essays contained in this volume requires a word of explanation. It was hoped that it might be possible to include contributions from adherents of both the great traditions represented in Indian religious thought. With this view, besides philosophers known to be attached to Hinduism, several Moslems were approached, but for different reasons excused themselves, and it has been found necessary to proceed with this, which it is hoped may be merely a first edition, without further attempt to fill the gap.

The order of the contributions is alphabetical with the exception that Gandhi and Rabindranath Tagore have been given the place of honour at the beginning in consideration of their world-wide fame in fields other than that of technical philosophy.

GENERAL EDITOR
of the LIBRARY OF PHILOSOPHY

M. K. GANDHI

Born October 2, 1869

M. K. GANDHI

I HAVE been asked by Sir S. Radhakrishnan to answer the following three questions:

(1) What is your Religion?
(2) How are you led to it?
(3) What is its bearing on social life?

My religion is Hinduism which, for me, is Religion of humanity and includes the best of all the religions known to me.

I take it that the present tense in the second question has been purposely used instead of the past. I am being led to my religion through Truth and Non-violence, i.e. love in the broadest sense. I often describe my religion as Religion of Truth. Of late, instead of saying God is Truth I have been saying Truth is God, in order more fully to define my Religion. I used, at one time, to know by heart the thousand names of God which a booklet in Hinduism gives in verse form and which perhaps tens of thousands recite every morning. But nowadays nothing so completely describes my God as Truth. Denial of God we have known. Denial of Truth we have not known. The most ignorant among mankind have some truth in them. We are all sparks of Truth. The sum total of these sparks is indescribable, as-yet-Unknown-Truth, which is God. I am being daily led nearer to It by constant prayer.

The bearing of this religion on social life is, or has to be, seen in one's daily social contact. To be true to such religion one has to lose oneself in continuous and continuing service of all life. Realisation of Truth is impossible without a complete merging of oneself in, and identification with, this limitless ocean of life. Hence, for me, there is no escape from social service, there is no happiness on earth beyond or apart from it. Social service here must be taken to include every department of life. In this scheme there is nothing low, nothing high. For, all is one, though we *seem* to be many.

THE RELIGION OF AN ARTIST

by RABINDRANATH TAGORE

Born 1861

THE RELIGION OF AN ARTIST

I

I WAS born in 1861, that is not an important date of history,
but it belongs to a great epoch in Bengal, when the currents
of three movements had met in the life of our country. One of
these, the religious, was introduced by a very great-hearted man
of gigantic intelligence, Raja Rammohan Roy. It was revolutionary, for he tried to reopen the channel of spiritual life which
had been obstructed for many years by the sands and debris
of creeds that were formal and materialistic, fixed in external
practices lacking spiritual significance. People who cling to an
ancient past have their pride in the antiquity of their accumula-
tions, in the sublimity of time-honoured walls around them.
They grow nervous and angry when some great spirit, some lover
of truth, breaks open their enclosure and floods it with the sun-
shine of thought and the breath of life. Ideas cause movement
and all forward movements they consider to be a menace to
their warehouse security.

This was happening about the time I was born. I am proud
to say that my father was one of the great leaders of that movement, a movement for whose sake he suffered ostracism and
braved social indignities. I was born in this atmosphere of the
advent of new ideals, which at the same time were old, older
than all the things of which that age was proud.

There was a second movement equally important. Bankim
Chandra Chatterjee, who, though much older than myself, was
my contemporary and lived long enough for me to see him, was
the first pioneer in the literary revolution, which happened
in Bengal about that time. Before his arrival our literature had
been oppressed by a rigid rhetoric that choked its life and
loaded it with ornaments that became its fetters. Bankim Chandra
was brave enough to go against the orthodoxy which believed
in the security of tombstones and in that finality which can only
belong to the lifeless. He lifted the dead weight of ponderous

forms from our language and with a touch of his magic wand
aroused our literature from her age-long sleep. A great promise
and a vision of beauty she revealed to us when she awoke in
the fulness of her strength and grace.

There was yet another movement started about this time called
the National. It was not fully political, but it began to give voice
to the mind of our people trying to assert their own personality.
It was a voice of impatience at the humiliation constantly
heaped upon us by people who were not oriental, and who had,
especially at that time, the habit of sharply dividing the human
world into the good and the bad according to the hemispheres
to which they belong.

This contemptuous spirit of separatedness was perpetually
hurting us and causing great damage to our own world of culture.
It generated in our young men a distrust of all things that had
come to them as an inheritance from their past. The old Indian
pictures and other works of art were laughed at by our students
in imitation of the laughter of their European schoolmasters of
that age of philistinism.

Though later on our teachers themselves had changed their
mind, their disciples had hardly yet fully regained confidence
in the merit of our art. They have had a long period of encouragement in developing an appetite for third-rate copies of French
pictures, for gaudy oleographs abjectly cheap, for the pictures
that are products of mechanical accuracy of a stereotyped
standard, and they still considered it to be a symptom of superior
culture to be able disdainfully to refuse oriental works of
creation.

The modern young men of that period nodded their heads
and said that true originality lay not in the discovery of the
rhythm of the essential in the heart of reality but in the full
lips, tinted cheeks and bare breasts of imported pictures. The
same spirit of rejection, born of utter ignorance, was cultivated
in other departments of our culture. It was the result of the
hypnotism exercised upon the minds of the younger generation
by people who were loud of voice and strong of arm. The national
movement was started to proclaim that we must not be indis-

criminate in our rejection of the past. This was not a reactionary movement but a revolutionary one, because it set out with a great courage to deny and to oppose all pride in mere borrowings.

These three movements were on foot and in all three the members of my own family took active part. We were ostracised because of our heterodox opinions about religion and therefore we enjoyed the freedom of the outcast. We had to build our own world with our own thoughts and energy of mind.

I was born and brought up in an atmosphere of the confluence of three movements, all of which were revolutionary. My family had to live its own life, which led me from my young days to seek guidance for my own self-expression in my own inner standard of judgment. The medium of expression doubtless was my mother tongue. But the language which belonged to the people had to be modulated according to the urge which I as an individual had.

No poet should borrow his medium ready-made from some shop of orthodox respectability. He should not only have his own seeds but prepare his own soil. Each poet has his own distinct medium of language—not because the whole language is of his own make, but because his individual use of it, having life's magic touch, transforms it into a special vehicle of his own creation.

The races of man have poetry in their heart and it is necessary for them to give, as far as is possible, a perfect expression to their sentiments. For this they must have a medium, moving and pliant, which can freshly become their very own, age after age. All great languages have undergone and are still undergoing changes. Those languages which resist the spirit of change are doomed and will never produce great harvests of thought and literature. When forms become fixed, the spirit either weakly accepts its imprisonment within them or rebels. All revolutions consist of the fight of the within against invasion by the without.

There was a great chapter in the history of life on this earth when some irresistible inner force in man found its way out into the scheme of things, and sent forth its triumphant mutinous voice, with the cry that it was not going to be overwhelmed from outside by the huge brute beast of a body. How helpless it appeared at the moment, but has it not nearly won? In our social life also, revolution breaks out when some power concentrates itself in outside arrangements and threatens to enslave for its own purpose the power which we have within us.

When an organisation which is a machine becomes a central force, political, commercial, educational or religious, it obstructs the free flow of inner life of the people and waylays and exploits it for the augmentation of its own power. To-day, such concentration of power is fast multiplying on the outside and the cry of the oppressed spirit of man is in the air which struggles to free itself from the grip of screws and bolts, of unmeaning obsessions.

Revolution must come and men must risk revilement and misunderstanding, especially from those who want to be comfortable, who put their faith in materialism, and who belong truly to the dead past and not to modern times, the past that had its age in distant antiquity when physical flesh and size predominated, and not the mind of man.

Purely physical dominance is mechanical and modern machines are merely exaggerating our bodies, lengthening and multiplying our limbs. The modern mind in its innate childishness delights in this enormous bodily bulk, representing an inordinate material power, saying: "Let me have the big toy and no sentiment which can disturb it." It does not realise that in this we are returning to that antediluvian age which revelled in its production of gigantic physical frames, leaving no room for the freedom of the inner spirit.

All great human movements in the world are related to some great ideal. Some of you may say that such a doctrine of spirit has been in its death-throes for over a century and is now moribund; that we have nothing to rely upon but external forces and material foundations. But I say, on my part, that your doctrine was obsolete long ago. It was exploded in the springtime of life, when mere size was swept off the face of the world, and was replaced by man, brought naked into the heart of creation, man with his helpless body, but with his indomitable mind and spirit.

When I began my life as a poet, the writers among our educated community took their guidance from their English textbooks which poured upon them lessons that did not fully saturate their minds. I suppose it was fortunate for me that I never in my life had the kind of academic training which is considered proper for a boy of respectable family. Though I cannot say I was altogether free from the influence that ruled young minds of those days, the course of my writings was nevertheless saved from the groove of imitative forms. In my versification, vocabulary and ideas, I yielded myself to the vagaries of an untutored fancy which brought castigation upon me from critics who were learned, and uproarious laughter from the witty. My ignorance combined with my heresy turned me into a literary outlaw.

When I began my career I was ridiculously young; in fact, I was the youngest of that band who had made themselves articulate. I had neither the protective armour of mature age, nor enough English to command respect. So in my seclusion of contempt and qualified encouragement I had my freedom. Gradually I grew up in years—for which, however, I claim no credit. Steadily I cut my way through derision and occasional patronage into a recognition in which the proportion of praise and blame was very much like that of land and water on our earth.

What gave me boldness when I was young was my early acquaintance with the old Vaishnava poems of Bengal, full of the freedom of metre and courage of expression. I think I was only twelve when these poems first began to be reprinted. I surreptitiously got hold of copies from the desks of my elders. For the edification of the young I must confess that this was not right for a boy of my age. I should have been passing my examinations and not following a path that would lead to loss of marks. I must also admit that the greater part of these lyrics was erotic and not quite suited to a boy just about to reach his teens. But my imagination was fully occupied with the beauty of their forms and the music of their words; and their breath, heavily laden with voluptuousness, passed over my mind without distracting it.

My vagabondage in the path of my literary career had another reason. My father was the leader of a new religious movement, a strict monotheism based upon the teachings of the Upaniṣads. My countrymen in Bengal thought him almost as bad as a Christian, if not worse. So we were completely ostracised, which probably saved me from another disaster, that of imitating our own past.

Most of the members of my family had some gift—some were artists, some poets, some musicians and the whole atmosphere of our home was permeated with the spirit of creation. I had a deep sense almost from infancy of the beauty of Nature, an intimate feeling of companionship with the trees and the clouds, and felt in tune with the musical touch of the seasons in the air. At the same time, I had a peculiar susceptibility to human kindness. All these craved expression. The very earnestness of my emotions yearned to be true to themselves though I was too immature to give their expression any perfection of form.

Since then I have gained a reputation in my country, but till very late a strong current of antagonism in a large section of my countrymen persisted. Some said that my poems did not spring from the national heart; some complained that they were incomprehensible, others that they were unwholesome. In fact, I have never had complete acceptance from my own people, and that too has been a blessing; for nothing is so demoralising as unqualified success.

This is the history of my career. I wish I could reveal it more clearly through the narration of my own work in my own language. I hope that will be possible some day or other. Languages are jealous. They do not give up their best treasures to those who try to deal with them through an intermediary belonging to an alien rival. We have to court them in person and dance attendance on them. Poems are not like market commodities transferable. We cannot receive the smiles and glances of our sweetheart through an attorney, however diligent and dutiful he may be.

I myself have tried to get at the wealth of beauty in the literature of the European languages, long before I gained a full right to their hospitality. When I was young I tried to approach Dante, unfortunately through an English translation. I failed utterly, and felt it my pious duty to desist. Dante remained a closed book to me.

I also wanted to know German literature and, by reading Heine in translation, I thought I had caught a glimpse of the beauty there. Fortunately I met a missionary lady from Germany and asked her help. I worked hard for some months, but being rather quick-witted, which is not a good quality, I was not persevering. I had the dangerous facility which helps one to guess the meaning too easily. My teacher thought I had almost mastered the language, which was not true. I succeeded, however, in getting through Heine, like a man walking in sleep crossing unknown paths with ease, and I found immense pleasure.

Then I tried Goethe. But that was too ambitious. With the help of the little German I had learnt, I did go through *Faust*. I believe I found my entrance to the palace, not like one who has keys for all the doors, but as a casual visitor who is tolerated in some general guest-room, comfortable but not intimate. Properly speaking, I do not know my Goethe, and in the same way many other great luminaries are dusky to me.

This is as it should be. Man cannot reach the shrine if he does not make the pilgrimage. So, one must not hope to find anything true from my own language in translation.

In regard to music, I claim to be something of a musician myself. I have composed many songs which have defied the canons of orthodox propriety and good people are disgusted at the impudence of a man who is audacious only because he is untrained. But I persist, and God forgives me because I do not know what I do. Possibly that is the best way of doing things in the sphere of art. For I find that people blame, but also sing my songs, even if not always correctly.

Please do not think I am vain. I can judge myself objectively and can openly express admiration for my own work, because I am modest. I do not hesitate to say that my songs have found their place in the heart of my land, along with her flowers that are never exhausted, and that the folk of the future, in days of joy or sorrow or festival, will have to sing them. This too is the work of a revolutionist.

If I feel reluctant to speak about my own view of religion, it is because I have not come to my own religion through the portals of passive acceptance of a particular creed owing to some accident of birth. I was born to a family who were pioneers in the revival in our country of a religion based upon the utterance of Indian sages in the Upaniṣads. But owing to my idiosyncrasy of temperament, it was impossible for me to accept any religious teaching on the only ground that people in my surroundings believed it to be true. I could not persuade myself to imagine that I had religion simply because everybody whom I might trust believed in its value.

My religion is essentially a poet's religion. Its touch comes to me through the same unseen and trackless channels as does the inspiration of my music. My religious life has followed the same mysterious line of growth as has my poetical life. Somehow they are wedded to each other, and though their betrothal had a long period of ceremony, it was kept secret from me. I am not, I hope, boasting when I confess to my gift of poesy, an instrument of expression delicately responsive to the breath that comes from depth of feeling. From my infancy I had the keen sensitiveness which always kept my mind tingling with consciousness of the world around me, natural and human.

I had been blessed with that sense of wonder which gives a child his right of entry into the treasure-house of mystery which is in the heart of existence. I neglected my studies because they rudely summoned me away from the world around me, which was my friend and my companion, and when I was thirteen I freed myself from the clutch of an educational system that tried to keep me imprisoned within the stone walls of lessons.

I had a vague notion as to who or what it was that touched my heart's chords, like the infant which does not know its mother's name, or who or what she is. The feeling which I always had was a deep satisfaction of personality that flowed into my nature through living channels of communication from all sides.

It was a great thing for me that my consciousness was never dull about the facts of the surrounding world. That the cloud was the cloud, that a flower was a flower, was enough, because they directly spoke to me, because I could not be indifferent to them. I still remember the very moment, one afternoon, when coming back from school I alighted from the carriage and suddenly saw in the sky, behind the upper terrace of our house, an exuberance of deep, dark rain-clouds lavishing rich, cool shadows on the atmosphere. The marvel of it, the very generosity of its presence, gave me a joy which was freedom, the freedom we feel in the love of our dear friend.

There is an illustration I have made use of in another paper, in which I supposed that a stranger from some other planet has paid a visit to our earth and happens to hear the sound of a human voice on the gramophone. All that is obvious to him, and most seemingly active, is the revolving disk; he is unable to discover the personal truth that lies behind, and so might accept the impersonal scientific fact of the disk as final—the fact that could be touched and measured. He would wonder how it could be possible for a machine to speak to the soul. Then if in pursuing the mystery, he should suddenly come to the heart of the music through a meeting with the composer, he would at once understand the meaning of that music as a personal communication.

Mere information of facts, mere discovery of power, belongs to the outside and not to the inner soul of things. Gladness is the one criterion of truth as we know when we have touched Truth by the music it gives, by the joy of the greeting it sends forth to the truth in us. That is the true foundation of all religions, it is not in dogma. As I have said before, it is not as ether waves that we receive light: the morning does not wait for some scientist for its introduction to us. In the same way, we touch the infinite reality immediately within us only when we perceive the pure truth of love or goodness, not through the explanation of theologians, not through the erudite discussion of ethical doctrines.

I have already confessed that my religion is a poet's religion; all that I feel about it, is from vision and not from knowledge. I frankly say that I cannot satisfactorily answer questions about the problem of evil, or about what happens after death. And yet I am sure that there have come moments when my soul has touched the infinite and has become intensely conscious of it through the illumination of joy. It has been said in our Upaniṣads that our mind and our words come away baffled from the supreme Truth, but he who knows That, through the immediate joy of his own soul, is saved from all doubts and fears.

In the night we stumble over things and become acutely conscious of their individual separateness, but the day reveals the great unity which embraces them. And the man, whose inner vision is bathed in an illumination of his consciousness, at once realises the spiritual unity reigning supreme over all differences of race and his mind no longer awkwardly stumbles over individual facts of separateness in the human world, accepting them as final; he realises that peace is in the inner harmony which dwells in truth, and not in any outer adjustments; and that beauty carries an eternal assurance of our spiritual relationship to reality, which waits for its perfection in the response of our love.

II

The renowned Vedic commentator, Sayanāchārya, says:

*Yajñe hutāśishṭasya odanasya sarvajagatkāraṇabhūta
Brahmābhedena stutih kriyate.*

"The food offering which is left over after the completion of sacrificial rites is praised because it is symbolical of Brahma, the original source of the universe."

According to this explanation, Brahma is boundless in his superfluity which inevitably finds its expression in the eternal world process. Here we have the doctrine of the genesis of creation, and therefore of the origin of art. Of all living creatures

in the world, man has his vital and mental energy vastly in
excess of his need, which urges him to work in various lines of
creation for its own sake. Like Brahma himself, he takes joy in
productions that are unnecessary to him, and therefore representing his extravagance and not his hand-to-mouth penury.
The voice that is just enough can speak and cry to the extent
needed for everyday use, but that which is abundant sings,
and in it we find our joy. Art reveals man's wealth of life, which
seeks its freedom in forms of perfection which are an end in
themselves.

All that is inert and inanimate is limited to the bare fact of
existence. Life is perpetually creative because it contains in
itself that surplus which ever overflows the boundaries of the
immediate time and space, restlessly pursuing its adventure of
expression in the varied forms of self-realisation. Our living
body has its vital organs that are important in maintaining its
efficiency, but this body is not a mere convenient sac for the
purpose of holding stomach, heart, lungs and brains; it is an
image—its highest value is in the fact that it communicates its
personality. It has colour, shape and movement, most of which
belong to the superfluous, that are needed only for self-expression
and not for self-preservation.

This living atmosphere of superfluity in man is dominated
by his imagination, as the earth's atmosphere by the light. It
helps us to integrate desultory facts in a vision of harmony and
then to translate it into our activities for the very joy of its
perfection, it invokes in us the Universal Man who is the seer
and the doer of all times and countries. The immediate consciousness of reality in its purest form, unobscured by the shadow
of self-interest, irrespective of moral or utilitarian recommenda-
tion, gives us joy as does the self-revealing personality of our
own. What in common language we call beauty which is in
harmony of lines, colours, sounds, or in grouping of words or
thoughts, delights us only because we cannot help admitting a
truth in it that is ultimate. "Love is enough," the poet has said;
it carries its own explanation, the joy of which can only be
expressed in a form of art which also has that finality. Love

gives evidence to something which is outside us but which intensely exists and thus stimulates the sense of our own existence. It radiantly reveals the reality of its objects, though these may lack qualities that are valuable or brilliant.

The *I am* in me realises its own extension, its own infinity whenever it truly realises something else. Unfortunately, owing to our limitations and a thousand and one preoccupations, a great part of our world, though closely surrounding us, is far away from the lamp-post of our attention: it is dim, it passes by us, a caravan of shadows, like the landscape seen in the night from the window of an illuminated railway compartment: the passenger knows that the outside world exists, that it is important, but for the time being the railway carriage for him is far more significant. If among the innumerable objects in this world there be a few that come under the full illumination of our soul and thus assume reality for us, they constantly cry to our creative mind for a permanent representation. They belong to the same domain as the desire of ours which represents the longing for the permanence of our own self.

I do not mean to say that things to which we are bound by the tie of self-interest have the inspiration of reality; on the contrary, these are eclipsed by the shadow of our own self. The servant is not more real to us than the beloved. The narrow emphasis of utility diverts our attention from the complete man to the merely useful man. The thick label of market-price obliterates the ultimate value of reality.

The fact that we exist has its truth in the fact that everything else does exist, and the "I am" in me crosses its finitude whenever it deeply realises itself in the "Thou art." This crossing of the limit produces joy, the joy that we have in beauty, in love, in greatness. Self-forgetting, and in a higher degree, self-sacrifice, is our acknowledgment of this our experience of the infinite. This is the philosophy which explains our joy in all arts, the arts that in their creations intensify the sense of the unity which is the unity of truth we carry within ourselves. The personality in me is a self-conscious principle of a living unity; it at once comprehends and yet transcends all the details of facts that are individually mine, my knowledge, feeling, wish and will, my memory, my hope, my love, my activities, and all my belongings. This personality which has the sense of the *One* in its nature, realises it in things, thoughts and facts made into units. The principle of unity which it contains is more or less perfectly satisfied in a beautiful face or a picture, a poem, a song, a character or a harmony of interrelated ideas or facts and then for it these things become intensely real, and therefore joyful. Its standard of reality, the reality that has its perfect revelation in a perfection of harmony, is hurt when there is a consciousness of discord— because discord is against the fundamental unity which is in its centre.

All other facts have come to us through the gradual course of our experience, and our knowledge of them is constantly undergoing contradictory changes through the discovery of new data. We can never be sure that we have come to know the final character of anything that there is. But such a knowledge has come to us immediately with a conviction which needs no arguments to support it. It is this, that all my activities have their source in this personality of mine which is indefinable and yet about the truth of which I am more certain than anything in this world. Though all the direct evidence that can be weighed and measured support the fact that only my fingers are producing marks on the paper, yet no sane man ever can doubt that it is not these mechanical movements that are the true origin of my writings but some entity that can never be known, unless known through sympathy. Thus we have come to realise in our own person the two aspects of activities, one of which is the aspect of law represented in the medium, and the other the aspect of will residing in the personality.

Limitation of the unlimited is personality: God is personal where he creates.

He accepts the limits of his own law and the play goes on, which is this world whose reality is in its relation to the Person. Things are distinct not in their essence but in their appearance; in other words, in their relation to one to whom they appear. This is art, the truth of which is not in substance or logic, but

in expression. Abstract truth may belong to science and metaphysics, but the world of reality belongs to Art.

The world as an art is the play of the Supreme Person revelling
in image making. Try to find out the ingredients of the image
—they elude you, they never reveal to you the eternal secret of
appearance. In your effort to capture life as expressed in living
tissue, you will find carbon, nitrogen and many other things
utterly unlike life, but never life itself. The appearance does not
offer any commentary of itself through its material. You may
call it *Māyā* and pretend to disbelieve it, but the great artist, the
Māyāvin, is not hurt. For art is *Māyā*, it has no other explanation but that it seems to be what it is. It never tries to conceal
its evasiveness, it mocks even its own definition and plays the
game of hide-and-seek through its constant flight in changes.

And thus life, which is an incessant explosion of freedom, finds
its metre in a continual falling back in death. Every day is a
death, every moment even. If not, there would be amorphous
desert of deathlessness eternally dumb and still. So life is *Māyā*,
as moralists love to say, it *is* and *is not*. All that we find in it is
the rhythm through which it shows itself. Are rocks and minerals
any better? Has not science shown us the fact that the ultimate
difference between one element and another is only that of
rhythm? The fundamental distinction of gold from mercury lies
merely in the difference of rhythm in their respective atomic
constitution, like the distinction of the king from his subject
which is not in their different constituents, but in the different
metres of their situation and circumstance. There you find
behind the scene the Artist, the Magician of rhythm, who imparts
an appearance of substance to the unsubstantial.

What is this rhythm? It is the movement generated and regulated by harmonious restriction. This is the creative force in the
hand of the artist. So long as words remain in uncadenced prose
form, they do not give any lasting feeling of reality. The moment
they are taken and put into rhythm they vibrate into a radiance.
It is the same with the rose. In the pulp of its petals you may
find everything that went to make the rose, but the rose which is
Māyā, an image, is lost; its finality which has the touch of the

infinite is gone. The rose appears to me to be still, but because of its metre of composition it has a lyric of movement within that stillness, which is the same as the dynamic quality of a picture that has a perfect harmony. It produces a music in our consciousness by giving it a swing of motion synchronous with its own. Had the picture consisted of a disharmonious aggregate of colours and lines, it would be deadly still.

In perfect rhythm, the art-form becomes like the stars which in their seeming stillness are never still, like a motionless flame that is nothing but movement. A great picture is always speaking, but news from a newspaper, even of some tragic happening, is still-born. Some news may be a mere commonplace in the obscurity of a journal; but give it a proper rhythm and it will never cease to shine. That is art. It has the magic wand which gives undying reality to all things it touches, and relates them to the personal being in us. We stand before its productions and say: I know you as I know myself, you are real.

A Chinese friend of mine, while travelling with me through the streets in Peking, suddenly, with great excitement, called my attention to a donkey. Ordinarily a donkey does not have any special force of truth for us, except when it kicks us or when we need its reluctant service. But in such cases, the truth is not emphasised in the donkey but in some purpose or bodily pain exterior to it. The behaviour of my Chinese friend at once reminded me of the Chinese poems in which the delightful sense of reality is so spontaneously felt and so simply expressed.

This sensitiveness to the touch of things, such abundant delight in the recognition of them is obstructed when insistent purposes become innumerable and intricate in our society, when problems crowd in our path clamouring for attention, and life's movement is impeded with things and thoughts too difficult for a harmonious assimilation.

This has been growing evident every day in the modern age, which gives more time to the acquisition of life's equipment than to the enjoyment of it. In fact, life itself is made secondary to life's materials, even like a garden buried under the bricks gathered for the garden wall. Somehow the mania for bricks and

mortar grows, the kingdom of rubbish dominates, the days of
spring are made futile and the flowers never come.

Our modern mind, a hasty tourist, in its rush over the miscel-
laneous, ransacks cheap markets of curios which mostly are
delusions. This happens because its natural sensibility for simple
aspects of existence is dulled by constant preoccupations that
divert it. The literature that it produces seems always to be
poking her nose into out-of-the-way places for things and effects
that are out of the common. She racks her resources in order to
be striking. She elaborates inconstant changes in style, as in
modern millinery; and the product suggests more the polish of
steel than the bloom of life.

Fashions in literature that rapidly tire of themselves seldom
come from the depth. They belong to the frothy rush of the
surface, with its boisterous clamours for the recognition of the
moment. Such literature, by its very strain, exhausts its inner
development and quickly passes through outer changes like
autumn leaves—produces with the help of paints and patches
an up-to-dateness shaming its own appearance of the immediately preceding date. Its expressions are often grimaces, like
the cactus of the desert which lacks modesty in its distortions
and peace in its thorns, in whose attitude an aggressive dis-
courtesy bristles up suggesting a forced pride of poverty. We
often come across its analogy in some of the modern writings
which are difficult to ignore because of their prickly surprises
and paradoxical gesticulations. Wisdom is not rare in these
works, but it is a wisdom that has lost confidence in its serene
dignity, afraid of being ignored by crowds which are attracted by
the extravagant and the unusual. It is sad to see wisdom struggling
to seem clever, a prophet arrayed in caps and bells before an
admiring multitude.

But in all great arts, literary or otherwise, man has expressed
his feelings that are usual in a form that is unique and yet not
abnormal. When Wordsworth described in his poem a life
deserted by love, he invoked for his art the *usual* pathos expected
by all normal minds in connection with such a subject. But the
picture in which he incarnated the sentiment was unexpected

and yet every sane reader acknowledges it with joy when the image is held before him of

> . . . a forsaken bird's nest filled with snow
> Mid its own bush of leafless eglantine.

On the other hand, I have read some modern writing in which the coming out of the stars in the evening is described as the sudden eruption of disease in the bloated body of darkness. The writer seems afraid to own the feeling of a cool purity in the star-sprinkled night which is *usual*, lest he should be found out as commonplace. From the point of view of realism the image may not be wholly inappropriate and may be considered as outrageously virile in its unshrinking incivility. But this is not art; this is a jerky shriek, something like the convulsive advertisement of the modern market that exploits mob psychology against its inattention. To be tempted to create an illusion of forcefulness through an over-emphasis of abnormality is a sign of anaesthesia. It is the waning vigour of imagination which employs desperate dexterity in the present-day art for producing shocks in order to poke out into a glare the sensation of the unaccustomed. When we find that the literature of any period is laborious in the pursuit of a spurious novelty in its manner and matter, we must know that it is the symptom of old age, of anaemic sensibility which seeks to stimulate its palsied taste with the pungency of indecency and the tingling touch of intemperance. It has been explained to me that these symptoms mostly are the outcome of a reaction against the last century literature which developed a mannerism too daintily saccharine, unmanly in the luxury of its toilet and over-delicacy of its expressions. It seemed to have reached an extreme limit of refinement which almost codified its conventions, making it easy for the timid talents to reach a comfortable level of literary respectability. This explanation may be true; but unfortunately reactions seldom have the repose of spontaneity, they often represent the obverse side of the mintage which they try to repudiate as false. A reaction against a particular mannerism is liable to produce its own mannerism in a militant fashion, using the toilet preparation of the war paint, deliberately manufactured style of primitive rudeness. Tired of the elaborately planned flower-beds, the gardener proceeds with grim determination to set up everywhere artificial rocks, avoiding natural inspiration of rhythm in deference to a fashion of tyranny which itself is a tyranny of fashion. The same herd instinct is followed in a cult of rebellion as it was in the cult of conformity and the defiance, which is a mere counteraction of obedience, also shows obedience in a defiant fashion. Fanaticism of virility produces a brawny athleticism meant for a circus and not the natural chivalry which is modest but invincible, claiming its sovereign seat of honour in all arts.

It has often been said by its advocate that this show of the rudely loud and cheaply lurid in art has its justification in the unbiased recognition of facts as such; and according to them realism must not be shunned even if it be ragged and evil-smelling. But when it does not concern science but concerns the arts we must draw a distinction between realism and reality. In its own wide perspective of normal environment, disease is a reality which has to be acknowledged in literature. But disease in a hospital is realism fit for the use of science. It is an abstraction which, if allowed to haunt literature, may assume a startling appearance because of its unreality. Such vagrant spectres do not have a proper modulation in a normal surrounding; and they offer a false proportion in their features because the proportion of their environment is tampered with. Such a curtailment of the essential is not art, but a trick which exploits mutilation in order to assert a false claim to reality. Unfortunately men are not rare who believe that what forcibly startles them allows them to see more than the facts which are balanced and restrained, which they have to woo and win. Very likely, owing to the lack of leisure, such persons are growing in number, and the dark cellars of sex-psychology and drug-stores of moral virulence are burgled to give them the stimulus which they wish to believe to be the stimulus of aesthetic reality.

I know a simple line sung by some primitive folk in our neighbourhood which I translate thus: "My heart is like a pebble-bed hiding a foolish stream." The psycho-analyst may classify it as an instance of repressed desire and thus at once degrade it to a mere specimen advertising a supposed fact, as it does a piece of coal suspected of having smuggled within its dark the flaming wine of the sun of a forgotten age. But it is literature; and what might have been the original stimulus that startled this thought into a song, the significant fact about it is that it has taken the shape of an image, a creation of a uniquely personal and yet universal character. The facts of the repression of a desire are numerously common; but this particular expression is singularly uncommon. The listener's mind is touched not because it is a psychological fact, but because it is an individual poem, representing a personal reality, belonging to all time and place in the human world.

But this is not all. This poem no doubt owed its form to the touch of the person who produced it; but at the same time with a gesture of utter detachment, it has transcended its material —the emotional mood of the author. It has gained its freedom from any biographical bondage by taking a rhythmic perfection which is precious in its own exclusive merit. There is a poem which confesses by its title its origin in a mood of dejection. Nobody can say that to a lucid mind the feeling of despondency has anything pleasantly memorable. Yet these verses are not allowed to be forgotten, because directly a poem is fashioned, it is eternally freed from its genesis, it minimises its history and emphasises its independence. The sorrow which was solely personal in an emperor, was liberated directly it took the form of verses in stone, it became a triumph of lament, an overflow of delight hiding the black boulder of its suffering source. The same thing is true of all creation. A new drop is a perfect integrity that has no filial memory of its parentage.

When I use the word creation, I mean that through it some imponderable abstractions have assumed a concrete unity in its relation to us. Its substance can be analysed but not this unity which is in its self-introduction. Literature as an art offers us the mystery which is in its unity.

We read the poem:

> Never seek to tell thy love
>   Love that never told can be;
> For the gentle wind does move
>   Silently, invisibly.
>
> I told my love, I told my love,
>   I told all my heart;
> Trembling cold in ghastly fears
>   Ah, she did depart.
>
> Soon as she was gone from me
>   A traveller came by;
> Silently, invisibly,
>   He took her with a sigh.

It has its grammar, its vocabulary. When we divide them part by part and try to torture out a confession from them the poem which is *one*, departs like the gentle wind, silently, invisibly. No one knows how it exceeds all its parts, transcends all its laws, and communicates with the person. The significance which is in a unity is an eternal wonder.

As for the definite meaning of the poem, we may have our doubts. If it were told in ordinary prose, we might feel impatient and be roused to contradict it. We would certainly have asked for an explanation as to who the traveller was and why he took away love without any reasonable provocation. But in this poem we need not ask for an explanation unless we are hopelessly addicted to meaning-collection which is like the collection mania for dead butterflies. The poem as a creation, which is something more than as an idea, inevitably conquers our attention; and any meaning which we feel in its words, is like the feeling in a beautiful face of a smile that is inscrutable, elusive and profoundly satisfactory.

The unity as a poem introduces itself in a rhythmic language in a gesture of character. Rhythm is not merely in some measured blending of words, but in a significant adjustment of ideas, in a music of thought produced by a subtle principle of distribution, which is not primarily logical but evidential. The meaning which

the word character contains is difficult to define. It is comprehended in a special grouping of aspects which gives it an irresistible impetus. The combination it represents may be uncouth,
may be unfinished, discordant; yet it has a dynamic vigour in
its totality which claims recognition, often against our wishes
for the assent of our reason. An avalanche has a character,
which even a heavier pile of snow has not; its character is in
its massive movement, its incalculable possibilities.

It is for the artist to remind the world that with the truth
of our expression we grow in truth. When the man-made world
is less an expression of man's creative soul than a mechanical
device for some purpose of power, then it hardens itself, acquiring
proficiency at the cost of the subtle suggestiveness of living
growth. In his creative activities man makes nature instinct
with his own life and love. But with his utilitarian energies he
fights Nature, banishes her from his world, deforms and defiles
her with the ugliness of his ambitions.

This world of man's own manufacture with its discordant
shrieks and swagger, impresses on him the scheme of a universe
which has no touch of the person and therefore no ultimate
significance. All the great civilisations that have become extinct
must have come to their end through such wrong expression of
humanity; through parasitism on a gigantic scale bred by
wealth, by man's clinging reliance on material resources; through
a scoffing spirit of denial, of negation, robbing us of our means of
sustenance in the path of truth.

It is for the artist to proclaim his faith in the everlasting
YES—to say: "I believe that there is an ideal hovering over
and permeating the earth, an ideal of that Paradise which is
not the mere outcome of fancy, but the ultimate reality in which
all things dwell and move."

I believe that the vision of Paradise is to be seen in the
sunlight and the green of the earth, in the beauty of the human
face and the wealth of human life, even in objects that are
seemingly insignificant and unprepossessing. Everywhere in this
earth the spirit of Paradise is awake and sending forth its voice.
It reaches our inner ear without our knowing it. It tunes our

harp of life which sends our aspiration in music beyond the finite, not only in prayers and hopes, but also in temples which are flames of fire in stone, in pictures which are dreams made everlasting, in the dance which is ecstatic meditation in the still centre of movement.

PRINCIPAL PUBLICATIONS

Gītāñjali.   Macmillan & Co.
Sādhana.   Macmillan & Co.
Creative Unity.   Macmillan & Co.
Personality.   Macmillan & Co.
Greater India.   Macmillan & Co.
The Religion of Man.   George Allen & Unwin.
The Child.   George Allen & Unwin.
Letters to a Friend.   George Allen & Unwin.
The Golden Boat.   George Allen & Unwin.

HINDU PHILOSOPHY IN INDIA

by SWĀMI ABHEDĀNANDA

Born October 2, 1866; Educated Oriental Seminary, Calcutta

BIOGRAPHICAL

I was born in Calcutta, October 2, 1866. My father, late Rasick Lal Chandra, was a student of philosophy and teacher of English in the Oriental Seminary in Calcutta, for twenty-five years from 1838 to 1863. I was educated first in a Sanskrit School, then in a Bengali Vernacular School and afterwards in the Oriental Seminary, from which I successfully passed the Entrance Examination at the age of eighteen.

From my childhood I wanted to know the cause of everything and used to ask questions about the "Why" and "How" of all events. When for the first time I read in Wilson's *History of India*, that Śaṁkarācārya was a great philosopher, I had a thrilling sensation, and I wanted to become a philosopher and to study his philosophy. At that time, I was a student in the drawing class of the Seminary and was learning to paint from nature. Suddenly, a thought came to my mind that I did not want to be a painter but I would be a philosopher; and so I gave up the study of the art of drawing and painting.

When I was in the preparatory class I studied Sanskrit, which was my second language. At home, I studied "Mugdhabodha," the Sanskrit Grammar, thoroughly, and acquired such a command of the Sanskrit language that I could compose verses in it.

At that time, I found a copy of the *Bhagavat Gītā* in my father's private library and began to study it. When my father saw me reading that book, he took it away from me, saying that the *Bhagavat Gītā* was not for boys: "It would make you insane." But his remarks could not stop me from reading it.

In my youth, I was fond of listening to discourses on Hindu philosophy and used to hear lectures on various phases of different religions. I attended the sermons on Christ and Christianity by Christian missionaries like the Rev. Dr. Macdonald, the Rev. Kali Laran Banerjee and others, who spoke regularly, every Sunday, at the Beadon Square on Chitpur Road in Calcutta. There, I also heard many anti-Christian lectures which were based upon the higher criticism of the Bible and free thought. I had the privilege of hearing Keshab Chandra Sen and Protap Chandra Mazoomder, the celebrated leaders of the Brahmo Samaj.

In 1883 the noted Hindu philosopher, Pundit Sasadhar Tarkachudamani, delivered a series of public lectures on the six Systems of Hindu philosophy at the Albert Hall, under the presidentship of late Bankim Chandra Chatterjee, the great scholar and writer. I attended the lectures on *Vaisesika* and *Sāmkhya* philosophies in

which the Punditji explained the atomic theory of Kaṇāda, and
the evolution theory of Kapila, and compared them with similar
theories of the ancient Greek philosophers as well as with the modern
theory of Evolution. Those discourses aroused my interest in the
study of Western philosophies of ancient and modern Europe.
Furthermore, when I heard Panditji's lectures on "Yoga" philosophy
of Patañjali, I became interested in Hindu Psychology as well as
in the practical methods of the Yoga system.

I studied Patañjali's system under the direction of the great
philosopher, late Kalibara Vedantavagish, who at that time was
translating the Yoga Sutras and was making an elaborate commentary on them in Bengali. After completing the study of the
Yoga Sutras of Patañjali, I turned to analyse my own mind, to gain
self-control and to enter into *Nirvikalpa Samādhi* through the
practice of Hatha Yoga and Rāja Yoga.

Then, I studied *Śiva Saṁhitā*, a treatise on the practical methods
of Rāja Yoga. But I was told not to practise any of those methods
described in the Yoga Sastras without being instructed by a competent Yogi preceptor (Guru). Then my great anxiety was to find
a suitable teacher or guru. My class-fellow, Jajneswar Bhattacharya,
directed me to go to the great Rāmakrishna Paramahamsa who
lived at Dakshineswar, a suburban town about four miles north
of Calcutta.

One Sunday morning, I reached the Temple Garden at
Dakshineswar, where I met the great Yogi, Rāmakrishna Paramahamsa, and asked him whether he could teach me the practical
methods of "Yoga Philosophy." He replied, "Yes," and after reading
of my past life, he said, "You were a great Yogi in your past
incarnation. Come, my boy! I will teach you how to practise Yoga."
Then, he initiated me and gave me instructions in concentration
and meditation. He touched my chest and aroused my "Kundalini,"
the "Serpent Power" at the base of my spinal column, and I went
into Samādhi, the state of superconsciousness. In him I found the
embodiment of the Absolute Truth of the highest philosophy, as
well as of the Universal Religion which underlies all sectarian religions
of the world, and became his humble disciple. I had the good fortune
to be with him and to serve for two years. There, I met his other
disciples, among whom Swami Vivekānanda was the most brilliant.
I was attracted to him and became his close companion. Frequently,
I used to discuss with him various abstruse points of Epistemology,
Ontology and Metaphysics of India and of Europe.

At that time, I began to devote myself to self-education and
studied Ganot's *Physics*, Herschel's *Astronomy*, John Stuart Mill's
Logic, and *Three Essays on Religion*, Herbert Spencer's *First*

Principles, and *Psychology*, Hamilton's *Philosophy*, Lewes' *History of Philosophy* and attended the courses of lectures at the "Science Association," which had been established by Dr. Mohendra Lall Sircar, the famous Homoeopath. With Swami Vivekananda I studied the Buddhistic Philosophy as well as the principles of the *Advaita* or the non-dualistic philosophy of Vedānta.

From Sri Rāmakrishna I learnt that "Dwaita," or Dualistic philosophy, leads to the Visista-Advaita philosophy of Rāmānuja in search after the Ultimate Truth of the universe, which is one and the absolute (Brahman); and that the search after Truth ends in the realisation of the oneness of the *Jīva* (individual soul), Jagat (World), and Īśvara (God) in Brahman as taught in the Advaita philosophy of Vedānta; and that they are the different steps in the path of the realisation of the absolute Truth or Brahman.

In 1886, after the departure of Sri Rāmakrishna, I renounced the world and became a *Saññyāsin* monk along with Swami Vivekānanda and other co-disciples (*Gurubhais*). As this was our second birth, we gave up our former names. From that time I have been known by my present name. I continued my self-education by studying Pāṇini's grammar, six systems of Hindu philosophy, the Upaniṣads and Vedānta Sūtras, with the commentaries of Śaṃkara, Rāmānuja, Sribhāṣya, Nimbārka, Vallabhāchārya and others.

I travelled bare-footed from place to place, depending entirely on alms cooked or uncooked, whatever chance would bring to me. I always held in my mind the thought that the phenomenal world was transitory and unreal; that I was a spectator like the unchangeable Ātman of Vedānta which always remains a witness (Sākshi) of the games which the people were playing in the world. In this manner I endured all sorts of privation and hardship, practised austerities of all kinds, walked up to the sources of the Jamuna and the Ganges, where I stayed for three months in the caves of the Himalayas at the altitude of nearly 14,000 feet above the sea level, spending most of my time in contemplation of the Absolute, I realised that the phenomenal world was like a dream. Thus wandering for ten years all over India, and visiting sacred places like Kedarnath and Badarīnārāyana, Dwāraka and Rāmeswaram, Jagannāth and Pūri, etc., I met great sages and saints like "Trailainga Swāmi," "Swāmi Bhāskarānanda" at Benares, Pavahari Baba at Gazipur, many Vaishnava saints at Brindāban and great Vedānta philosophers at Rishikesh, where I studied monistic Vedānta Philosophy under the great scholar "Dhanaraj Giri," who was the eminent Advaita Vedāntist of those days.

In 1896 Swāmi Vivekānanda, who after his successful lectures in U.S.A. on Vedānta and Rāja Yoga, given in the three years following his appearance at the Parliament of Religions in Chicago in 1893, had come over to London and had delivered several lectures on Jñāna Yoga and Rāja Yoga in that great city, invited me to assist him in his work there.

I accepted his invitation and sailed from Calcutta to London in August 1896. My first lecture was before the Christo-Theosophical Society of London, on the Advaita philosophy of "Pañcadaśi." Swāmi Vivekānanda entrusted me with the charge of conducting his classes on Vedānta and Rāja Yoga there, and left for India in 1897. I continued my class lectures on Jñāna Yoga, Rāja Yoga, and delivered public lectures in churches and before religious and philosophical societies in London and its suburbs for one year. When I was in London Swāmi Vivekānanda took me to meet Professor Max Müller and Professor Paul Deussen of Kiel University, who had translated sixty Upaniṣads into the German language and who was the author of the *Philosophy of the Upaniṣads*. I had conversations with them in Sanskrit. But Professor Max Müller could neither speak in Sanskrit nor understand Sanskrit words when spoken, because, as he said, his ears and tongue were not trained in the sounds of Sanskrit utterances. So, I exchanged my views with him in English. He was deeply interested in the life and teachings of Rāmakrishna and said, "Rāmakrishna was an original thinker, for he was never brought up within the precincts of any university and, therefore, his teachings were new and original." This remark created a deep impression upon my mind. Later on, he published the *Life and Sayings of Rāmakrishna*.

In 1897, at the request of Swāmi Vivekānanda, I crossed the Atlantic and landed at New York, to take charge of the Vedānta Society which he had started in New York City. There, in six months I delivered ninety public lectures before large audiences on Vedānta Philosophy and Yoga Philosophy of Patañjali; organised the Society, and held regular classes on *Bhagavat Gītā*, *Katha Upaniṣad*, and various other Upaniṣads on the *Secret of Death*, *Self-Knowledge*,[1] *Sānkhya* and *Yoga Philosophy*, for nearly twenty years under the auspices of the Vedānta Society of which I was the president.

In 1898, Professor William James held a discussion with me in his house on the problem of the "Unity of the Ultimate Reality." This discussion lasted for nearly four hours, in which Professor

---

[1] "Self-Knowledge" includes the following subjects: Spirit and Matter; Knowledge of the Self; Prana and the Self; Search after the Self; Realisation of the Self; Immortality of the Self.

These were afterwards published by the Vedānta Society of New York, U.S.A.

Royce, Professor Lanman, Professor Shaler and Dr. James, the
Chairman of Cambridge philosophical conferences, took my side and
supported my arguments in favour of "Unity."

I travelled extensively all through the United States, Canada,
Alaska and Mexico, and delivered addresses on various phases of
the Vedānta Philosophy in all the principal cities of those countries.
I delivered a series of public lectures on "Krishna and His Teachings";
"Zoroaster and His Teachings"; "Taoism"; "Laotze and His Teach-
ings"; "Lamaism in Tibet"; "Shintoism in Japan"; "Buddha and
His Teachings"; "Christ and His Teachings"; "Mahomet and His
Teachings"; "Rāmakrishna and His Teachings"; under the title
of the "Great Saviours of the World."

In 1921, I sailed from San Francisco and crossed the Pacific Ocean,
breaking my voyage at Honolulu, where I was a delegate from India
at the Pan-Pacific Educational Conference. Then, I came to Japan
and studied Japanese culture, philosophy and religion, stopping at
Shanghai, Hongkong, Canton, Manila and Singapore, where I
delivered the message of Vedānta Philosophy in popular lectures.
From Singapore I was invited to Kuala-Lumpur in Malaya States,
where I gave a series of lectures on "Confucianism," "Buddhism"
and "Taoism" before Chinese and Hindu audiences. From there I
was invited to Rangoon, whence, after delivering several public
lectures on the "Message of Buddha" and on "Religion of the
Hindus," I returned to Calcutta.

In 1922 I went to Tibet from Kashmere, crossing the Himalayas
on foot, to study the manners, customs and Buddhistic philosophy
and Lamaism which prevail among the Tibetan Lamas. I went
along Yarkand Road, the highway to Europe, and stopped at "Leh,"
the capital of Ladak, in western Tibet. My destination was "Hemis
Monastery," about twenty-five miles north of the City of "Leh."

In 1923, after returning from Tibet, I established "The Rāmakrishna Vedānta Society" in Calcutta of which I am the President.
In 1924 I opened a branch of this Society at Darjeeling under the
name of "Rāmakrishna Vedānta Ashram."

This short sketch of my life will give the reader some idea of the
different influences which have moulded my convictions.

HINDU PHILOSOPHY IN INDIA

WHAT IS VEDĀNTA?

THE popular belief is that "Vedānta philosophy" means the "Philosophy of the Upaniṣads" confined exclusively to the Vedas or the sacred Scriptures of the Hindus in India. But the term "Veda" in the present case is used to signify, not any particular book, but "Knowledge," being derived from the Sanskrit root verb "vid" to know; while the English word "end" is derived from Sanskrit "Anta." Vedānta, therefore, implies literally "End of knowledge"; and the philosophy is called "Vedānta" because it explains what that "End" is, and how it can be attained. All relative knowledge ends in the realisation of the unity of the individual soul with the ultimate truth of the universe, which is the infinite ocean of absolute knowledge, the universal spirit or Brahman. As rivers running from various sources ultimately end in the ocean, so the rivers of relative knowledge starting from various view-points and flowing through different stages of the phenomena, ultimately end in the infinite ocean of absolute Existence, and infinite knowledge—*Satyam, Jñānam, Anantam Brahma*—the ultimate Reality of the universe. It is the absolute Substance which is beyond subject and object, which is the infinite Source of knowledge, of consciousness and blissfulness, and which is not many, but one. It is the same as the "Good" of Plato, the "Substantia" of Spinoza, the "Ding-an-sich" or the transcendental thing-in-itself of Kant, the "Over-soul" of Emerson, and the "Unknowable" of Herbert Spencer. It is the Noumenon which pervades the phenomena of the universe.

The system of Vedānta is more critical than the Kantian system, because it shows the phenomenal nature of the Kantian ego, of his forms of intuition and of his categories of thought. It is also more sublime than the philosophy of Kant, because it recognises and proves the identity of the objective reality of the universe with the subjective reality of the ego. Kant

did not realise that the Thing-in-itself (Ding-an-sich) of the
objective world and the "Ding-an-sich" of the subjective world
are one. In no other philosophy has this oneness been so clearly
explained and so strongly emphasised as it is in Vedānta. "This
constituted the unique character of Vedanta, unique compared
with every other philosophy of the world which has not been
influenced by it, directly or indirectly."[1] In Europe there have
been many idealistic philosophies which have denied the existence
of the external world, but not one of them ventured to deny
the apparent reality of the ego, of the senses, of the mind and
of their inherent forms. In this respect, Vedānta holds a unique
position among the philosophies of the world. The self or ātman,
the true nature of the ego or *Jīvātma* is one with the essence of
Divinity (Brahman) which is absolutely pure, perfect, immortal,
unchangeable and one. No philosopher, not even Plato, Spinoza,
Kant, Hegel or Schopenhauer has reached that height of
philosophic thought.[2]

Starting from the ultimate conclusions of ancient and modern
science, Vedānta says that the absolute Truth is one and not
many, yet there can be varieties of expressions and manifold
manifestations of the one Truth. Furthermore, it maintains that
the aim of the higher philosophy is not merely to ascertain the
established conjunctions of events which constitute the order of
the universe, or to record the phenomena which it exhibits to our
observation and refer them to the general laws, but also to lead
the human mind from the realm of the knowable to that which
is beyond the knowable. We are now living in the realm of the
knowable, but that which teaches simply the laws which govern
the knowable phenomena is not the highest kind of philosophy.
We must know the laws of the knowable, yet at the same time

---

[1] *The Six Systems of Indian Philosophy*, p. 223, by Professor Max Müller.
[2] Professor Max Müller declares: "None of our philosophers, not excepting
Heraclitus, Plato, Kant or Hegel, has ventured to erect such a spire, never
frightened by storms or lightnings. Stone follows on stone in regular
succession after once the first step has been made, after once it has been
clearly seen that in the beginning there can have been but One, as there
will be but One in the end, whether we call it Ātman or Brahman." *The
Six Systems of Philosophy*, p. 239.

we should aspire to go beyond the knowable and plunge into the realm of the Infinite. If any philosophy can help us in this attempt, then it must be higher than the ordinary system which keeps us within the limits of time, space and causality of these knowable phenomena. The monistic Vedānta philosophy guides us above all knowable objects of perception and directs our soul toward the Eternal absolute Being, where we find the solution of all problems and the answer to all questions. Its attempt is to trace the origin of all phenomena objective and subjective, physical and mental, not by any unscientific method, but by the most rigorous processes of logic and reason starting from the ultimate generalisations of the various branches of science.

TRUE PHILOSOPHY

True philosophy must construct a theory which will be the simplest in its nature and yet at the same time will explain all the vital problems which the science of the phenomenal can never explain and which will harmonise with the highest form of the universal religion without destroying the loftiest aspirations of the human soul. True philosophy in the widest sense must perform three great functions. First, it must co-ordinate the ultimate results arrived at by special branches of knowledge which we call sciences, and taking up those conclusions, it must form the widest generalisations possible. When it does this, it is called Phenomenology. Herbert Spencer's philosophy performs this function, but it leaves out the vital problems which perplex the minds of the greatest philosophers as unsolvable mysteries. Secondly, true philosophy must investigate the realm of knowledge and trace its source. A philosophy which does this is called Epistemology. The philosophy of Kant, Hegel, Fichte and others has sought to perform this function. George Croom Robertson says: "Epistemology is just philosophy, because it deals with things, deals with beings; it deals with things going beyond bare experience, but it treats of them in relation to the fact of knowing. Thus an Epistemologist cannot help being an Ontologist, because his theory of knowledge must treat about things also as being. He must also be a metaphysician, because he is concerned with the whole range of things beyond the physical; he must be a philosopher in being other and more than a man of science, or concerned with things in a way to which science is not."[1]

The third function which true philosophy performs is that of leading our minds into the realm of the Absolute or the Unknown, and then it solves the problems of life and death. It explains the origin of the universe and of individual existence and the purpose of evolution. On the plane of relativity, the perfect solution of these vital problems can never be found. Furthermore, when this phase of true philosophy directs our minds towards the Infinite, it helps us in becoming free from all limitations of ignorance and selfishness. These limitations are the greatest bondages that we are now suffering from, and by performing this function, true philosophy lays the foundation of the highest form of monistic religion. No philosophy in the world performs these three functions so satisfactorily as the Vedānta philosophy. Hence we may say that Vedānta is the most complete system.

Philosophy and religion must always be in perfect harmony. Ernest Haeckel, in his *Riddle of the Universe*, tried to give a foundation to monistic religion, but his monism is one-sided, because he says that the ultimate substance of the universe is unintelligent. His insentient substance may be compared with Kapila's *Prakriti* which is eternal and unintelligent. According to Vedānta, however, the final reality of the universe is Brahman which is Sat-Chit-Ānanda, or absolute Existence-Intelligence-Bliss. It teaches that that which is the substance of our souls must possess intelligence, consciousness and blissfulness. Thus, Vedānta lays the true foundation of a universal religion which is monistic or non-dualistic.

RELIGION OF VEDĀNTA

The monistic religion of Vedānta does not admit the Sānkhyan theory of the plurality of individual souls, which are eternal and

[1] *Elements of General Philosophy.*

infinite by nature, but on the contrary, by following the strict rules of Logic, it establishes that the Infinite must be one and not many. From one many have come into existence, and the individual souls are but so many images or reflections of the Absolute Brahman. From this Absolute Brahman the phenomenal universe rises and in the end returns into the Brahman.

The religion of Vedānta admits that Brahman has two aspects, the one is without any attribute "Nirguṇa" and the other is with attributions "Saguṇa," who is called Īśvara or the Ruler of the universe. He is the personal God, who is the first-born Lord of the universe, who starts the evolution of *Prakriti* which forms His Body. The God of Vedānta is both the efficient and the material cause of all phenomena. He loves all living creatures who live and move and have their being in Him, and can be loved and be worshipped in return. In Vedānta the *Prakriti* of the Sānkhya philosophy is called *Māyā*, which is the divine energy of the Absolute Brahman. Māyā does not mean illusion, as some scholars think, but it is that power which produces time, space and causation, as also the phenomenal appearances which exist on the relative plane. Thus we see that the system of Vedānta is both philosophy and religion. Of the tree of knowledge, true philosophy is the flower and "religion" is the fruit, so they must go together. Religion is nothing but the practical side of philosophy and philosophy is the theoretical side of Religion.

In India, a true philosopher is not a mere speculator but a spiritual man. He does not believe in certain theories which cannot be carried into practice in everyday life; what he believes he lives up to; and, therefore, practical philosophy still exists among the Hindus in India. The followers of Vedānta live spiritual lives and strive to attain God-consciousness. In India, if anyone writes voluminous speculative philosophy and lives a worldly life, he is not considered a true philosopher.

The philosophy and religion of Vedānta embrace all the sciences, philosophies and religions of the world by accepting their ultimate conclusions, and classifying them according to their order of merit. Consequently, the universality of Vedānta is unique and unparalleled. The religion of Vedānta teaches:

"That which exists is one, men call it by various names"—Rig Veda. No other philosophy or religion is based upon this fundamental truth of the unity of existence under a variety of names and forms than Vedānta, and therefore it offers, as can no other, an adequate foundation of all the different phases of dualistic, qualified-non-dualistic and monistic systems of religious thought. Thus it establishes a "Universal Religion" which embraces all the special religions of the world. It has many phases.

The dualistic phase of Vedānta includes the fundamental principles of all the dualistic or monotheistic systems, such as Zoroastrianism, Judaism, Christianity, Islam and all other systems that advocate the worship of the personal God under any name or form, or devotion to any divine ideal.

The qualified non-dualistic phase embraces all the systems which teach the immanency and transcendency of God. It includes all such ideas as "God dwells in us as well as in the universe"; "The Kingdom of Heaven is within you"; "We live and move and have our being in God"; "He is the soul of our souls, and the Life of our lives"; "We are parts of one stupendous Whole"; "We are the sons of God, the children of Immortal Bliss," etc.

The monistic phase of Vedānta is the most sublime of all. Very few thinkers can appreciate the grandeur of spiritual oneness. Yet, herein lies the solution of the deepest problems of science, philosophy and metaphysics and the final goal of all religions. It alone explains how it is possible for one to say, "I and my Father are one"; "I am He"; "That thou art"; "*Analhaq*," as a Mahommedan Sufi says.

The system of Vedānta harmonises with the religious ideals of the human mind and shows the various paths by which a man may attain to God-consciousness and emancipation from the bondages of ignorance, selfishness and all other imperfections, and eventually becomes as perfect as the Father in Heaven is perfect. Its notable feature is that it does not prescribe to all one special path by which to reach the ultimate goal of all religions. On the contrary, it recognises the varying tendencies of different minds, and guides each along the way best suited to it. It classifies human tendencies into four great divisions

which together with their subdivisions cover almost all classes
of people; and then it sets forth the methods which may be
helpful to everyone. Each of these methods is called in Sanskrit
"Yoga."

First is "Karma Yoga"—the path of work. It is for the active
man; for those who like to work and are always ready to do
something for the help of others. In short, it is for the busy,
everyday working man or woman. Karma Yoga reveals the
"Secret of Work" and opens the way to complete Self-Mastery.

The next method is "Bhakti Yoga." It is for such as are of
devotional and emotional nature. It teaches how ordinary
emotions can bring forth spiritual unfoldment of the highest
kind and lead to the realisation of the ultimate ideal of all
religions. In a word, it is the path of devotion and love.

The third is "Rāja Yoga"—the path of concentration and
meditation. The field of Rāja Yoga is very vast. It covers the
whole psychic plane and describes the processes by which the
psychic powers are developed, such as thought-reading, clair-
voyance, clairaudience, the evolving of finer perceptions, the
communication with departed spirits, the going out of the body,
the curing of diseases through mental power and the performing
of all such acts as are ordinarily called miracles. All psychic
powers which were displayed by Jesus of Nazareth and his
followers, and which have been manifested by the Yogis of
India from time immemorial, are described rationally in Rāja
Yoga. Furthermore, the marvellous powers achieved by the
practice of *Prāṇāyāma*, the control of breath, and by the awakening of the "Serpent power," or "Kundalini," are scientifically
explained in this system of Rāja Yoga. The principal aim
of Rāja Yoga is to lead the seeker after Truth through the
path of concentration and meditation to the highest state of
superconsciousness, where individual soul communes with
the universal Spirit and realises the unity of both on the
spiritual plane.

Jñāna Yoga is the fourth method. It is the path of right knowledge and discrimination. This is for those who are intellectual,
discriminative and of a philosophical nature. He who travels

through this "Path of wisdom" burns the vast forest of the trees of phenomenal names and forms (Nāma Rūpa) by starting in it the fire of right knowledge. All these names and forms are produced by Māyā, the inscrutable power of Brahman. It is inseparable from Brahman as the power of burning is inseparable from fire. A Jñāna Yogi, in his search after the Absolute Truth, should reject all names and forms by saying "Not this," "Not this" (*Neti, Neti*), until he realises the one nameless, formless and absolute Being of the universe, where the subject and the object, the knower, knowledge and its object losing their relativity merge into the ocean of the absolute Brahman. Thus, we see how universal is the scope of Vedānta.

ETHICS OF VEDĀNTA

Standing on the rock of the spiritual oneness of the universe, Vedānta explains the basis of Ethics. If we injure, hate or cheat others, we injure, hate or cheat ourselves first. For this spiritual oneness we should love our neighbours as ourselves. Because love means the expression of oneness. When we begin to love others as we love our own self, we are truly ethical. Then we do not think that we have fulfilled the highest end and aim of life by eating, drinking and begetting children like lower animals, but that the fulfilment of the purpose of life consists in loving others disinterestedly without seeking any return of love as we love our own self. Animal nature, which is extremely selfish, must be conquered by moral nature through unselfish love for the real Self of others. Moral perfection consists in the destruction of selfishness. Having attained perfect freedom from the limitations of the animal self, the individual soul must strive to gain spiritual perfection which is the ultimate goal of evolution.

Spiritual perfection is the manifestation of the true nature of Spirit or Ātman which is immortal, free, divine and one with the Universal Spirit or God. Evolution attains to the highest fulfilment of its purpose when the Spirit manifests itself in its pristine purity and full glory. Each individual soul according to Vedānta is bound to become perfect in the end. As this cannot be gained in one life we shall have to admit the truth of the theory of Reincarnation.

Reincarnation explains the gradual evolution of the soul from the minutest *amoeba* to the highest man, through many lives and various forms until perfection is reached. The theory of Reincarnation is a logical necessity for the completion of the theory of evolution. They supplement each other. The Vedāntic theory of Reincarnation rejects the one-birth theory of Christianity, Islam and other religions. It is not the same as the theory of Metempsychosis or Transmigration of Souls, which was accepted by the Greek philosophers like Pythagoras, Plato and their followers. In the Platonic theory the idea of progress, growth or gradual evolution of the soul from lower to higher stages of existence, is entirely excluded, and the law of *Karma* is ignored. The theory of Reincarnation on the contrary admits the gradual evolution of each soul which is potentially divine, and which rises higher and higher in the process of the unfoldment of the latent powers, passing through various births and rebirths, always reaping the results of its own actions, being governed by the *Law* of *Karma*.

The Law of Karma includes the laws of causation, of action and reaction, of compensation and of retribution. Through this Law of Karma, Vedānta explains rationally the inequalities and diversities of nature which the theory of heredity has failed to explain. The doctrine of Karma denies the dogma that God punishes the wicked with eternal damnation and rewards the virtuous with celestial felicity. This is a dogma which makes God partial and unjust. In the doctrine of Karma there is no room for a Satan, the creator of Evil.

According to Vedānta all evil proceeds from ignorance, which is the mother of all sins and wickedness. God never punishes the wicked, nor rewards the virtuous, but the wicked punish themselves and the virtuous reward themselves by their own thoughts and deeds. The law of Karma, eternal as it is, predestines nothing and no one; but on the contrary making every soul a free agent for action, shows the way out of the world of misery through unselfish thoughts and good deeds.

We create our own destiny, mould our future, determine our character by our own thoughts and deeds. We cannot blame God or Satan for our own misery and sufferings for which we ourselves are responsible; because what we deserve we have got now, and what we shall make, we shall receive in future. Our present was determined by our past and our future will be determined by our present. This is the eternal Law.

PRINCIPAL PUBLICATIONS BY SWĀMI ABHEDĀNANDA

Reincarnation (1900).
Spiritual Unfoldment (1902).
Philosophy of Work (1903).
How to be a Yogi (1903).
Divine Heritage of Man (1903).
Self-Knowledge (1905).
The Gospel of Rāmakrishna (1905).
India and Her People (1905–6).
Nine Lectures (Parts 1 and 2) (1909).
The Sayings of Rāmakrishna (1910).
Great Saviours of the World (1912).
Human Affection and Divine Love (1912).

Published by the Vedānta Society of New York, U.S.A.

Lectures and Addresses in India (1906).
Travels in Kashmere and Tibet (Bengali, 1922).

THE CONCEPT OF PHILOSOPHY

by K. C. BHATTACHARYYA

Born 1875; Professor of Philosophy in Calcutta University

THE CONCEPT OF PHILOSOPHY

1. An explication of the concept of philosophy appears to me more important than the discussion of any specific problem of philosophy. The possibility of philosophy as a body of knowledge distinct from science is nowadays called in question. I may indicate my general position by stating wherein I differ from the Kantian view of the subject.

I. ORIENTATION TO KANT

2. With regard to the knowability of the self as a metaphysical entity, Kant holds that the self is a necessity of thought and is the object of moral faith, but is not in itself knowable. My position is, on the one hand, that the self is unthinkable and on the other that while actually it is not known and is only an object of faith, though not necessarily only of moral faith, we have to admit the possibility of knowing it without *thinking*, there being a demand, alternative with other spiritual demands, to realise such knowledge. This is practically reopening the entire epistemological question of the meaning of thought and knowledge.

3. In taking the self to be unthinkable, I understand Kant's Idea of the Reason to be not only not knowledge, but to be not even thought in the literal sense. The so-called extension of thought beyond experience and the possibility of experience means to me only the use of the verbal form of thought as a symbol of an unthinkable reality, such symbolising use not being thinking. I go further and hold that a form of thought as understood by itself in logic and apart from its symbolising use is not literally thought. Some present-day positivists who deny not only meta-physical knowing, but also metaphysical thinking, would not go so far as to deny logic itself to be a body of thought. They rely in fact on logic, which they take to be pure thinking, in order to deny metaphysical thinking. I take logic to be a philosophical and not a scientific subject: the logical forms are shadows of

C

metaphysical symbolisms and are as such themselves to be understood as symbolisms.

4. On the negative side then I go much further than Kant. On the positive side, however, I would tone down his agnosticism. That the self is believed in and is yet actually unknown is itself to me ground for holding that it is knowable without thinking and has to be so known. The self or freedom is taken to be a moral postulate, but why is a moral postulate formulated at all? Neither morality nor metaphysical theory gains anything by the formulation in theoretic form. A moral postulate is not simply an Idea of the Reason, nor is it a construct of the aesthetic imagination. It appears to me to be formulated for the contemplation of it not as a moral good or as an enjoyable value but as a truth to be known. Such contemplation cannot be a spiritual luxury or make-believe, but must have behind it the faith that it is just the process of reaching the truth without thinking. It is not indeed a duty to contemplate, but the contemplation being already there, it demands fulfilment in knowledge. The contemplation of the self as truth may start from consciousness other than the moral, nor need moral consciousness develop into it. A distinctively spiritual activity comes spontaneously and has no necessary origin. The contemplation of the self as truth demands fulfilment in knowledge only by one in whom this activity has already started. It is an absolute demand co-ordinate with other absolute demands.

5. What applies to the self applies with necessary alterations to other metaphysical entities. Metaphysics, or more generally, philosophy including logic and epistemology, is not only not actual knowledge, but is not even literal thought; and yet its contents are contemplated as true in the faith that it is only by such contemplation that absolute truth can be known.

II. GRADES OF THEORETIC CONSCIOUSNESS

6. Whether philosophy is knowledge or embodies literal thinking may be open to dispute. But in any case it presents beliefs that are speakable or systematically communicable and is like science

an expression of the theoretic consciousness. Theoretic consciousness at its minimum is the understanding of a speakable. What is spoken must be in the first instance believed. What is disbelieved must be, to start with, a believed content. The meaning of a sportive combination of words like the "hare's horn" or "square circle" is only not believed and cannot even be said to be disbelieved. Nor is such combination said to be spoken except as an example of what is not spoken. To speak is to formulate a belief. Even imperative or exclamatory speech expresses some kind of belief of the speaker, though the belief is not primarily intended to be communicated. A lie which is not believed by the speaker is not felt by him to be informatively spoken, being felt to be spoken only as incorporated in the implied prefix of all speech, viz. the imperative "believe me." It is the believed content that is spoken and it is the understanding of what can be spoken that constitutes the theoretic consciousness.

7. Such understanding may not be knowledge, but it involves belief in something as known or to be known. The belief may not be explicitly an awareness of the actual or possible known-ness, but it can always be made explicit as such. The belief in knowledge may be implied in the explicit awareness of unknown-ness. The agnostic or the anti-rationalist or the absolute sceptic is primarily conscious of unknown-ness, but to be conscious of unknown-ness is to be conscious of known-ness also. They may not be said to *know* the unknown as such but they *believe* it and impliedly believe also in something as known, even though it may be speakable only as unspeakable. They are said to present a philosophy so far as they express the theoretic consciousness which implies belief in something as known.

8. All forms of theoretic consciousness as involving the understanding of a speakable are sometimes called thought. Of these, as will appear presently, only one form is literal thought, the others being symbolistic thought which should not be called thought at all. Four forms or grades of thought may be distinguished. They may be roughly called empirical thought, pure objective thought, spiritual thought and transcendental thought. Empirical thought is the theoretic consciousness of a content

involving reference to an object that is perceived or imagined to be perceived, such reference being part of the meaning of the content. There are contents that are objective but have no necessary reference to sense-perception and the consciousness of such contents may be called pure objective or contemplative thought. The content of spiritual thought is no object, nothing that is contemplated in the objective attitude, being subjective in the sense of being appreciated in a subjective or "enjoying" attitude. Transcendental thought is the consciousness of a content that is neither objective nor subjective, the further characterisation of which will come later. The contents of the four grades of thought may be provisionally called fact, self-subsistence, reality and truth. Science deals with fact, the content of empirical thought. Philosophy deals with the last three, the contents of pure thought in the objective, subjective and transcendental attitudes.

9. All contents of the theoretic consciousness are speakable. The so-called grades of thought are really grades of speaking. Fact in science is spoken of as information and understood without reference to the spoken form. It is what need not be spoken to be believed. Speakability is a contingent character of the content of empirical thought, but it is a necessary character of the content of pure or philosophic thought. In philosophy, the content that is spoken is not intelligible except as spoken. Pure thought is not thought of a content distinguishable from it and is accordingly sometimes regarded as a fiction, philosophy being rejected as a disease of speech. Philosophical contents are indeed believed to be self-evident and the self-evident means what is independent of the spoken belief of an individual mind. This independence of speaking is, however, a part of their meaning. It is not part of the meaning of a scientific content which is understood without reference at all to the linguistic expression of it.

10. Now a believed content that has necessary reference to the speaking of it is not spoken of as information. Self-subsistence or enjoyed reality or truth is not assertable as fact. Belief in it may be expressed in the form of a judgment but the form would

be only artificial or symbolic. Fact is always expressible as a judgment of the form "A is thus related to B," this being the only judgment-form that is literally intelligible. A judgment of the form "X is," if it expresses belief in a fact of science, is only a periphrasis for a judgment of the above relational form. In "X is," if X stands for "A as related to B," the assertion means either only that A is related to B or that A that is thus related is related to something else. Fact is always a fact related to facts. If anywhere "X is" means something other than the relational assertion, it means that X is self-subsistent, real or true, which is only an apparent judgment. The subject is here understood as presupposing the predicate. The predicate does not, as in a judgment proper, amplify or explicate the meaning of a subject that is already believed. The subject is here believed as a self-evident elaboration of the predicate that is already believed to be self-evident.

11. Philosophy is such self-evident elaboration of the self-evident and is not a body of judgments. The self-evident is spoken, but is not spoken *of*. Of what is only spoken and contains a necessary reference to the speaking of it there are three forms according as it is spoken in the objective, subjective or transcendental attitude. The difference between the first two forms is the difference between the imports of the apparent judgments "The object (-in-general) is" and "I am." In a judgment proper "A *is* thus related to B," if the word *is* by itself means anything, if in other words the assertion means any content more than "A related to B," the content as isolated would be objectivity. It may be expressed as an apparent judgment "the relation of A and B is." In a judgment proper, the word "is" expresses only the objective attitude of the subject, but in this apparent judgment, "is" means an objective content which is self-subsistent but not fact. To express or formulate this content is still to retain the objective attitude. The attitude is explicitly dropped in saying "I am." The content here also is spoken and not spoken *of*, but it is explicitly understood as not objective and as only apparently objective or symbolised by objectivity. What the word "am" means is not contemplated in the objective attitude,

but is subjectively enjoyed and only spoken *as though* it were objectively contemplated. If fact is spoken of and the self-subsistent object is only spoken—both being spoken as *meant*, reality is spoken not as meant but as only *symbolised*.

12. All the three are literally speakable. To say that the object is not the subject and that the latter is symbolised by the former is still to speak literally. The word that is used as symbol is not indeed literally understood, but what is symbolised by it (and that it is symbolised) is literally spoken. The subjective is a positive entity through which the objective is understood. The concept of the object is not reached through a generalisation of the objective facts of science. Were it not for the direct consciousness and speakability of the subject *I*, the concept of the object would never be precipitated. The first person *I* is the primary instance of a content that necessarily refers to the speaking of it. It is in fact the spoken that is understood as the same as the speaking function. In "I am" then, the predicate is a symbol of a literally spoken subject. What is taken as self-subsistent or real is literally spoken and understood. What, however, is taken as true is not literally understood.

13. How then is truth as beyond reality spoken? To answer the question, the connection between the notions of fact, self-subsistence and reality has to be further elucidated. The denial of each of these is possible. The judgment "A is thus related to B" may be denied in the form "that A is so related is not fact," "That A is so related" is no judgment, but what is nowadays called a proposition. The enunciation and denial of it are possible because we have already a belief in the self-subsistent. If the proposition is understood as not fact, it is because we cannot deny it self-subsistence.[1] So we may deny the self-subsistent in the form "object is not," meaning "What is other than the subjective is not a definite or self-identical content for contemplation"—a recognised philosophical view that is not *prima*

---

[1] The term self-subsistence instead of subsistence is used because we *mean* only in reference to a belief. The believed subsistent is the self-subsistent as meant. A meaning that is not a believed content of one grade is a believed content of a higher grade.

facie meaningless. The denial is possible because we already believe in the subjective as enjoyed reality. We may also deny reality in the form "I (as individual subject) am not." This too is *prima facie* intelligible and it represents a new grade of negation, for the individual subject is understood to be real as subject and not as object though it may be individual through some sort of identification with the object. Even as individual, the *I* is enjoyingly believed and the denial of such a content is possible because we have already the notion of truth beyond reality.

14. Taking a sentence of the form "X is," it is a judgment proper if "X," "is" and their combination (or the judgment-form) are each literally understood. Where X stands for the self-subsistent, both X and *is* are literally understood but the combination is not, since X is intelligible only through *is*. Where X stands for the (individual) self as enjoyed, it is literally understood, but the word *is* is only an objective symbolism for enjoyed reality and the combination therefore is also symbolic. Where X stands for the negation of the (individual) self, it is not literally understood, because no positive is understood as equivalent to it. The self is unintelligible except as the subject *I* or as what the subject *I* is not. There is no consciousness of an absolute or transcendental self without reference to the subject *I*. If such a self is understood, it is only as the implication of the enjoyed *I* and never by itself. It is indeed positively believed, but there is no positive formulation of it independent of the notion of *I*. Thus here X is only symbolically understood and consequently the word *is* and the judgment-form also are symbolically understood. "Object is" is no judgment, being tautologous as a judgment and "I am" is no judgment because *am* is only symbolism, but both are literally spoken because the subject is literally understood as positive. But the sentence "the absolute self is" is not only no judgment but is not even literally spoken. Still, it is not meaningless, and symbolises what is positively believed, viz. truth. What is believed and is not literally speakable (and is as such undeniable) is truth.

15. So there are the four grades of speakables. There is the primary distinction between what is only symbolically speakable

and what is literally speakable. The literally speakable comprises what is spoken of as information and what is only spoken and not spoken *of*. Of these, what is only spoken is spoken either as symbolised or as meant. Truth is only symbolically spoken, reality is literally spoken as symbolised and the self-subsistent is literally spoken as meant. None of these are spoken *of* as information, while fact is spoken of as information. These correspond to what were roughly called empirical, contemplative, enjoying and transcendental thought. It is only what is spoken of as information or fact that is or can be meant literally. In contemplative, enjoying and transcendental thought, the content is not spoken *of* but is only spoken. If it is put in the judgment form "X is," the form is only symbolical. In the first two, X being literally understood, the content though not literally thought is still said to be literally spoken. In contemplative thought, the judgment-form is only symbolical, even in enjoying thought, the word *is* is also used symbolically. In transcendental thought, X also being symbolical, "X is" is not only not literally thought but not also literally spoken.

16. A content that can be literally spoken of is the content of a judgment. The content of a judgment is information or fact that is intelligible without reference to the speaking of it. A content that is necessarily understood in reference to the speaking of it is in some respect at least symbolically understood and is not information, fact or content of judgment. Beliefs in science alone are formulable as judgments and literally thinkable. If a content is literally thinkable in a judgment, the belief in it as known is actual knowledge. If it is only symbolically thinkable, it is said not to be known but to be only believed as known.

17. Theoretic consciousness was said to be belief in a speakable content involving belief in a content as known. When the content is spoken symbolically, it may not be believed as known, but is at least understood as pointing to what is believed to be known. In science, the content is spoken literally, and is just the content that is believed to be known and is as such actually known. In philosophy, the content is spoken as at least partially symbolised. The self-subsistent content meant by "object is" where the

judgment-form is symbolical is not actually known and demands to be known in absorbed contemplation (or intuited) as simply "object." The real *I* similarly demands to be known not only without the judgment-form, but also without the objective intuitive attitude, i.e. in pure enjoyment. Yet in all these cases something is literally spoken and there is no demand to know the content without the speaking attitude. Truth, however, which is not literally speakable at all demands to be known without even the speaking attitude. The speaking function is the final form of individual subjectivity and even the pure form of spiritual thought implies it. Transcendental consciousness starts by regarding all speaking as only symbolising, and is accordingly conceived as completed when this symbolising speech also is dispensed with. What transcendental consciousness amounts to and whether it remains consciousness at all when it frees itself from speech or individual subjectivity we do not know, for absolute or impersonal consciousness is only conceivable in a negative way. All that can be said is that truth which consciousness starts by symbolising continues to be believed and becomes more and more self-evident as the symbolising accomplishes its purpose.

18. Theoretic consciousness is embodied in science and philosophy. Science alone speaks in genuine judgments, the content of which is fact intelligible without reference to speaking and is alone actually known and literally thought. Philosophy deals with contents that are not literally thinkable and are not actually known, but are believed as demanding to be known without being thought. Such contents are understood as self-subsistent object, real subject and transcendental truth. We have accordingly three grades of philosophy which may be roughly called philosophy of the object, philosophy of the subject and philosophy of truth.

III. SCIENCE AND METAPHYSICS

19. The philosophy of the object requires to be further distinguished from science. Both deal with the object understood as what is believed to be known in the objective attitude as

c*

distinct from the subjective, enjoying or spiritual attitude. The object in science, however, is understood as fact and not as self-subsistent. By fact is meant what is perceivable or has necessary reference to the perceivable, is speakable in the form of a literal judgment and is believed without reference to the speaking of it. The self-subsistent is an object that has no necessary reference to the perceivable, is not literally expressible in a judgment and is believed only as it is spoken. A speakable is understood in necessary reference either to sense-perception or to the speaking of it. What is believed and understood in necessary reference to the speaking of it is, however, believed as self-evident or independent of the belief of any individual mind. As understood in the objective attitude, the self-evident is the self-subsistent. Fact in science is not believed as self-subsistent, as what would be even if no one believed it.

20. The self-subsistent object is a concept of philosophy, and it is not only not a concept of science, but may be even denied by science. Science has no interest to formulate the concept of the self-subsistent object; and it apparently believes that the object *must* be knowable or usable. The self-subsistence of the object implies that the object *may be* in its very nature inaccessible to the mind. To contemplate the object as what would be if there were no subject to know it is to believe that it may be unknowable, that in any case it is not known as of right. Science would not only take this suggestion to be gratuitous but would positively deny it. The notion that truth freely reveals itself and is in itself a mystery or even that it is its very nature to reveal itself would be scouted by science as obscurantist or anthropomorphic. To science, there is nothing in the object to make it known; it is just what is known and though it may be unknown, there is no question of its being unknowable.

21. The implicit belief of science then is that the object is knowable and usable *as of right*. This belief is at least questioned in philosophy to which it is an expression of solipsistic self-sufficiency on the part of the subject. In normal practical life, nature is not consciously exploited as a tool but is negotiated in the primitive spirit of sociableness. It is the arrogant exploiting

attitude of science towards the object that provokes a self-healing reaction of the spirit in the form of philosophy or some cognate discipline. The spiritual demand is that nature should be contemplated and not merely used or manipulated. Science even as theory is evolved in a practical interest. What is more significant is that its very intellectual method is practical, being the use of actual or ideal *contrivances*. It is the wrong spiritual attitude of science towards the object rather than the so-called contradictions and problems left unsolved in scientific theory—as imagined by the philosopher but never felt by the scientist—that suggests the need for a speculative theory of the object. The concept of the self-subsistent object is the first corrective that philosophy offers of the predatory outlook of the scientific intellect. Realism is a philosophical faith among faiths: the creed of science, if formulated, would be a pragmatist form of solipsistic idealism.

22. The relation between science and the philosophy of the object may be brought out by a reference to certain problems which have been wrongly taken to be philosophical. There is the problem of piecing together the results of the sciences into a world-view. The synthesis wanted is sometimes imagined to be the generalisation of the primary laws of the sciences into more comprehensive laws. To suppose, however, that it can be accomplished by philosophy without the employment of the distinctive technique and methods of science would be nothing short of a presumptuous folly. If a law as distinct from a loose descriptive concept could be thus established, philosophy might well take in hand the entire work of science. All that can be achieved in this direction is an imaginative description of the world, which would be not only not actual knowledge, but not even a hypothesis that is intended to be turned into knowledge. Nor could it claim the *a priori* certitude of a theory of logic or of metaphysics. Philosophical contents, if not known, are at least theoretically believed, but a world-view of this kind cannot even be claimed to be believed. It can be only an aesthetic view, having at best a suggestive value for science and an illustrative value for philosophy.

23. As an example of such speculation, I may refer to what is called evolutionary philosophy as distinct from the scientific account of evolution. Metaphysics may discuss the general concept of evolution which is but the concept of life and its materialistic, spiritualistic or other interpretations. For this, however, it does not require to piece together the results of science, all the data needed—matter, life and mind—being presented in the knowledge of oneself as in the body. The details and specific generalisations of science are utilised in the so-called philosophy of evolution not as evidence but as only illustrative material intended for visualising the metaphysical theory on the subject. The scientific account of evolution is knowledge or hypothesis, the metaphysic of life in relation to matter and mind is believed, if not known, but the so-called philosophy of evolution, so far as it is different from either, is only an organised presentation of the known or supposed facts of evolution *as though* they constituted the history of a single cosmic life. Cosmic life is not known as a fact, but may still be believed as self-subsisting. The single significant history of this life, however, as rounding off the jagged groupings of facts in science and bridging over the gaps left by it, is only imagined, and is understood to be neither self-evident nor verifiable. The significant story of cosmic evolution then is neither science nor philosophy, but only a species of imaginative literature.

24. There is another problem, viz. the formulation of the postulates or structural concepts of science, which used to be regarded as a philosophical problem. Pure physics, for example, was taken by Kant as a branch of knowable metaphysic established by deduction from the *a priori* principles of synthetic knowledge. There is a similar confusion of thought at the present day in the romantic philosophy that has sprung up round the physico-mathematical theory of relativity, although here the confusion is of science with philosophy and not of philosophy with science as in the other case. In both the impassable gulf between fact and the self-subsistent is ignored. The so-called axioms of science are but postulates, the formulation of which is the work of science itself. The postulates are hypotheses of

a kind which are intended not for the anticipation of facts, but for the organisation of them into a system. They admit of rival hypotheses and may be rejected though not as contradicted by fact, but only as clumsier and less expeditious to work with than the rival hypotheses. Again there is no passage from a postulate of science to a concept of the object in itself. Whether the real world is four-dimensional or is intrinsically indeterminate in its behaviour can never be determined from the basic conceptual devices that happen to organise the facts of science at the present day. The postulates of science neither lead to nor are deducible from any metaphysical conception of the object.

IV. PHILOSOPHY OF THE OBJECT

25. What then has philosophy to say about the object? The objective attitude is understood only in contrast with the subjective or enjoying attitude. What is believed in the objective attitude, viz. the object, need not, however, be understood in reference to the subject. Where the reference to the subject is no part of the meaning of the object, the object is called fact and is dealt with in science. Philosophy deals with the object that is intelligible only in reference to the subject. By subject is meant the individual subject or *I* which is understood in the theoretic consciousness as the speaking function that is symbolised by itself as spoken. The object that has necessary reference to the speaking of it is the self-subsistent object for philosophy.

26. Philosophy formulates and elaborates the concept of the self-subsistent object. What is common to such object and scientific fact is objectivity which is itself no fact, being only the circumstance of being understood in the objective attitude. This is just the form of the object, the self-subsistent form that is elaborated in logic. It is indeed the form of spoken fact, but as it is the form of the self-subsistent object also, it cannot be said to have necessary reference to fact or the perceivable. Logic as the study of this form is thus no science, but a branch of the philosophy of the object. The form is itself a pure object and is also the form of pure object. The pure object of which logic

is the form or shadow is the metaphysical object. The two branches of the philosophy of the object then are logic and metaphysics.

27. Logical form or objectivity is not a concept reached by a comparison of the objects or facts of science. The concept of the object is reached in the first instance by contrast with the subject as the self-evident content of the spiritual consciousness. It is in the theoretic consciousness of the spiritual grade that one is first explicitly conscious of the object as such. In the consciousness of "I am," one appreciates the objective attitude of judgment as distinct from the enjoying attitude and understands it to be assumed only as a necessary make-believe. The consciousness of the asserted being (*am*) or object as such here emerges as the consciousness of a necessary symbol of the subject *I*. That object is symbol of subject implies that object is not subject. The consciousness of negation as such in fact emerges only in this symbolising consciousness. One may be conscious of the object without being explicitly conscious of the subject, but object has no meaning except as the negation and the symbol of the subject. The symbolism here is necessary, and hence when the reference to the subject is only implicit, the object appears as the immediacy of the subject, as implicitly real. Thus object is understood as self-subsistent before fact is understood as object. Hence objectivity or the form of the object is intelligible in reference to the object that is taken to be implicitly real or what is called metaphysical object. Logic in this sense presupposes metaphysics.

28. Metaphysics is philosophy of the object and involves theoretic consciousness in the objective attitude. There is properly speaking no metaphysic of the subject. What passes as such is either the metaphysic of the mind understood as a particular type of object or is no metaphysic but a self-symbolising form of spiritual activity. Metaphysics elaborates the concept of the object in reference to the subject. The rationale of any distinction of metaphysical contents is to be found in an introspectively appreciable distinction within spiritual experience. Even the crude division of the object into matter, life and mind

is not intelligible as an inductive classification of fact. That these are *all that is* can at least never be known by induction. The notion of the objective universe is that of an infinite singular and not of a universal; and an *exhaustive* division of such a singular into items that are *all positive* can only be reached if the singular self-evidently unfolds itself in them, if in other words each item means every other item or means the entire system. Such a system is self-evident only as the symbol of an introspective or enjoyed content, as the symbolic analysis of the simple or unitary consciousness of oneself living in the body. The analysis is symbolic because the so-called constituents of the content—matter, life and mind—are intelligible not by themselves but only in reference to this consciousness. Their difference is such as is immediately felt and every apparently factual characterisation of them is understood in reference to this feeling.

29. No metaphysical concept is intelligible without reference to the subject or spirit which itself goes beyond metaphysics. The characteristic abstractions of metaphysics which are supposed on the one hand to be of an "extra high grade," and on the other to be only diseases of speech are really symbolic meanings which derive their whole value for belief from the spiritual experiences that they symbolise. There are no judgments, accordingly, in metaphysics and, paradoxical as it may sound, the metaphysical beliefs are not reached by inference. The elaborate parade of deductive proof in metaphysics is only a make-believe, unless proof is taken, as it is sometimes taken, as the exposition of an unperceived tautology. Metaphysical reasoning is only the *systematic exposition of symbolic concepts*, concepts that are implicitly taken as symbols of contents that are enjoyingly believed.

30. Fact and the self-subsistent are both literally spoken and in both the believed content is figured by being spoken. Fact is understood as independent of this figuration while the self-subsistent is presented as constituted by it. What is common to these spoken contents is this speech-created form. There are accidental forms of speech, but there are also certain structural

forms that are unavoidable in the communication of belief and which are believed to belong to the understood content and not to the speech only. When a fact is spoken, there is a peculiar dualism in the understood content of the meant and the believed, the latter being meant as beyond meaning or as perceivable. When a self-subsistent is spoken, the dualism lapses, the meant and the believed being coincident. The unavoidable forms of speech are constitutive of the meaning. Logic presents a system of speech-created forms of meaning. There may be alternative systems, for logic presupposes metaphysic which presents alternative theories. The fundamental disputes in logic are unavowed metaphysical disputes. Apart from the question of accidental inconsistency within a logical system, whether one logical system is better than another is settled not by logic but by metaphysic. Metaphysical dispute, however, is not settled by logic, for apparently every metaphysical system has its distinctive logic.

31. The suspicion that the subject is not believed in in the same sense as the metaphysical object does not arise within metaphysics. Metaphysics is unaware of the distinction between the self-subsistent and the real. There seems to be nothing wrong, for instance, in the characterisation of matter or mind as real. The distinction is suggested by a contrast of logic with metaphysics. The forms of meaning as discussed in logic are a kind of entity that must be said to be believed in, but it would be absurd to say that they are real. They are believed in as not real and yet not nothing or in other words as self-subsistent. If logical form or objectivity is self-subsistent, has the object of metaphysics any higher status? The distinction of abstract and concrete has meaning only within fact and hence the object cannot mean anything more than objectivity. The metaphysical object is defined, in contrast with fact, as objectivity or self-subsistent meaning. Metaphysic defines itself into logic.

V. PHILOSOPHY OF THE SPIRIT

32. The suggested distinction of self-subsistence and reality is explicitly verified in the spiritual or enjoying consciousness

of objectivity as a symbol of the real subject. As already pointed out, in "I am," *am* meaning self-subsistent being as understood in the objective attitude is the symbol of *I* as understood in the subjective attitude. Enjoying understanding of a content in fact is the consciousness of it as symbolised by an objectively contemplated meaning. Without such a symbolism, the subject would be enjoyed but not enjoyingly understood. It is not only understood like the self-subsistent in necessary reference to the speaking of it: it is understood further as symbolised by its spoken form. This enjoying understanding is what we mean or should mean by introspection. Introspection proper is a form of the theoretic consciousness that implies an abjuration of the objective attitude. Its content is not understood as objective fact nor even as self-subsistent object. The content is not the "interior" of the body which is fact nor is it the "mental" which as unintelligible without reference to the speaking of it is a self-subsistent object. The content is *I* or implies *I*, and although it is spoken as though it were an object, it is understood as what object is not, as the speaking subjectivity.

33. To introspect is actually or ideally to speak in the first person. To speak in the first person may not be to be explicitly conscious of the *I* as what the object is not. When it involves such consciousness, it amounts to introspection. Again introspective speaking may or may not involve the explicit conscious-ness of *being* what is spoken. When it involves such consciousness, it may be called spiritual introspection. The consciousness of being what is spoken (*I*) is itself a new achievement of the subject, its realisation or deepening of being. All introspection involves such achievement: introspection cannot be like the knowledge of objective fact, which leaves the fact unaffected in being. But there is a form of introspection which *apparently* leaves the content thus unaffected, where really there is an alteration of subjective being which is enjoyed only in the non-theoretic way. This may be taken to be an implicit form of spiritual introspec-tion. Sometimes there is a conscious suspension of theoretic consciousness about such alteration, a deliberate exclusion of it from introspection. In such a case, introspection tends to

degenerate into objective consciousness of the mind as distinct from the *I*—what is ordinarily called psychological introspection.

34. The subject *I* is never accepted by itself in spiritual introspection. Something else is always enjoyed along with the subject and enjoyed in reference to it. This may be of three grades. There is in the first place the explicit consciousness of the subject as *unaccountably* embodied, this being the same as the consciousness of the subject as what the object including the mind is not. Next there is the consciousness of personal relation to other selves. Lastly there is the consciousness of the over-personal self. The over-personal self is enjoyingly understood not only in reference to the subject *I* but as implying the specific experience of communion, the felt form of identity with the *I*. Such enjoying identity is what is called concrete identity or identity-in-difference, a relation that is unintelligible in the objective attitude. Identity in the philosophy of the object is conceived as abstract identity of the form "A is A" and there is no place for the *relation* of identity in the sphere of fact. The consciousness of the over-personal self as thus one with the *I* is the religious form of the spiritual consciousness. The study of all contents enjoyed in explicit reference to the subject *I* may be called the philosophy of the spirit.

35. Spiritual consciousness is not mere consciousness of reality but is reality itself. Except in the specifically religious form of it, however, it involves some consciousness of reality as distinct from what may be called empty subjectivity. In the enjoying consciousness of the self as embodied or symbolised by the object, the object is conceived not as self-subsistent, but only as a shadow or symbol of the *I*, the consciousness of the shadow as such being said to be empty. In the consciousness of personal relations—the moral consciousness, for example—*I* and the other person are each not the other, each the symbol of the other, there being an alternation of symbolisms. The other person is to me "another *I*" which taken literally is a contradiction through which alone, however, he is understood. Or I (first person) am aware of being "this person" (third person) to him, which too is symbolising by a contradiction. Each alternative is real in being

but contradictory or empty in meaning or theory. The experience of religious communion or worship is the consciousness of the over-personal reality as symbolised by *I*. The conscious symbolising by *I* is a non-theoretic experience of self-abnegation: it is consciously *being* nought and not consciousness *of I* as nought. What emerges to theoretic religious consciousness is the over-personal reality alone. In this sense the religious consciousness is said to outgrow all empty subjectivity and to be the enjoyed fulness of being.

36. Religious experience as conscious fulness of being is simple and admits of no variation within itself. There is, however, an infinite plurality of unique religious experiences. Their relation is determined by themselves and not by any external reflection. Each experience by its self-deepening gets opposed to or synthesised with other experiences. One experience may enjoy another as a stage outgrown or as in absolute conflict with it, where a third experience may emerge as adjusting them to one another. There is no possibility of systematising them by secular reason and so far as they systematise themselves, they present themselves in many alternative systems. Each experience in fact is a revelation and we believe in a system only so far as it is actually revealed. Extensive internally coherent systems with indefinite boundaries are actually revealed, though there is no *a priori* necessity of a system and still less of a system admitting of no alternative systems. The Hegelian notion of a single and exclusive gradation of religions would appear from this standpoint to be intrinsically irreligious.

37. The theoretic form of a religious system is a philosophy of religion, there being as many forms of this philosophy as there are religious systems. This form expresses itself in the lower grades of philosophy—in the theory of the sub-religious spirit, in the metaphysic of the object and even in logic. Every system of religious philosophy has its distinctive theory of the spirit, metaphysic and logic. The fundamental differences within logical theory are, as has been suggested, implicitly metaphysical, those in metaphysic are implicitly spiritual and those in the theory of the secular spirit are implicitly religious. Religions may

indefinitely multiply and indefinitely get synthesised. So is there indefinite scope for differences and syntheses in philosophical theory in general. There is no question of philosophy progressing towards a single unanimously acceptable solution. All philosophy is systematic symbolism and symbolism necessarily admits of alternatives.

VI. PHILOSOPHY OF TRUTH

38. In religion, there can be no theoretic denial of the subject I. In worship, indeed, the subject abnegates itself but the abnegation is there an affair of enjoyed being and not of theory. There is, however, a theoretic consciousness of "I am nought," of the possibility at any rate of the subject or the individual self being unreal. The denial of the I is possible because we already believe that the absolute is. The absolute is not the same as the over-personal reality that is enjoyed in religion. It means what the subject I is not, but the reality of religious experience while it is enjoyed and symbolised by I does not mean such theoretic negation of I. What is called the absolute is a positively believed entity that is only negatively understood. It is an entity that cannot be understood as it is believed, and is speakable only by way of symbolism. Reality as apprehended in religion is indeed symbolised by I, but so far as it is expressed as a self, it is expressed literally. The positive character of the absolute, however, is expressible only by the negation of I (or more accurately by "what I am not") and as such is not literally expressible at all. If then we say that the absolute *is*, we mean by *is* not reality but truth. Reality is enjoyed but truth is not. The consciousness of truth as what is believed in but not understood either in the objective or in the subjective attitude, as not literally speakable at all but speakable only in the purely symbolistic way, is extra-religious or transcendental consciousness.

39. What is believed in and understood as literally unspeakable may be said to be self-revealing. Reality is still literally speakable and may be taken to depend on the speaking for its revelation, though the speaking (which means the I) is not there empty

subjectivity. Truth is believed or revealed *as* independent of it,
as *self*-revealing, what is true being spoken as what the speaking
I is not. At the same time, to be even symbolically spoken, it
has to be believed as a distinct. As a positive to which even the
I is but a symbol and therefore nought in itself, it has nothing
to be distinguished from and is absolute. If, then, truth as absolute
is distinguished, it can only be distinguished from itself. The
self-distinction of the absolute cannot mean self-identity as it
appears in the religious consciousness in which the identity-in-
difference is conceived to be necessary. There is no necessity
in this self-distinction. The absolute may be truth or it may be
what truth is not or it may be their mere distinction without
any unity in the background, which means their indeterminate
togetherness which cannot be denied to be either of them. What
truth is not and is yet positive is the absolute freedom beyond
being (the absolute freedom of the will) and what is indeter-
minately either truth or freedom is absolute value. There is no
sense in speaking of the absolute as the unity of truth, freedom
and value. It is *each* of them, these being only *spoken* separately
but not *meant* either as separate or as one. The theoretic consciousness of truth, then, is the consciousness of truth as distinct
from itself as freedom and from this identity-less self-distinction
or value. The absolute as transcending the enjoyed reality of
religion is positive being (truth) or positive non-being (freedom)
or their positive indetermination (value). The absolute is conceived rigorously as truth in (Advaita) Vedānta. What is loosely
called nihilistic Buddhism apparently understands the absolute
as freedom. The Hegelian absolute may be taken to represent
the indetermination, miscalled *identity*, of truth and freedom
which is value. All these views belong to what may be called
the transcendental grade of philosophy.

40. This triple absolute is apparently the prototype of the
three subjective functions—knowing, willing and feeling. These
functions are primarily the self-distinction of the transcendental
consciousness. The distinction of the functions does not emerge
in the spiritual consciousness. Spiritual experience is simple and
integral in its very nature. The consciousness of *I* is not only

not the consciousness of a complex unity of these functions, it is not even the consciousness of a unity revealing itself in each of them. It not only does not analyse itself: it supplies no motive for such analysis. The tripartite elaboration of consciousness is not introspective but transcendental. The absolutes reveal themselves and the *I* appears trinal only as their shadow or symbolism. As the absolutes are not related into a unity, neither can their subjective shadows be said to be related. The simple *I* has no enjoyed elements or aspects to be related. Nor are the so-called functions intelligible as pure acts or interests *of the I*. They cannot be defined in subjective terms nor can they be taken as unique subjective experiences, being not presented as distinct to introspection at all. Their whole meaning is derived from the self-revealed absolutes.

41. The theory of truth is the theory of the other two absolutes also. At the same time it recognises the possibility of elaborating a primary theory of each of them in reference to the other absolutes. We have shadows of these primary theories in the lower grades of philosophy. The theory of truth, for example, as conceived in its explicit transcendental form has its shadow in the theory of knowledge which belongs to the philosophy of the spirit and in the theory of objective categories which is somewhere intermediate between metaphysics and logic in the philosophy of the object.

COMMON-SENSE EMPIRICISM

by G. C. CHATTERJI

Born March 4, 1894. Professor of Philosophy, Government College, Lahore

COMMON-SENSE EMPIRICISM

AFTER some twenty years during which one's main intellectual concern has been the study and teaching of Philosophy, one should have thought that one would have worked out a fairly complete and well-rounded system of Philosophical beliefs. When I take stock of my philosophical knowledge, I find that I have nothing like a complete and systematic Philosophy to offer, but instead only a few disconnected and disjointed bits of doctrine, which perhaps can hardly be strung together into a common fabric, and which in any case will leave large gaps and openings through which the cold blast of doubt, and the frost of scepticism, can easily penetrate my philosophic soul. This lack of anything like a philosophical system is not the outcome of mere indolence of spirit and temperamental inaptitude, but is largely the outcome of the course of philosophical study and training I have undergone, and the general trend in which philosophical doctrines themselves have tended to move during the last twenty years that I have been interested in them. But more than anything else it is the experience of my own life and of the world in which my daily lot has been cast, which has helped to shape and mould my attitude on general philosophical problems.

In my early days of philosophical study I was attracted to Pluralistic Theism under the influence of James Ward and William James. Later the study of Bradley's *Appearance and Reality* made me a convert to the doctrine of the absolute, and I was an adherent of this school when at the age of 21 I went to Trinity College, Cambridge, and came under the influence of the great triumvirate of Cambridge, McTaggart, Moore and Russell. Of these three McTaggart was my director of studies for three years and I naturally saw a great deal of him. These were the years of the Great War in which McTaggart seemed to be immersed in intellectual coma, induced by excess of patriotism. He was more concerned to perform his duties as a special constable with zeal and so contribute his share to the national endeavour than to pursue either his own speculations about the nature of existence, or to encourage the youthful philosophical enquiries of a young disciple. McTaggart's mental apathy, more than amply compensated for by his later *Nature of Existence* which came out soon after the war, sent me with a rebound to the opposite camp of Moore and Russell, who, each in his own way, seemed to uphold for me the ideal of philosophical integrity. Moore seemed to be wholly unconcerned with the war, and went on investigating the status of sense-data with a meticulous care which made you doubt that there was a great war in progress, or that only last night a contingent of German aeroplanes had passed over the hooded lights of Cambridge on their way to London. Russell on the other hand was as much absorbed in the war as McTaggart was, only in a different way. He was publishing his essays on *Justice in War Time,* organising the Union of Democratic Control, championing the cause of conscientious objectors, and in a hundred other ways bringing his philosophical learning and analytical genius to the study of social problems, and allaying the fever of patriotism which seemed to threaten the mental balance of war-time England. It was thus that my young soul was weaned from Philosophical Idealism to Realism, for in actual practice the Idealist's Philosophy seemed to me less concerned with ideal ends than the Realist's, and the future not only of Philosophy but of a better life for the individual seemed to lie with them.

The loyalties then engendered have never been shaken, for though I no longer believe that Moore's defence of common sense is either very common or very intelligible, or that Russell's Logical Atomism is anything but a series of barren formulae, I can never return to a faith in a timeless Absolute whose logical perfection can lull us to a spirit of happy acquiescence in the intellectual, social and moral muddle in which man from his finite point of view appears to be involved.

This brief sketch of my own philosophical development is only appended here in order that it may help to throw some light on the all too incomplete fragments of my own Philosophy which I wish now to introduce to my readers. What, then, are the cardinal principles of my own Philosophy?

Philosophy, I believe, springs from some abiding human need or purpose. There is some deep-laid desire, need or craving in man to reflect upon the world and his experience, and to form some sort of a general intelligible plan or explanation of it. By this I do not mean to posit any so-called philosophical instinct in man, nor do I suggest that all men need to be, or even attempt to be philosophers. The prime need or function of life is living itself. At first man is so occupied with the mere maintenance and continuance of life, that he cannot be supposed to squander any of his fitful intelligence on solving the problem of the Universe or on his place and destiny in its midst. But as he advances and does not need to spend all his waking hours in the search for food, or sexual satisfaction, or clothing and warmth, he has periods in which his mind is no longer occupied with practical concerns, and he turns his intellectual powers to two main pursuits, Art and Philosophy. Art is the product of the free imagination, Philosophy that of the freed intellect. Between these there is no hard-and-fast distinction or separation, for in Art the imagination makes subsidiary use of the intellect, and in Philosophy the intellect frequently seeks the aid of the imagination. But they are different in their goal or purpose chiefly, for Art seeks to create the beautiful, whereas Philosophy seeks to apprehend the true.

Philosophy, as I understand it, is thus a natural activity of man which springs from the actual conditions of his being and which is intended to satisfy some abiding and permanent need of his nature. This need is theoretical, the need to know and understand himself and the world of which he is a part, and is different from other needs which are practical in character or spring from the free play of imagination.

If this be accepted, it follows that Philosophy cannot divorce itself from life, without risk of becoming a series of sterile formalisms, the indulgence in which becomes mere mental gymnastics. The most fruitful periods of philosophic thought have been those in which Philosophy has remained in intimate contact with life, as witness the great days of Greek Philosophy, whereas Philosophy has always fallen into disrepute wherever it has divorced itself from the real problems of life and devoted itself to artificial subtilities of the intellect, as in the scholas- ticism of Mediaeval Europe. Much of modern philosophic thought seems to me to be a species of barren formalism, which has no bearing whatsoever on the essential task of Philosophy, which is to reflect upon life and seek to guide and illumine it. I believe that Philosophy is more and more called upon to fulfil this purpose as traditional faiths decline and customary morality loses its hold on the new generation.

The foregoing remarks must not be interpreted as implying any Pragmatic or Humanistic standpoint in Philosophy. I believe that Philosophy is essentially theoretic activity. It is human need and human interest which set the problems which Philosophy must attempt to solve, but any consideration of the nature of the need or interest, and of what will most satisfy that need, has no bearing upon the actual solution of its problems. Philosophy begins in concrete experience, and must return to concrete experience in the character of guide or mentor, but in the actual solution of its problems it must remain unbiased by considerations of utility or subjective satisfaction.

I believe that experience is not only the starting-point of Philosophy, but in a certain sense it is also the criterion and touchstone of every Philosophy. By experience here and elsewhere I mean the actual concrete experience of some finite individual or subject of experience and primarily the philosopher's own and not some Absolute or Universal experience, to the assumption of which he may be led from an analysis and examination of his own experience or by some abstract process of logical construction. Even if such an absolute experience is posited by Philosophy, it is my contention that the starting- point for such an hypothesis is the philosopher's own experience, and the test and criterion of its validity is again his own immediate experience. For if such an hypothesis implies that something which is an actual experience of mine cannot really be what I experience it to be, but something totally different,

I contend that such an hypothesis is thereby finally condemned and declared unwarranted. Philosophy cannot legislate to reality, for its business is to examine and investigate the nature of reality, not to create it, out of some supposed imperative of Reason. I reject the Hegelian dictum that the Real is the Rational, if this dictum is interpreted to mean that by examining the supposed requirements of Reason we can arrive at any solution of the problem as to what reality actually is. Hegel calls his Metaphysical system Logic, implying thereby that it is an *a priori* system, built up through the sole force of Reason. My contention is that Logic supplies the skeleton into which any metaphysical system must be fitted, but that it cannot supply the material, the body of metaphysics, which experience alone can yield.

While I believe that my own experience supplies the raw material for my philosophical speculation and also acts as the criterion or test by which my philosophical constructions have to be finally judged, I do not for a moment believe that my experience is itself the sole Reality, or even that Reality itself can consist of nothing but experiences or psychical matters of fact. In other words, I am neither a subjective nor an objective idealist. I believe that Reality does not consist solely of my own experience, because my experience itself is sufficient warrant for the belief that there are other realities besides itself. Every experience that I have is related to some object other than itself, and in the absence of such another could not be what it is. If I am perceiving, or remembering, or desiring, or having an emotion, there is always something that I perceive, or remember, or desire, or have an emotion towards. My experiences are not self-contained or self-generated, but directed towards some object other than themselves, with which they are related by the subject-object relation. I believe that such a theory as that of Hume, which resolves all reality into a flux of immediate experiences, is totally false to experience itself, for every immediate experience contains a reference to something outside itself, in the absence of which the experience itself could not be what it is. What exactly that object or entity is with which

each concrete experience of mine brings me in contact, varies
with the nature of each individual experience, and it is the
business of Philosophy and scientific enquiry to examine and
explore the nature of those varied realities. But that such
extra immediate realities do exist is warranted by each and every
experience. The objects that I cognise, which stir me emotionally,
or towards which I strive or aspire, are not constituted by the
acts of my cognising, feeling or striving. For if this be denied,
then I can neither cognise nor feel, nor strive after, and my
experience cannot possess the character which it does, as a
matter of fact, actually possess. If I am perceiving a blue patch
of colour, then the analysis of my perceptual experience cannot
merely consist of the actual content of my act of awareness,
for in that case I would not be perceiving a blue patch of
colour, but my awareness of it, which is a totally different
thing. Further, I can never express the difference between my
perception of a blue patch of colour and a red patch of colour
merely in terms of awareness. The difference between those
two acts lies, not in the nature or character of the acts themselves but in the objects to which each is directed. If there are
no patches of blue and red colours, but merely my awareness
of them, then I can never have an experience of now perceiving
blue, now red, and now some other colour. What distinguishes
one act of perception from the other is not the mental processes
involved but the variety of objects to which they are directed.
Perception thus itself implies the existence of extra-immediate
entities or objects.

What I have attempted to demonstrate about perception
can equally be demonstrated with regard to other forms of
experience, but I will take specially the case of feeling, as it
is chiefly to this form of experience that self-sufficiency and
immediacy have generally been ascribed. For example, Bradley
and others who have admitted the duality of subject-object,
have urged that this is a peculiar defect of the finite consciousness,
and have in fact employed it as a ground for rejecting that
consciousness as a mere appearance and not an ultimate reality.
They have posited an Absolute consciousness in which the

distinction of subject and object has disappeared, and to which
they have ascribed a state of consciousness analogous to feeling
in ourselves, in which they contend that subjectivity or immediacy
is more patent, and in which the distinction of subject and object
is practically obliterated. I do not know what feeling as experienced by the Absolute may be like, but as experienced
by myself I am absolutely certain that it is invariably directed
towards an object, and in the absence of such an object it
simply could not exist. In the first place I would like to urge
that philosophical discussions about feeling are generally
directed towards some abstract feeling of pure pleasure or pure
pain, which it has not been my privilege to experience. All the
feelings that I experience are usually extremely complicated
and confused, and though they may have elements of pleasure
and pain mixed up in them, are never solely constituted by
what is called pure feeling tone. I prefer, therefore, to speak
of emotions rather than of feelings. The emotions I experience
are very varied in range, extending from the primitive instinctive
emotions of fear, anger, disgust and so on, to highly complex
and derivative emotions such as those which are generally
described as aesthetic, moral and religious emotions. In every
case, whether the feeling be primitive or derived, there is always
some object in relation to which I have that emotion, and in
the absence of which I could not continue to have that emotion.
If I am angry, it is always someone or something which has
made me angry, and if you could only convince me that such
a person or thing does not exist, my anger must of necessity
evaporate. If I could only believe that no person or circumstance
is obstructing the gratification of my wishes, the consummation
of my ambitions, anger would be a passion wholly unknown
to me. Similarly, if there was nothing besides my own immediate
consciousness, I could experience neither love nor hate, nor
aesthetic appreciation, nor moral indignation or fervour, nor
religious ecstasy and devotion. Such a consciousness would
indeed be an evaporation of experience itself, an absence of
consciousness, a state of nothingness, "a dreamless sleep and
a forgetting," which indeed I am told is the goal and ambition

of many a mystic especially in the East, but which at any rate I have never experienced, and which, if it does exist, must indeed be mute, unutterable, unponderable, and that of which Philosophy can have no cognisance. It is not for me to deny the existence of such obscure and abnormal experiences, whether generated artificially by the administration of certain drugs, or the practice of certain religious exercises and rites, or occurring spontaneously without external aid, but I would urge that unless such experiences can be brought under the scope of scientific psychology for investigation and explanation, they cannot be cited as evidence in support of any particular theory of the general nature of reality. Philosophy at the present moment can only take into account such experiences as are the common possession of ordinary humanity, and it is on the basis of such experiences alone that any rational or scientific theory of the world can be constructed. Experience then gives us sufficient warrant to escape from the coils of solipsism, or subjective idealism. On the basis of my experience I am entitled to believe that a world extraneous to my own consciousness exists, for at each point of my consciousness this larger world of external reality breaks in upon the chamber of my inner consciousness, disturbs and determines its flow, and it is towards this that my own emotions and strivings are constantly directed. What is the nature of this trans-subjective world, and in what manner the world of my own subjective experience is related to it, is the essential problem of Philosophy.

A little earlier in this paper I made two denials, firstly that reality consists solely of my own experience, and secondly that the world of external reality consists solely of other psychical matters of fact. It is to this second denial that I must now turn. No theory has been so generally held in Philosophy as the theory of Idealism, which holds that Reality is essentially spiritual in character, and that nothing but spirits and their experiences exist. Such Idealistic theories have been either singularistic, like those of Hegel, Bradley and others, or Pluralistic, such as that of Leibniz, while others seem to have adopted a midway position difficult to define, such as Lotze and Ward, who have attempted to build a bridge between Singularism and Pluralism. Into the various controversies between the different schools of Idealism I do not propose to enter, since what I am concerned to deny is the assumption which all schools of Idealism make in common, namely, that reality is mental, or psychical matter of fact and nothing which is not mental can ever be real. Arguments urged in support of this view in the past were generally directed against the doctrine of materialism as held by eighteenth-century mechanical science. These may be called negative arguments for Idealism. There are also certain positive arguments for Idealism which do not merely rely upon the alleged non-existence of matter, but also bring forward certain positive considerations in favour of the belief that nothing but mind can exist. Most Idealists, however, make use of both types of argument, and in what follows I shall make no hard-and-fast distinction between them. We may take the arguments used by Berkeley as typical of one school of Idealists. He urges that what I directly know in perception are merely sensations, and sensations being mental, I have no direct knowledge of any supposed physical reality which may be accepted as their cause. He admits that sensations are not spontaneous or self-caused, but holds that their cause cannot be a non-mental material substance which Locke had described as a "We know not what," but must also be mental, viz., ideas in the mind of God. He does not deny an objective world order but holds that this order and arrangement is nothing, but the ideas which God is presenting to finite minds. But Berkeley's argument if strictly enforced leads to Hume's Phenomenalism and not to his own pan-psychism. It starts with a fundamentally wrong analysis of perception, namely that any act of perception is to be simply analysed into a mental content and implies no reference to an object external to itself. It is true that Berkeley contradicts himself when he proceeds to posit an external cause or source of sensations, even though he regards this cause to be mental. Against his view I can only urge that when I perceive a blue patch of colour, what I am perceiving is a patch of blue colour, and that this is quite different from my act of perceiving, and also totally different

D

from any act of perception on the part of any other being. I do not perceive, as Berkeley seems to imply, an idea of a blue patch of colour in the mind of God. I have ideas myself, and I am sometimes aware that other people also have certain ideas. But neither my own ideas nor those of other people when known to me appear as "this patch of colour" which I am now seeing, "this hard surface" I am now touching, and so on. It is conceivable that a Being such as God exists, it is conceivable, further, that God has experiences similar to my own, but if God perceives the world, I would contend, as I did in the case of my own experiences, that God could only do so if the world as a fact extraneous to his act of awareness of it actually existed. If the world of nature is identified with God's act of perceiving it, then it follows that there is no world which he can perceive, and consequently there cannot even be the act of perceiving it, and so God's mind is empty, which contradicts the assumption from which we began. Berkeley's argument, therefore, fails to prove that the world of nature which I perceive is really mental. Certain other philosophers, such as Hegel, and, following him, Bradley, Taylor and others, have urged that Reality must be mental or spiritual, because the very concept of matter, space, time and other categories in terms of which we try to interpret an extra-mental reality are self-contradictory. These contentions seem to me unconvincing, because not only are the contradictions pointed out by these philosophers largely of their own invention, but what is more, they condemn with equal emphasis the categories in terms of which we seek to interpret mental and spiritual phenomena in so far as they come within the range of our own experience. Bradley, for example, by pointing out contradictions in our concept of time, of discursive reasoning, of self and not-self, good and evil, and so on, arrives at the conclusion that finite experience and the finite self also are mere appearances. I consider, therefore, that in his Philosophy Matter and Mind are really on a par, and the Absolute which he posits is no more a spiritual or psychical Being than he is a chunk of boundless space. I have already urged that I am not prepared to accept any such hypothesis which constrains me to regard my own experience as an illusion and to substitute in its place some supposed reality for which I can find no warrant in my experience. In the present connection I would only urge that Absolute Idealism is not a Pan-Psychical theory but one which is indifferent alike to Materialism and Idealism, and really more akin to what Mr. Russell calls Neutral Monism.

My denial of Idealism must not be interpreted as implying any adherence to the opposed doctrine of materialism. I believe that experience reveals to me in Perception that external nature exists, but that the very variety and richness of this experience also implies a plurality of attributes in the objects of nature, which cannot be reduced either to my own ideas or to those of some other mind or minds, nor merely to qualitatively simple atoms behaving in accordance with simple mechanical laws. The determination of the exact properties and laws of external nature I believe is the task of Physical Science, and Philosophy has no direct concern with it. Philosophy is concerned with Physical Science only in the sense in which it is concerned with each and every science. This concern is twofold: firstly in a formal respect, since every science must conform to certain logical standards, which standards are arrived at after philosophical analysis of the concepts and categories employed by a science, and secondly in a more material respect, since Philosophy must interpret the generalisations and conclusions of every science in terms of the actual experience from which their scientific investigation first originates. Each phase of my concrete experience, therefore, gives rise to certain scientific as well as to certain philosophical problems. In every phase of my experience I am in contact with some reality extraneous to my own experience, and it is the business of the several sciences to investigate in detail the nature of these realities, and the business of Philosophy to interpret the conclusions of each individual science, as well as to form a synthesis of the conclusions of the different sciences so as to form some consistent and harmonious theory of my experience as a whole. The philosophy of Nature, therefore, is really the Philosophy of Physical Science, and can only be built upon the body of detailed knowledge which physical

science is accumulating from day to day. Since scientific knowledge is itself progressive and unstable, any Philosophy of Nature
which we build upon this foundation must itself be tentative
and capable of adjustment to new discoveries.

What I have said with regard to external nature applies
equally to the world of Mind. Just as perceptual experience
reveals that there exists a world of nature extraneous to
itself, so do I know through experience that other selves
similar to my own exist, influence my experiences, and in turn
are influenced by what I experience. The knowledge of other
minds has involved Philosophy in difficulties even greater than
those connected with external nature. It has been urged that
if I know nature at best at second-hand, my knowledge of
other minds is still more remote, for I know them only through
their bodies, which are part of the already doubtful world of
external reality. The problem has become still more complicated
by difficulties with regard to the relation of body and mind,
for it has been urged that since body and mind are totally
divergent from each other, and interaction between them
inconceivable, it is still more impossible that the knowledge of
my neighbour's body could convey to me any knowledge with
regard to his mind. I believe, however, that all those difficulties
are of the philosopher's own making.

I will begin by admitting that so far as my experience goes,
my knowledge of other minds is dependent upon knowledge of
their bodies. Your bodies are the media through which I know
that you are here, that you are listening to me, approving or
disapproving of what I say. It is true that if there was a remitting
apparatus here, others whose bodies I cannot see could be
"listening in" to what I am saying. But in this case also the
communication of one mind with another is through some
bodily organ or other, and through the aid of some external
agents. It is my lips which utter my thoughts, the air waves
which communicate the movement to the transmitting and
receiving apparatus, and the listener's ears which in the last
resort convey my thoughts to his mind. It has been urged that
there are instances in which one mind can communicate with

another without the intervention of any bodily media, such as is claimed in telepathy or alleged communications received from disembodied spirits. Such phenomena, however, are admittedly outside the range of normal everyday experience, and still await the verdict of scientific psychology. At any rate, they do not afford any solution of our ordinary knowledge of other selves, for we all claim to possess such knowledge, while we do not lay any claim to telepathic or other forms of supernatural contacts with living or departed spirits. If we believe that we know other minds we must admit that we know them through our own and their bodies and consequently that minds can act upon bodies and vice versa. I believe, therefore, that the difficulties urged against interaction of body and mind are imaginary, and result from false abstractions with regard to the nature of body and of mind, and a misconception with regard to what is really meant by interaction in this connection. I contend that we ought to make our start from the fact of inter-action of body and mind and so proceed to conceive of body and of mind, as to permit of such interaction. In other words, the experience of body and mind relation is the datum from which we should start and proceed to form our notions of the living body and the human mind. Why philosophers have found the Body-Mind problem insoluble, is because they have started from an abstract conception of what physical bodies are and what mind is, and have so defined each of them, that their interaction is made impossible. At all grades of its manifestation, mind so far as it comes within human ken, be it the mind of a frog or that of a philosopher, seems to be embodied, and it is only through the medium of its body that it can communicate with other minds or receive communications from them.

I believe that the hypothesis of Emergent Evolution does enable us to approach the problem of body-mind interaction in a more hopeful attitude than under the guidance of the old-fashioned theories of materialism or Idealism. If we conceive of nature as a procession of events beginning with simple elements, we can conceive how, at different stages of nature's evolution, new characteristics should emerge in complex wholes which were not discernible nor predictable from a mere consideration of the simple elements, of which such wholes are composed. We can then regard life as an *emergent* property of inorganic nature and mind as an *emergent* property of organic nature.

Such a view of nature is fully in harmony with the teachings of modern Physics, which no longer conceives of matter as inert homogeneous stuff distributed at various points in space, possessing indestructible properties, to which time can bring neither dissolution nor change. In place of this static world, modern science conceives of nature as a realm of ceaseless activity, with no passive substratum, composed of self-identical bits of matter. Instead of a space which is empty, and time which is irrelevant, it regards nature as a progression of events in space-time, which may be isolated for purposes of observation and abstraction, but which are woven together in an indissoluble stream pressing forward to eternity. Science merely takes cross sections of this eternal stream of moving events, isolating a set of agitations which betray a superficial stability and in the observation of which it can ignore the influence exerted upon them by environmental conditions.

Emergence of new attributes is a common feature of our everyday experience. The butterfly emerges from the cocoon, the completed house from the bricks and mortar, the finished symphony from the conflicts and struggles of the composer's soul. Here is indeed the creative evolution of Bergson, but not conceived as a process of pure change somehow entangled in an illusory matter, but more after the pattern of Aristotle where form is something which emerges in matter, and without matter would remain unrealised and merely potential.

I use the concept of *emergence* as descriptive rather than explanatory. That new and unpredictable properties emerge in nature through the intermingling of previously known elements is a conclusion forced upon us by the facts observed in experience. But as to why such properties as *life* and *mind* should emerge in the evolutionary progression of nature, we are not in a position to explain. It is true that Lloyd Morgan and others who have introduced the conception of Emergence and emphasised the creative element in nature have used it as an argument for the teleological character of the Universe as a whole, and have urged that such a Universe must necessarily imply the existence of a Creator who is himself outside the evolutionary process, but whose purpose the Universe embodies. Such a conclusion seems to me very inadequately grounded on the extremely narrow range of phenomena actually observed, and further to gloss over fundamental difficulties inherent in the very conception of a timeless reality, which is yet indissolubly bound up with the spatio-temporal order. Given the Deity eternal and immutable, there seems no reason why the world of finite experience should exist at all. The inevitable consequence of such an assumption is the rejection of my own immediate experience as illusory, thus destroying the very foundation on which all philosophical construction must necessarily rest. The concept of Emergence, while it does not close the possibility of some form of Theism as a possible hypothesis of the origin of the Universe, does not logically imply any Theistic assumptions, and in any case would involve a complete recasting of Theological Dogma, just as it requires a modification of the categories of Physics and Psychology.

In what manner the theory of Emergent Evolution requires us to modify our previous notions of space, time, matter, mind and evolution are problems of supreme importance which cannot be touched upon here. I give preference to it only because, unlike its alternatives, it does not require me to reject the verdict of my experience, but merely to modify the concepts in terms of which I have been wont to explain that experience.

The detailed study of Mind is the subject matter of Psychology, just as the detailed study of nature is the subject of Physical Science. Psychology I regard as an independent science, but one which gives rise to philosophical problems similar to those of other sciences. But Psychology is in a sense more intimately connected with Philosophy, since its subject matter is that experience which is also the starting-point of philosophical reflection and the criterion of philosophical construction. But Psychology cannot take the place of Philosophy, for it deals

merely with the mental life of the individual, while experience
implies realities beyond and outside that experience and of
which Philosophy must take note.

I turn now to a third aspect of the world of my experience,
the aspect of value. My experience not only convinces me that
there is an external nature which I contemplate, and other
selves with whom I communicate, but I also *approve* or *disapprove*
of things which I experience, persons whom I know, acts which
I perform, or observe others performing. This attitude of
appraisement is quite distinct from the attitude of contemplation
or cognitive awareness. When I ask does "X" exist, I am asking
a question which is quite different from the question, ought
"X" to be, or is "X" good or bad. The attributes of value in
terms of which I appraise things are moral as well as aesthetic.
I attribute goodness to certain things, badness to others, beauty
to certain things, ugliness to others. With regard to these value
judgments of mine, there are two points which I wish to make
clear from the very beginning. In the first place I do not believe
that value is in any way derivative from existence. That is,
I do not believe that if a thing really exists it follows from the
fact of its existence that it is good or beautiful. Conversely,
I also believe that existence is not derivative from value. If I
hold that something is good, and rightly hold that it is so, it
does not follow from this that therefore that thing necessarily
exists. If I believe that "X" exists, it does not follow from this
that "X" is good. If on the other hand I believe that "X" is
good, it does not follow from this that "X" necessarily exists.
To take a concrete illustration, Mill believed that all men do
as a matter of fact always desire pleasure. He proceeded to
infer from this that therefore all men ought to desire pleasure.
But because all men do actually desire pleasure, it does not
follow that they ought to do so. I can admit the first part of
Mill's so-called proof of Hedonism, while totally denying his
conclusion. Following Professor G. E. Moore, we may call this
kind of fallacy the Naturalistic Fallacy. But many philosophers
have committed an opposite fallacy, which is to infer existence
from goodness. That is, they have tried to show that such and

such a conclusion about reality is very good if true, and have proceeded to assume that therefore reality must actually be so, or that such and such a conclusion about reality is extremely bad, and must therefore be false. Thus it has been urged that if human life does not survive after death, the world would be a very bad place, and therefore we are entitled to believe that human life does survive after death.

The attempt to ground existential conclusions in value premises is parallel with the Naturalistic Fallacy and might be called the Ethical Fallacy. Just as moralists have often committed the Naturalistic Fallacy, so have metaphysicians frequently committed the ethical fallacy.

The second point which I wish to make clear is that when I attribute goodness or beauty to anything, the goodness or beauty is not something in my mind, but in the object which I judge to be good or beautiful. That is, I believe that value is an objective and not a subjective property. Many philosophers have held that value is subjective, in the mind of the person who makes the judgment and not in the things which he values. Many kinds of arguments have been used by philosophers in support of this view, but they have chiefly relied upon the variability of Ethical and Aesthetic standards. That a Zulu's idea of what ought to be done or not done, what ought to be admired or not admired, is very different from that of civilised man, is too obvious to be denied. But even in the same age and clime, and what is more, very often with the same individual, judgments of taste and approval show considerable variations. But this variability of value judgments does not prove that value is merely a subjective attitude, and connotes no objective properties in things.

It is admitted that man's Ethical and Aesthetic consciousness undergoes a process of evolution, just as his sensory consciousness has been gradually evolved through his prehuman ancestors. But just as the colours I see, the sounds I hear, are not merely mental contents, but objects apprehended by me, so also the goodness I approve of, or the beauty I admire, are not mere subjective feelings, but objective realities. To reduce value to

D*

a subjective state or feeling of the mind is to contend that valuation is an illusion, and that there is no sense in saying that Jesus Christ was a better man than Nero, or the Taj Mahal of Agra more beautiful than the latest excrescence of commercialised architecture.

Such a theory seems to me wholly false to that individual experience which I hold to be the starting-point and the criterion of all philosophising.

It has been urged that value is something which belongs to consciousness alone, and nothing but some experience, or person as the subject of experiences, can in the last resort be judged to be good or bad. Obviously such a theory cannot apply to beauty, for beauty is frequently ascribed to corporeal things, such as pictures, statues and other objects of art. It is, therefore, goodness alone which it is intended to confine to sentient experience. The question is to some extent purely academic, for I believe that the things at any rate of great intrinsic value are all connected with experience or are the subjects of experience, but at the same time I hold that the mind is itself embodied, and if the corporeal aspect of mind is divorced from it, I believe that the value of such wholes would greatly diminish if it did not altogether disappear. For example, I believe that love between persons is one of the greatest goods, but all the persons whom I love have a body, and I cannot myself differentiate between my love for their bodies and my love for their spiritual personalities. That I should love a person's spiritual being and at the same time hate or be indifferent to that person's physical being seems to me an impossibility.

The analysis and examination of men's evaluating experiences I regard as the subject matter of the sciences of Ethics and Aesthetics, and conceive the relation of these sciences with Philosophy on lines analogous to those I have already indicated with regard to the other sciences.

I will conclude with a brief reference to man's religious experience. By religion I mean the attitude which the individual adopts with regard to the ultimate reality of which he conceives himself to be a part, and with which he is related in all aspects of his being, be they cognitive, conative or affective. The object of Philosophy and of religion is the same, but whereas Philosophy is merely my theory of Reality, Religion is the total response of my whole personality towards this same reality.

This definition would include every positive religion, for all religions have a credal element, that is, consist of dogmas with regard to the nature of reality, inculcate an emotional attitude towards that ultimate reality, and evoke a particular conative attitude in relation to it. It would include also the attitude of many of those who while not adhering to any positive religion, yet claim that they have a religious life of their own. It would, however, exclude all people whose religion merely consists of conformity to certain traditional ritual and social practices, but whose thoughts, feelings and emotions are in no way deeply affected by such observances.

There are many who believe that religion can provide a short cut to reality which enables us to dispense with the devious and uphill path to which Philosophy points. In religion, it is claimed, we have an intuitive and immediate knowledge of that ultimate reality which Philosophy seeks. Such a claim may rest either on a direct experience of the protagonist of this view, or a claim on behalf of a religious leader or founder, to whom such truths are said to be revealed. I do not myself believe in the validity of such claims. I admit the place of intuition in my apprehensions of reality. But intuition is the starting-point for philosophical reflection, not its culminating and completing point. Perceptual experience is thus an intuition of external reality, and communication between minds an intuition of other selves. But such intuitions need to be analysed by the respective sciences of Physics and Psychology, and then interpreted by Philosophy before man's theoretic interest in the external world or in the world of mind can be satisfied. So also with religious intuitions. That there are specifically religious experiences which are genuine, must be admitted by all unbiased observers, but that the interpretation placed upon those experiences by the person experiencing them is necessarily valid is an extravagant claim which every adherent of any particular religion himself denies to all his rivals. I place religious experience on a par with the other aspects of human experience, so far as it claims to bring me knowledge of a reality extraneous to itself. It supplies the raw material of scientific and philosophical knowledge, but cannot dispense with their aid, any more than perception can dispense with the aid of physical science or a philosophy of nature. Religious experience, according to my view, is thus a fit subject for psychological study and investigation, after which the findings of the psychology of religion must be fitted into our synthetic view of reality as a whole, as in the case of the other sciences.

What then is the religious attitude I can maintain consistently with the Philosophy I have been advocating? Taking my start from my own experience, I have contended that experience brings me in contact with three phases of objective reality, which I have called external Nature, other Minds and Values. I have urged that our knowledge of these is the problem of special sciences, which themselves are incomplete, and that their interpretation and synthesis, which is the special task of Philosophy, must therefore itself be tentative and progressive. Our Philosophy must therefore be lacking in finality, for while rejecting certain theories as most decidedly irreconcilable with the dicta of experience, it can only express a provisional preference in favour of others which seem more in conformity with that experience. Thus we cannot offer any explanation of the origin, destiny and future of our own lives, or of that of the Universe of which we are a part. Our knowledge is everywhere incomplete, and both the world of inner experience, as well as the world of external nature, are like great books, of which humanity has as yet only scanned a few scattered pages somewhere in the middle. The cardinal dogma of our religion must therefore be a suspense of judgment on final issues, an ardent search for the advancement of that little knowledge of the great unknown which we already possess, and a determination to hold fast to whatever of truth we have perceived, whatever of goodness or of beauty our souls have grasped. Ours is but a little day, for out of the great unknown we come, and into a still vaster unknown we pass away. But in our little fitful day the gods have given us the gift of laughter, of human friendship, and the vision of beauty both in Nature and in Art. What if we ourselves are mortal, our laughter but the prelude of tears, love's brief transport the herald of approaching doom, and beauty but the echo of a dying song? Shall we refuse the gifts which the gods bring us, for brief must be the time in which we can enjoy them and mortality the fate of all we prize! Shall not our own mortality teach us to treasure all the more the good things that life brings us, and the very niggardliness of fortune enhance the value of its gifts? And if sorrow, or grief, or loss be our portion, these also we shall bear with what of fortitude we can summon, for these also are but transitory, and in any case rebellion and false expectation will but enhance our own afflictions. And if we have wooed with any ardour that coy maid, Philosophy, she also will come to our aid, and by teaching us to lose the personal in the impersonal pursuit of remoter ends, help us to preserve that sanity and forbearance, in the face of good fortune or ill fortune alike, which has been from times immemorial her reward to her devotees.

ON THE PERTINENCE OF PHILOSOPHY

by ANANDA K. COOMARASWAMY

BORN 1877, in Ceylon, of an English mother and Hindu father (the late Sir Muthu Coomaraswamy), educated in England, graduated at London University (D.Sc. in botany and geology), Fellow of University College, London; was Director of the Mineralogical Survey of Ceylon, 1903–6, and for the last seventeen years a member of the staff of the Museum of Fine Arts, Boston, being now "Fellow for Research in Indian, Persian and Muhammadan Art," and also a Vice-President of the India Society, London, the Indian Society of Oriental Art, Calcutta, and of the American Oriental Society, U.S.A., and a correspondent of the Archaeological Survey of India.

ON THE PERTINENCE OF PHILOSOPHY

"Wisdom uncreate, the same now as it ever was, and the same to be for evermore."—St. Augustine, *Confessions*, ix. 10.

"Primordial and present Witness."—Prakāśânanda, *Siddhântamuktâvali*, 44.

I. DEFINITION AND STATUS OF PHILOSOPHY, OR WISDOM

To discuss the "problems of philosophy" presupposes a definition of "philosophy." It will not be contested that "philosophy" implies rather the love of wisdom than the love of knowledge, nor secondarily that from the "love of wisdom," philosophy has come by a natural transition to mean the doctrine of those who love wisdom and are called philosophers.[1]

Now knowledge as such is not the mere report of the senses (the reflection of anything in the retinal mirror may be perfect, in an animal or idiot, and yet is not knowledge), nor the mere act of recognition (names being merely a means of alluding to the aforesaid reports), but is an abstraction from these reports, in which abstraction the names of the things are used as convenient substitutes for the things themselves. Knowledge is not then of individual presentations, but of types of presentation; in other words, of things in their intelligible aspect, i.e. of the being that things have in the mind of the knower, as principles, genera and species. In so far as knowledge is directed to the attainment of ends it is called practical; in so far as it remains in the knower, theoretical or speculative. Finally, we cannot say that a man knows wisely, but that he knows well; wisdom takes knowledge for granted and governs the movement of the will with respect to things known; or we may say that wisdom is the criterion of value, according to which a decision is made to act or not to act in any given case or universally. Which will apply not merely to external acts, but also to contemplative or theoretical acts.

Philosophy, accordingly, is a wisdom about knowledge, a

[1] It is not pretended to lay down a final definition of philosophy.

correction du savoir-penser. In general, philosophy (2)[1] has been held to embrace what we have referred to above as theoretical or speculative knowledge, for example, logic, ethics, psychology, aesthetic, theology, ontology; and in this sense the problems of philosophy are evidently those of rationalisation, the purpose of philosophy being so to correlate the data of empirical experience as to "make sense" of them, which is accomplished for the most part by a reduction of particulars to universals (deduction). And thus defined, the function of philosophy contrasts with that of practical science, of which the proper function is that of predicting the particular from the universal (induction). Beyond this, however, philosophy (1) has been held to mean a wisdom not so much about particular kinds of thought, as a wisdom about thinking, and an analysis of what it means to think, and an enquiry as to what may be the nature of the ultimate reference of thought. In this sense the problems of philosophy are with respect to the ultimate nature of reality, actuality or experience; meaning by reality whatever is in act and not merely potential. We may ask, for example, what *are* truth, goodness and beauty (considered as concepts abstracted from experience), or we may ask whether these or any other concepts abstracted from experience have actually any being of their own; which is the matter in debate as between nominalists on the one hand and realists, or idealists, on the other.[2] It may be noted that, since in all these applications philosophy means "wisdom," if or when we speak of philosophies in the plural, we shall mean not different kinds of wisdom, but wisdom with respect to different kinds of things. The wisdom may be more or less, but still one and the same order of wisdom.

[1] Our numbering of the philosophies in inverse order as (2) and (1) is because Aristotle's First Philosophy, viz. Metaphysics, is actually prior in logical order of thought, which proceeds from within outwards.

[2] This is, for example, the matter in debate as between Buddhist and Brahmanical philosophers. For the nominalist, the ultimate forms, ideas, images or reasons are merely names of the counters of thought and valid only as means of communication; for the realist (idealist) the ultimate forms are "realities" dependent upon and inherent in being, i.e. real in their being and nominal only in the sense "only logically distinguishable."

As to this order, if knowledge is by abstraction, and wisdom about knowledge, it follows that this wisdom, pertaining to things known or knowable, and attained by a process of reasoning or dialectic from experimental data, and neither being nor claiming to be a revealed or gnostic doctrine, in no way transcends thought, but is rather the best kind of thought, or, let us say, the truest science. It is, indeed, an excellent wisdom, and assuming a good will, one of great value to man.[1] But let us not forget that because of its experimental, that is to say statistical basis, and even supposing an infallible operation of the reason such as may be granted to mathematics, this wisdom can never establish absolute certainties, and can predict only with very great probability of success; the "laws" of science, however useful, do nothing more than resume past experience. Furthermore, philosophy in the second of the above senses, or human wisdom about things known or knowable, must be systematic, since it is required by hypothesis that its perfection will consist in an accounting for everything, in a perfect fitting together of all the parts of the puzzle to make one logical whole; and the system must be a *closed* system, one namely limited to the field of time and space, cause and effect, for it is by hypothesis about knowable and determinate things, all of which are presented to the cognitive faculty in the guise of effects, for which causes are sought.[2] For example, space being of indefinite and not infinite extent,[3] the wisdom about determinate things cannot have any application to whatever "reality" there may

---

[1] Common sense is an admirable thing, as is also instinct, but neither of these is the same as reason, nor the same as the wisdom that is not about human affairs, but "speculative," i.e. known in the mirror of the pure intellect.

[2] When a cause is discovered, this is called an explanation. But each cause was once an effect, and so on indefinitely, so that our picture of reality takes the form of a series of causes extending backward into the past, and of effects expected in the future, but we have no empirical experience of a now, nor can we explain empirically how causes produce effects, the assumption *post hoc propter hoc* being always an act of faith.

[3] As is very elegantly demonstrated by St. Thomas, *Sum. Theol.*, i, q. 7, a. 3, cf. q. 14, a. 12, *ad*. 3; his "relatively infinite" being our "indefinite" (*ananta*), incalculable (*asaṁkhya*) but not placeless (*adeśa*) nor wholly timeless (*akāla*).

or may not belong to non-spatial, or immaterial, modes, or similarly, to a non-temporal mode, for if there be a "now," we have no sensible experience of any such thing, nor can we conceive it in terms of logic. If it were attempted by means of the human wisdom to overstep the natural limits of its operation, the most that could be said would be that the reference "indefinite magnitude" (mathematical infinity) presents a certain analogy to the reference "essential infinity" as postulated in religion and metaphysics, but nothing could be affirmed or denied with respect to the "isness" (esse) of this infinite in essence.

If the human wisdom, depending upon itself alone ("rationalism"), proposes a religion, this will be what is called a "natural religion," having for its deity that referent of which the operation is seen everywhere, and yet is most refractory to analysis, viz. "life" or "energy." And this natural religion will be a pantheism or monism, postulating a soul (*anima*, "animation") of the universe, everywhere known by its effects perceptible in the movements of things; amongst which things any distinction of animate and inanimate will be out of place, inasmuch as animation can be defined rationally only as "that which is expressed in, or is the cause of, motion." Or if not a pantheism, then a polytheism or pluralism in which a variety of animations ("forces") is postulated as underlying and "explaining" a corresponding variety of motions.[1] But nothing can be affirmed or denied as regards the proposition that such animation or animations may be merely determinate and contingent aspects of a "reality" indeterminate in itself. Expressed more technically, pantheism and polytheism are essentially profane conceptions, and if recognisable in a given religious or metaphysical doctrine, are there interpolations of the reason, not essential to the religious or metaphysical doctrine in itself.[2]

[1] Science differs from animism only in this respect, that while science assumes forces in the sense of blind wills, animism (which is also a kind of philosophy) personifies these forces and endows them with a free will.

[2] Pantheism is more commonly predicated of a given doctrine merely by imputation, either with unconsciously dishonest intention or by customary usage uncritically perpetuated. In every case the observer

On the other hand, the human wisdom, not relying on itself alone, may be applied to a partial, viz. analogical, exposition of the religious or metaphysical wisdoms, these being taken as prior to itself. For although the two wisdoms (philosophy (2) and philosophy (1)) are different in kind, there can be a formal coincidence, and in this sense what is called a "reconciliation of science and religion." Each is then dependent on the other, although in different ways; the sciences depending on revealed truth for their formal correction, and revealed truth relying upon the sciences for its demonstration by analogy, "not as though it stood in need of them, but only to make its teaching clearer."

In either case, the final end of human wisdom is a good or happiness that shall accrue either to the philosopher himself, or to his neighbours, or to humanity at large, but necessarily in terms of material well-being. The kind of good envisaged may or may not be a moral good.[1] For example, if we assume a good will, i.e. a natural sense of justice, the natural religion will be expressed in ethics in a sanction of such laws of conduct as most conduce to the common good, and he may be admired who sacrifices even life for the sake of this. In aesthetic (art being *circa factibilia*) the natural religion, given a good will, will justify the manufacture of such goods as are apt for human well-being, whether as physical necessities or as sources of sensible pleasure. All this belongs to "humanism" and is very far from despicable. But in case there is not a good will, the natural religion may equally be employed to justify the proposition "might is right" or "devil take the hindmost," and in manufacture the production of goods either by methods which are injurious to the common good, or which in themselves are immediately adapted to ends injurious to the common good; as in the cases of child-labour and the manufacture of poison gas.

presumed to be impartial should consider the doctrine itself, and not what is said of it by hostile critics. On the general impropriety of the term "pantheism" in connection with the Vedānta, see Lacombe, Avant-propos to Grousset, *Les Philosophies Indiennes*, p. xiv, note 1, and Whitby, Preface to Guénon, *Man and his Becoming*, p. ix.

[1] St. Thomas, *Sum. Theol.* i, q. 1, a. 6, *ad.* 2.

Revealed truth, on the contrary, demands a good will *a priori*, adding that the aid of the rational philosophy, as science or art, is required in order that the good will may be made effective.[1]

There is then another kind of philosophy (1), viz. that to which we have alluded as "revealed truth," which though it covers the whole ground of philosophy (2), does so in another way, while beyond this it treats confidently of "realities" which may indeed be immanent in time and space tissue, and are not wholly incapable of rational demonstration, but are nevertheless said to be transcendent with respect to this tissue, i.e. by no means wholly contained within it nor given by it, nor wholly amenable to demonstration. The First Philosophy, for example, affirms the actuality of a "now" independent of the flux of time; while experience is only of a past and future. Again, the procedure of the First Philosophy is no longer in the first place deductive and secondarily inductive, but inductive from first to last, its logic proceeding invariably from the transcendental to the universal, and thence as before to the particular. This First Philosophy, indeed, taking for granted the principle "as above, so below" and vice-versa,[2] is able to find in every microcosmic fact the trace or symbol of a macrocosmic actuality, and accordingly resorts to "proof" by analogy; but this apparently deductive procedure is here employed by way of demonstration, and not by way of proof, where logical proof is out of the question, and its place is taken either by faith (Augustine's *credo ut intelligam*) or by the evidence of immediate experience (*alaukika-pratyakṣa*).[3]

---

[1] Prudence is defined as *recta ratio agibilium*, art as *recta ratio factibilium*.

[2] E.g. *Aitareya Brāhmaṇa*, viii. 2.

[3] "Metaphysics can dispute with one who denies its principles, if only the opponent will make some concession; but if he concede nothing, it can have no dispute with him. . . . If our opponent believes nothing of divine revelation, there is no longer any means of proving the articles of faith by reasoning" (St. Thomas, *Sum. Theol.*, i, q. 1, a. 8 c.); and *ib.*, q. 46, a. 2: "The articles of faith cannot be proved demonstratively."

Similarly in India it is repeatedly and explicitly asserted that the truth of Vedic doctrine cannot be demonstrated but only experienced. *"By what* should one know the Knower of knowing" (*Bṛhadāraṇyaka Up.*, iv. 5. 15).

Our first problem in connection with the highest wisdom, considered as a doctrine known by revelation (whether through ear or symbolic transmission), consistent but unsystematic, and intelligible in itself although it treats in part of unintelligible things, is to distinguish without dividing religion from metaphysics, philosophy (2) from philosophy (1). This is a distinction without a difference, like that of attribute from essence, and yet a distinction of fundamental importance if we are to grasp the true meaning of any given spiritual act.

We proceed therefore first to emphasise the distinctions that can be drawn as between religion and metaphysics with respect to a wisdom that is one in itself and in any case primarily directed to immaterial, or rationally speaking, "unreal" things.[1] Broadly speaking, the distinction is that of Christianity from Gnosticism, Sunnī from Shi'a doctrine, Rāmânuja from Śaṁkara, of the will from the intellect, participation (*bhakti*) from gnosis (*jñāna*), or knowledge-of (*avidyā*) from knowledge-as (*vidyā*). As regards the Way, the distinction is one of consecration from initiation, and of passive from active integration; and as regards the End, of assimilation (*tadākāratā*) from identification (*tadbhāva*). Religion requires of its adherents to be perfected; metaphysics that they realise their own perfection that has never been infringed (even Satan is still virtually Lucifer, being fallen in grace and not in nature). Sin, from the standpoint of religion, is moral; from that of metaphysics, intellectual (mortal sin in metaphysics being a conviction or assertion of independent self-subsistence, as in Satan's case, or envy of the spiritual attainments of others, as in Indra's).

Religion, in general, proceeds from the being in act (*kāryâvasthā*) of the First Principle, without regard to its being in potentiality (*kāraṇâvasthā*);[2] while metaphysics treats of the Supreme

---

[1] Throughout the present essay it is assumed that sensibility means the perception of things by the senses, not a cognition but a reaction; reason, the activity of the intelligence with respect to the causal series of accidents, sometimes called the chain of fate, or in other words an intelligence with respect to things phenomenally known in time and space and called "material"; and intellect, the habit of first principles.

[2] Thus *Chāndogya Up.*, vi. 2. 1 asserts a religious point of view, as distinct from the metaphysical point of view that prevails in the Upaniṣads

Identity as an indisseverable unity of potentiality and act, darkness and light, holding that these can also and must also be considered apart when we attempt to understand their operation in identity in It or Him. And so religion assumes an aspect of duality,[1] viz. when it postulates a "primary matter," "potentiality" or "non-being" far removed from the actuality of God, and does not take account of the principal presence of this "primary matter" in, or rather "of" the First, as its "nature."[2]

Religions may and must be many, each being an "arrangement of God," and stylistically differentiated, inasmuch as the thing known can only be in the knower according to the mode of the knower, and hence as we say in India, "He takes the forms that are imagined by His worshippers," or as Eckhart expresses it, "I am the cause that God is God."[3] And this is why religious beliefs, as much as they have united men, have also divided men against each other, as Christian or heathen, orthodox or heretical.[4] So that if we are to consider what may be the most

generally, e.g. *Taittirīya Up.*, ii. 7. Christian philosophy maintains that God is "wholly in act." Metaphysics concurs in the definition of perfection as a realisation of all the possibilities of being, but would rather say of God that "He does not proceed from potentiality to act" than that He is without potentiality.

[1] Duality, as of "spirit and matter," "act and potentiality," "form and substance," "good and evil." This is avoided in Christianity metaphysically, when it is shown that evil is not a self-subsistent nature, but merely a privation, and can be known to the First Intellect only as a goodness or perfection *in potentia*. It is avoided in Sūfī metaphysic by considering good and evil as merely reflections in time and space of His essential attributes of Mercy and Majesty.

[2] "Matter" here must not be confused with the "solid matter" of everyday parlance; in Christian philosophy, "primary matter" is precisely that "nothing" with respect to which it is said *ex nihilo fit*. Such "matter" is said to be "insatiable for form," and the same is implied when in the *Jaiminīya Up. Brāhmaṇa*, i. 56, it is said that "In the beginning, the woman (= Urvaśī, Apsaras) went about in the flood seeking a master" (*icchantī salile patim*).

[3] The physical analogy is represented in the assertion of the anthropologist that "God is man-made"; a proposition perfectly valid within the conditions of its own level of reference.

[4] That is mainly, of course, in Europe from the thirteenth century onwards. In Hinduism, a man is regarded as a true teacher who gives to any individual a better access to that individual's *own* scriptures; for

urgent *practical* problem to be resolved by the philosopher, we can only answer that this is to be recognised in a control and revision of the principles of comparative religion, the true end of which science, judged by the best wisdom (and judgment is the proper function of applied wisdom), should be to demonstrate the common metaphysical basis of all religions and that diverse cultures are fundamentally related to one another as being the dialects of a common spiritual and intellectual language; for whoever recognises this, will no longer wish to assert that "My religion is best," but only that it is the "best for me."[1] In other words, the purpose of religious controversy should be, not to "convert" the opponent, but to persuade him that his religion is essentially the same as our own. To cite a case in point, it is not long since we received a communication from a Catholic friend in which he said "I've been ashamed for years at the superficiality and cheapness of my attempt to state a difference between Christians and Hindus." It is noteworthy that a pronouncement such as this will assuredly strike a majority of European readers with a sense of horror. We recognise in fact that religious controversy has still generally in view to convince the opponent of error rather than of correctness in our

"the path men take from every side is Mine" (*Bhagavad Gītā*, iv. 11). Clement of Alexandria allows that "There was always a natural manifestation of the one Almighty God amongst all right-thinking men" (*Misc.*, bk. v); Eckhart says almost in the words of the *Bhagavad Gītā*, cited above, "In whatever way you find God best, that way pursue," Dante will not exclude all the pagan philosophers from Heaven; in the Grail tradition, Malory says that "Merlyn made the round table in tokenyng of the roundenes of the world for by the round table is the world sygnifyed by ryghte. For all the world crysten and hethen repayren vnto the round table" (*Mort d'Arthur*, xiv. 2); these may be contrasted with the position taken in the Song of Roland where, when Saragossa has been taken, "A thousand Franks enter the synagogues and mosques, whose every wall with mallet and axe they shatter . . . the heathen folk are driven in crowds to the baptismal font, to take Christ's yoke upon them."

[1] The "best for me" need not be "truest absolutely" as judged by absolute metaphysical standards. Nevertheless, the metaphysician will not suggest that the follower of a "second best" religion should abandon it for another (cf. *Bhagavad Gītā*, iii. 26, *na buddhibhedaṁ janayed ajñānam*), but rather that he go *farther in* where he already is, and thus verify as "true" his own images, not by those of another pattern, but rather by the prior form that is common to both.

eyes; and one even detects in modern propagandist writing an undertone of fear, as though it would be a disaster that might upset our own faith, were we to discover essential truth in the opponent; a fear which is occasioned by the very fact that with increasing knowledge and understanding, it is becoming more and more difficult to establish fundamental differences as between one religion and another. It is one of the functions of the First Philosophy to dissipate such fears. Nor is there any other ground whatever upon which all men can be in absolute agreement, excepting that of metaphysics, which we assert is the basis and norm of all religious formulations. Once such a common ground is recognised, it becomes a simple matter to agree to disagree in matters of detail, for it will be seen that the various dogmatic formulations are no more than paraphrases of one and the same principle.[1]

Few will deny that at the present day Western civilisation is faced with the imminent possibility of total functional failure nor that at the same time this civilisation has long acted and still continues to act as a powerful agent of disorder and oppression throughout the rest of the world. We dare say that both of these conditions are referable in the last analysis to that impotence and arrogance which have found a perfect expression in the dictum "East is East and West is West, and never the twain shall meet," a proposition to which only the most abysmal ignorance and deepest discouragement could have given rise. On the other hand, we recognise that the only possible ground upon which an effective entente of East and West can be accomplished is that of the purely intellectual wisdom that is one and the same at all times and for all men, and is independent of all environmental idosyncrasy.[2]

We had intended to discuss at greater length the differentia of religion and metaphysics, but shall rather conclude the present section by an assertion of their ultimate identity. Both, considered

----

[1] "Diverse dogmatic formulations," i.e. *dharma-paryāya* as this expression is employed in the *Saddharma Puṇḍarīka*.
[2] In this context the reader is recommended to René Guénon, *L'Orient et l'Occident*, Paris, 1932.

as Ways, or praxis, are means of accomplishing the rectification, regeneration and reintegration of the aberrant and fragmented individual consciousness, both conceive of man's last end (*puruṣârtha*) as consisting in a realisation by the individual of all the possibilities inherent in his own being, or may go farther, and see in a realisation of all the possibilities of being in any mode and also in possibilities of non-being, a final goal. For the Neo-Platonists and Augustine, and again for Erigena, Eckhart and Dante, and for such as Rūmī, Ibnu'l Arabī, Śaṁkarâcārya, and many others in Asia, religious and intellectual experience are too closely interwoven ever to be wholly divided;[1] who for example would have suspected that the words "How can That, which the Comprehending call the Eye of all things, the Intellect of intellects, the Light of lights, and numinous Omnipresence, be other than man's last end," and "Thou hast been touched and taken! long has Thou dwelt apart from me, but now that I have found Thee, I shall never let Thee go," are taken, not from a "theistic" source, but from purely Vedântic hymns addressed to the Essence (*ātman*) and to the "impersonal" Brahman?

II. HOW DIVERS WISDOMS HAVE CONSIDERED IMMORTALITY

Let us now consider the application of different kinds of wisdom to a particular problem of general significance. The pertinence of philosophy to the problem of immortality is evident, inasmuch as wisdom is primarily concerned with immaterial things, and it is evident that material things are not immortal as such (in *esse per se*), nor even from one moment to another, but are continually in flux, and this is undeniable, regardless of whether

[1] Cf. Erigena, *De div. naturae*, i. 66, *Ambo siquidem ex una fonte, divina scilicet sapientia, manare dubium non est*, and *Bhagavad Gītā*, v. 4–5, "It is the children of this world, and not the men of learning who think of gnosis and works as different. . . . He sees in truth who sees that gnosis and works are one" (for Sāṁkhya and Yoga aṣ meaning gnosis and works respectively, see *ib.*, iii. 3). That the Way of Gnosis and the Way of Participation have one and the same end becomes evident when we consider that love and knowledge can only be conceived of as perfected in an identity of lover and beloved, knower and known.

there may or may not be in such perpetually becoming things some immortal principle. Or to regard the matter from another angle, we may say that whatever, if anything, there may be immortal in phenomenal things must have been so since time began, for to speak of an immortal principle as having become mortal is the same thing as to say it was always mortal.

It needs no argument to demonstrate that human wisdom, rationalism, our philosophy (2), will understand by "immortality," not an everlasting life on earth, but an after-death persistence of individual consciousness and memory and character, such as in our experience survives from day to day across the nightly intervals of death-like sleep. Rational wisdom then will take up either one of two positions. It may in the first place argue that we have no experience of nor can conceive of the functioning of consciousness apart from the actual physical bases on which the functioning seems to rest, if indeed consciousness be in itself anything whatever more than a function of matter in motion, that is to say of physical existence; and will not therefore conceive the possibility of any other than an immortality in history, viz. in the memories of other mortal beings. In this sense there can also be postulated the possibility of a kind of resurrection, as when memory is refreshed by the discovery of documentary proofs of the existence of some individual or people whose very names had been forgotten it may be for millennia. Or human wisdom may maintain, rightly or wrongly, that evidences have been found of the "survival of personality," viz. in communications from the "other world," of such sort as to prove either by reference to facts unknown to the observer, but which are afterwards verified, or by "manifestations" of one sort or another, a continuity of memory and persistence of individual character in the deceased who is assumed to be in communication with the observer. If it is then attempted to rationalise the evidence thus accepted, it is argued that there may be kinds of matter other and subtler than those perceptible to our present physical senses, and that these other modalities of matter may very well serve as the suppositum of consciousness functioning on other planes of being.

It will be readily seen that no spiritual or intellectual distinction can be drawn between the two rationalistic interpretations, the only difference between them being as regards the amount or kind of time in which the continuity of individual character and consciousness can be maintained in a dimensioned space and on a material basis, theories of "fourth dimensions" or of "subtle matter" changing nothing in principle. Both of the rationalistic interpretations are rejected *in toto*, equally by religion and metaphysics.

Not that the possibility of an indefinite perdurance of individual consciousness upon indefinitely numerous or various platforms of being and in various temporal modes is by any means denied in religion or in metaphysics (it being rather assumed that individual consciousness even now functions on other levels than those of our present terrestrial experience),[1] but that a persistence in such modes of being is not, strictly speaking, an immortality, this being taken to mean an immutability of being without development or change and wholly un-eventful; while that which is thus presumed to subsist apart from contingency, viz. the soul, form or noumenal principle (*nāma*) of the individual, by which it is *what* it is, must be distinguished alike from the subtle and the gross bodies (*sūkṣma* and *sthūla śarīra*) which are equally phenomenal (*rūpa*), as being wholly intellectual and immaterial.[2]

For example, "things belonging to the state of glory are not under the sun" (St. Thomas, *Sum. Theol.*, iii., Sup., q. 1, a. 1), i.e. not in any mode of time or space; rather, "it is through the midst of the Sun that one escapes altogether" (*atimucyate*), (*Jaiminīya Up. Brāhmaṇa*, i. 3), where the sun is the "gateway of the worlds" (*loka-dvāra*), (*Chānd. Up.*, viii. 6. 6), Eckhart's "gate through which all things return perfectly free to their supreme felicity (*pūrṇânanda*) . . . free as the Godhead in its non-existence" (*asat*), the "Door" of John X, "Heaven's-gate

---

[1] "Even we ourselves as mentally tasting something eternal, are not in this world." St. Augustine, *De Trin.*, iv. 20.

[2] Therefore incapable of "proof," whether the phenomena adduced be "scientific" or "spiritualistic."

that Agni opens" (*svargasya lokasya dvāram avṛṇot*), (*Aitareya Brāhmaṇa*, iii. 42).[1] It is true that here again we shall inevitably meet with a certain and by no means negligible distinction of the religious from the metaphysical formulation. The religious concept of supreme felicity culminates as we have already seen in the assimilation of the soul to Deity in act; the soul's own act being one of adoration rather than of union. Likewise, and without inconsistency, since it is assumed that the individual soul remains numerically distinct alike from God and from other substances, religion offers to mortal consciousness the consolatory promise of finding there in Heaven, not only God, but those whom it loved on earth, and may remember and recognise.

Nor will metaphysics deny that even in a "Heaven," on the farther side of time, there may be, at least until the "Last Judgment," a knowledge-of (*avidyā*) rather than a knowledge-as (*vidyā*), though it will not think of him whose modality is still in knowledge-of as wholly Comprehending (*vidvān*) nor as absolutely Enlarged (*atimukta*). Metaphysics will allow, and here in formal agreement with religion, that there may or even must be states of being by no means wholly in time, nor yet in eternity (the timeless now), but aeviternal, "aeviternity" (Vedic *amṛtatva*) being defined as a mean between eternity and time;[2] the Angels,

---

[1] While it is shown here how the formulations of different religions may express the same conceptions in almost verbal agreement, it must not be supposed that we therefore advocate any kind of eclecticism, or conceive the possibility of a new religion compounded of all existing religions. Eclecticism in religion results only in confusion and caricature, of which a good example can be cited in "Theosophy."

[2] St. Thomas, *Sum. Theol.*, i, q. 10, a. 5. He says "states of being" in the plural deliberately (cf. René Guénon, *Les États multiples de l'Être*, Paris, 1932), although for purposes of generalisation it has been necessary to speak only of three, viz. the human, angelic and divine, that is those to which the literal, metaphorical and analogical understandings pertain respectively.

With the Christian "aeviternity," Indian *amṛtatva*, and the traditional concept of "humanity" and "Perfect Man" (e.g. Islamic *insanu'l kamīl*), cf. Jung, *Modern Man in Search of a Soul*, p. 215: "If it were permissible to personify the unconscious, we might call it a collective human being combining the characteristics of both sexes, transcending youth and age, birth and death, and from having at its command a human experience for example, as conscious intellectual substances, partaking of eternity as to their immutable nature and understanding, but of time as regards their accidental awareness of before and after, the changeability of their affections (liability to fall from grace, etc.), and inasmuch as the angelic independence of local motion (because of which Angels are represented as winged, and spoken of as "birds"),[1] whereby they can be anywhere, is other than the immanence of the First, which implies an equal presence everywhere. Nor is it denied by religion that "Certain men even in this state of life are greater than certain angels, not actually, but virtually" (St. Thomas, *Sum. Theol.*, i, q. 117, a. 2, *ad.* 3), whence it naturally follows that "Some men are taken up into the highest angelic orders" (Gregory, *Hom. xxxiv in Ev.*), thus partaking of an aeviternal being; all of which corresponds to what is implied by the familiar Hindu expression *devo bhūtvā*, equivalent to "dead and gone to Heaven." Precisely this point of view is more technically expressed in the critical text, *Bṛhadār. Up.*, iii. 2. 12, "When a man dies, what does not forsake (*na jahāti*) him is his 'soul' (*nāma*),[2] the soul is without end (*ananta*, 'aeviternal'), without

of one or two million years, almost immortal. If such a being existed, he would be exalted above all temporal change . . . he would have lived countless times over the life of the individual, or the family, tribe and people, and he would possess the living sense of the rhythm of growth, flowering and decay. It would be positively grotesque for us to call this immense system of the experience of the unconscious psyche an illusion." Here it may be noted that "unconscious" presents an analogy with "Deep-Sleep" (*susupti = samādhi = excessus* or *raptus*); on the other hand, the use of the word "collective" betrays a purely scientific, and not a metaphysical conception.

[1] "Intellect is the swiftest of birds" (*manaḥ javiṣtam patayatsu antaḥ, Ṛg. Veda*, vi. 9. 5). It is as birds that the Angels "celebrate in the Tree of Life their share of aeviternity" (*yatra suparṇā amṛtasya bhāgam . . . abhi svaranti, ib.*, i. 164. 21). The traditional expression "language of birds" (which survives in "a little bird told me") refers to angelic communications.

[2] *Nāma* is the correlative of *rūpa*, being the noumenal or intelligible part and efficient cause of the integration *nāma-rūpa*, viz. the individual as he is in himself; and therefore to be rendered not by "name" (for this is not a nominalist but a realist doctrine), but by "idea," "archetype," "form" or "soul" (as when it is said "the soul is the form of the body"); *ātman* on the other hand being "essence" rather than "soul" (*essentia,* that by which a substance has *esse* in whatever mode).

end is what the Several Angels are, so then he wins the world everlasting" (*anantam lokam*). Cf. Rūmī (xii in Nicholson's *Shams-i-Tabrīz*), "Every shape you see has its archetype in the placeless world, and if the shape perished, no matter, since its original is everlasting" (*lāmkān-ast*); and St. Thomas, *Sum. Theol.*, ii-i, q. 67, a. 2 c, "as regards the intelligible species, which are in the *possible* intellect, the intellectual virtues remain," viz. when the body is corrupted. This was also expounded by Philo, for whom "Le lieu de cette vie immortelle est le monde intelligible,"[1] that is to say the same as the "Intellectual Realm" of Plotinus, *passim*. If we now consider the implications of these dicta in connection with Böhme's answer to the scholar who enquires, "Whither goeth the soul when the body dieth?" viz. that "There is no necessity for it to *go* anywither. . . . For . . . whichsoever of the two (that is either heaven or hell) is manifested in it (now), in that the soul standeth (then) . . . the judgment is, indeed, immediately at the departure of the body,"[2] and in the light of *Bṛhadār. Up.*, iv. 4. 5-6, "As is his will . . . so is his lot" (*yat kāmam . . . tat sampadyate*) and " He whose mind is attached (to mundane things) . . . returns again to this world . . . but he whose desire is the Essence (*ātman*), his life (*prāṇāḥ*) does not leave him, but he goes as Brahman unto Brahman," it will be apparent that although the soul or intellect (Vedic *manas*) is immortal by nature (i.e. an individual potentiality that cannot be *annihilated*, whatever its "fate"), nevertheless the actual "fate" of an individual consciousness, whether it be destined to be "saved" or "liberated" (*devayāna*), or to enter into time again (*pitṛyāna*), or to be "lost" (*nirṛtha*), depends upon itself. And therefore we are told to "Lay up treasure in Heaven, where neither moth nor rust corrupt"; for evidently, if the conscious life of the individual be even now established intellectually (or in religious phraseology, "spiritually"), and the intellectual or spiritual world be aeviternal

---

[1] Bréhier, *Les Idées philosophiques et religieuses de Philon d'Alexandrie*, 1925, p. 240.

[2] Böhme, On Heaven and Hell (in Everyman's Library, volume entitled *Signatura Rerum*, etc.).

(as follows from the consideration that ideas have neither place nor date), this conscious life cannot be infringed by the death of the body, which changes nothing in this respect. Or if the consciousness be still attached to and involved in ends (whether good or evil) such as can only be accomplished in time and space, but have not yet been accomplished when the body dies, then evidently such a consciousness will find its way back into those conditions, viz. of space and time, in which the desired ends can be accomplished.[1] Or finally, if conscious life has been led altogether in the flesh, it must be thought of as cut off when its sole support is destroyed; that is, it must be thought of as "backsliding" into a mere potentiality or hell.

Space will not permit us to discuss the theory of "reincarnation" at any length. The fundamentals are given in the *Ṛg. Veda*, where it is primarily a matter of recurring manifestation, in this sense for example, Mitra *jāyate punaḥ* (x. 85. 19) and Uṣas is *punaḥpunar jāyamāna* (i. 92. 10). An individual application in the spirit of "Thy will be done" is found in v. 46. 1, "As a comprehending (*vidvān*) horse I yoke myself unto the pole (of the chariot of the year) . . . seeking neither a release nor to come back again (*na asyāḥ vimucaṁ na āvṛttam punaḥ*), may He (Agni) as Comprehender (*vidvān*) and our Waywise Guide lead us aright." The individual, indeed, "is born according to the measure of his understanding" (*Aitareya Āraṇyaka*, ii. 3. 2), and just as "the world itself is pregnant with the causes of unborn things" (Augustine, *De Trin.*, iii. 9) so is the individual pregnant with the accidents that must befall him; as St. Thomas expresses it, "fate is in the created causes themselves" (*Sum. Theol.*, i, q. 116, 2), or Plotinus, "the law is given in the entities upon whom it falls, . . . it prevails because it is within them . . . and sets up in them a painful longing to enter the realm to which they are bidden from within" (*Enneads*, iv. 3. 15); and similarly Ibnu'l 'Arabī, who says that while being is from God, modality is not directly from Him, "for He only wills what they have it in them to become" (Nicholson, *Studies* . . . ,

---

[1] It is the good purpose, for example, which operates in the return of a Bodhisattva, who is otherwise fit for Nirvāṇa.

E

p. 151). On the other hand, it may be taken as certain that the Buddhist and still more the modern Theosophical interpretations of causality (*karma*) or fate (*adṛṣṭa*), which assert the necessity of a return (except for one who is *mukta* or has "reached" *nirvāṇa*) to the very same conditions that have been left behind at death, involve a metaphysical antinomy; "You would not step twice into the same waters, for other waters are ever flowing in upon you" (Heracleitus). What is really contemplated in Vedic and other traditional doctrines is the necessity of a recurrent manifestation in aeon after aeon, though not again within one and the same temporal cycle,[1] of all those individual potentialities or forces in which the desire to "prolong their line" is still effective; every Patriarch (*pitṛ*) being, like Prajāpati himself, *prajā-kāmya*, and therefore willingly committed to the "Patriarchal Way" (*pitṛyāna*).

What is then from the standpoint of metaphysics the whole course of an individual potentiality, from the "time" that it first awakens in the primordial ocean of universal possibility until the "time" it reaches the last harbour? It is a return into the source and well-spring of life, from which life originates, and thus a passage from one "drowning" to another; but with a distinction, valid from the standpoint of the individual in himself so long as he is a Wayfarer and not a Comprehender, for, seen as a process, it is a passage from a merely possible perfection through actual imperfection to an actual perfection, from potentiality to act, from slumber (*abodhya*) to a full awakening (*sambodhi*). Ignoring now the Patriarchal Way as being a "round about" course, and considering only the straight Angelic Way (*devayāna*), with which the Ṛg. *Veda* is primarily and the individual *mumukṣu* specifically concerned, we may say that this Way is one at first of a diminishing and afterwards of an increasing realisation of all the possibilities intrinsic to

---

[1] In *Bhagavad Gītā*, vi. 41, for example, *śāsvatī samā* is very far from implying "forthwith." We doubt very much whether any Aupaniṣada passage could be cited as implying a re-embodiment otherwise than at the dawn of a new cycle, and then only as the growth of a seed sown in the previous aeon, or as a tendency with which the new age can be said to be pregnant.

the fact of being in a given mode (the human, for example),
and ultimately leads to the realisation of all the possibilities
of being in any or every mode, and over and beyond this of
those of being not in any mode whatever. We cannot do more
than allude here to the part that is taken by what is called
"initiation" in this connection; only saying that the intention
of initiation is to communicate from one to another a spiritual
or rather intellectual impulse that has been continuously trans-
mitted in *guru-paramparā-krama* from the beginning and is
ultimately of non-human origin, and whereby the contracted
and disintegrated individual is awakened to the possibility of
a reintegration (*saṁskarana*);[1] and that metaphysical rites, or
"mysteries" (which are in imitation of the means employed
by the Father to accomplish His own reintegration, the necessity
for which is occasioned by the incontinence of the creative
act), are, like the analogous traditional scriptures, intended to
provide the individual with the necessary preparatory education
in and means of intellectual operation; but the "Great Work,"
that of accomplishing the reunion of essence with Essence,
must be done by himself within himself.

We have so far followed the Wayfarer's course by the Angelic
Way to the spiritual or intellectual realm; and here, from the
religious point of view, lies his immortality, for indeed "the
duration of aeviternity is infinite" (St. Thomas, *Sum. Theol.*,
i, q. 10, a. 5, *ad.* 4). But it will be maintained in metaphysics, or
even in a religion or by an individual mystic such as Eckhart
(in so far as the religious experience is both devotional and intellectual in the deepest sense of both words) that an aeviternal
station (*pada*), such as is implied in the concept of being in a
heaven, is not the end, nor by any means a full return (*nivṛtti*),
but only a resting place (*viśrāma*).[2] And likewise, it will be

[1] See *Aitareya Āranyaka*, iii. 2. 6; *Aitareya Brāhmana*, vi. 27;
Śatapatha Brāhmana, vii. 1. 2. 1 and *passim*. Cf. also Guénon, "L'Initiation
et les Métiers," *Le Voile d'Isis*, No. 172, 1934.

[2] *Saddharma Puṇḍarīka*, v. 74. Similarly, the true end of the ritual
acts and appointed sacrifices of the Veda is not the attainment of a
temporary heaven, but the awakening of a desire to know the Essence
(*ātman*) (*Siddhāntamuktāvalī*, xxxiii, with Venis' note "Paradise is as it
were but the half-way house").

maintained that to conceive of the intellectual realm itself as a place of memories would be a derogation, for as Plotinus says of its natives, "if they neither seek nor doubt, and never learn, nothing being at any time absent from their knowledge . . . what reasonings, what processes of rational investigation, can take place in them? In other words, they have seen God and they do not recollect? Ah, no . . . such reminiscence is only for souls that have forgotten" (*Enneads*, iv. 4. 6);[1] and still more must we say respecting mundane memories (*vāsanā*) that "when the soul's act is directed to another order, it must utterly reject the memory of such things, over and done with now" (*ib.*, iv. 4. 8).

The metaphysical concept of Perfection, indeed, envisages a state of being that is, not *in*human since it is maintained that such a state is always and everywhere accessible to whoever will press inwards to the central point of consciousness and being on any ground or plane of being, nor "heartless" unless we mean by "heart" the seat of soulfulness and sentimentality; but assuredly *non*-human. For example, in *Chānd. Up.*, v. 10. 2 it is precisely as *amānava puruṣa*, "non-human person," that the Son and aeviternal *avatāra*, Agni,[2] is said to lead onward the Comprehending one who has found his way through the Supernal Sun to the farther side of the worlds, and this is the "pathway of the Angels" (*devayāna*) as contrasted with that of the Patriarchs (*pitryāna*) which does not lead beyond the Sun but to re-embodiment in a human mode of being. And it is foreseen that this *devayāna* must lead, whether sooner or later, to what is expressed in doctrinal mysticism as a "final death of the soul," or "drowning," the Sūfī *al-fanā 'an al-fanā*; by which is implied a passage

---

[1] Similarly in Dante, *Paradiso*, 29. 79–81, "their sight is never intercepted by any new perception, and so there is no need of memory, for thought has not been cleft."

[2] Agni(-Prajāpati), who in the Vedas is the Herdsman of the Spheres (*gopā bhuvanasya*), Waywise Leader (*vidvān pathaḥ puraeta*), Messenger and Herald (*dūta, arati*), and stands as the Pillar of Life at the Parting of the Ways (*āyor ha skambha . . . pathām visarge, Ṛg. Veda*, x. 5. 6) in cosmic crucifixion (*dharuṇeṣu sthitaḥ, ib.*), corresponding to the "dogmatic" Buddha, Christ as distinguished from Jesus, and to the "Idea of Muḥammad."

beyond even consciousness in deity as act, to a Supreme (Skt. *para, parātpara*) beyond all trace of even an exemplary multiplicity, nor in any way "intelligible." And there, so far that is from any possible "reminiscence" of any that have been known or loved in otherness, in the words of Eckhart, "No one will ask me whence I came or whither I went," or in Rūmī's, "None has knowledge of each who enters that he is so-and-so or so-and-so."[1]

If this appears to be a denial of ultimate significance to human love, the position has been altogether misunderstood. For all metaphysical formulations, assuming that an infallible analogy relates every plane of being to every other, have seen in human love an image of divine felicity (*pūrṇânanda*), imagined not as a contradiction of but as transformation (*parāvṛtti*) of sensual experience. This is the theory of "Platonic love," according to which, as Ibnu'l Farīd expresses it, "the charm of every fair youth or lovely girl is lent to them from Her beauty"; a point of view implicit too in Erigena's conception of the world as a theophany, and in the Scholastic doctrine of the *vestigium pedis*, the trace or footprint of divinity in time, which has its equivalent in Vedic and Zen symbolisms. What this means in actual tradition is that the beloved on earth is to be realised *there* not as she is in herself but as she is in God,[2] and so it is in the case of Dante and Beatrice, Ibnu'l 'Arabī and an-Niẓām,[3] and in that of Chandīdās and Rāmī.[4] The beauty of the Beloved *there* is no longer as it is here contingent and merely a participation or reflection, but that of the Supernal Wisdom, that of the One Madonna, that of the intrinsic being of the Bride, which "rains down flames of fire" (*Convivio*) and as *claritas* illuminates and guides the pure intellect. In that last and hidden station (*guhyam*

---

[1] Nicholson, *Shams-i-Tabrīz*, p. 61.

[2] Cf. *Tarjumān al-Ashwāq*, xl. 2, "She was exalted in majesty above time"; and Rūmī, " 'Tis love and the lover that live to all eternity" (xiii, in Nicholson, *Shams-i-Tabrīz*).
Another example could be cited in the *Shepherd of Hermas*.

[3] Whom Ibnu'l 'Arabī met at Mecca in 1201, see Nicholson, *Tarjumān al-Ashwāq*, 1911.

[4] Cf. "Sahaja" in our *Dance of Śiva*, 1917.

padam), nature and essence, Apsaras and Gandharva, are one
and indivisible, knowing nothing of a within or a without
(*na bāhyaṁ kiṁcana veda nântaram, Bṛhadār. Up.*, iv. 321),
and that is their supreme felicity, and that of every liberated
consciousness.

All this can only be described in terms of negation, in terms
of what it is *not*, and therefore we say again that metaphysics
can in no way be thought of as a doctrine offering consolations
to a suffering humanity. What metaphysic understands by
immortality and by eternity implies and demands of every
man a total and uncompromising denial of himself and a final
mortification, to be dead and buried in the Godhead. "Whoever
realises this, avoids contingent death (*punar mṛtyu*), death gets
him not, for Death becomes his essence, and of all these Angels
he becomes the One" (*Bṛhadār. Up.*, i. 2. 7). For the Supreme
Identity is no less a Death and a Darkness than a Life and a
Light, no less Asura than Deva: "His overshadowing is both
Aeviternity and Death" (*yasya chāyā amṛta, yasya mṛtyuḥ, Ṛg.
Veda*, x. 121. 2).[1] And this is what we understand to be the
final purport of the First Philosophy.

---

[1] Similarly, *Śatapatha Brāhmaṇa*, x. 4. 3. 1–3 *Eṣa vai mṛtyur yat
samvatsaraḥ . . . prajāpatiḥ*, "He, the Father, who is the Year and likewise
Death."
The Darkness and the Light, belonging to His *asuratva* and *devatva*
respectively, remain in Him, who is both *asura* and *deva*, Titan and angel,
sarpa and *āditya*; at the same time that from the Wayfarer's point of view
their reflections in time and space are evil and good. In Hinduism, "the
Darkness in Him is called Rudra" (*Maitri Up.*, vi. 2), and is represented
in the names and hues of Kālī and Kṛṣṇa; in Christian *yoga*, the Dark
Ray or Divine Darkness, Eckhart's "sable stillness" and "motionless
dark that no one knows but He in whom it reigns" (cf. the "Clouds and
thick darkness" of Deut. iv. 11), is spoken of already in the Codex Brucianus
and by Dionysius, and becomes the subject of the *contemplatio in caligine*.
Regarding the propriety of the expression "Christian *yoga*," we need only
point out that St. Bernard's *consideratio, contemplatio*, and *excessus* or
raptus correspond exactly to *dhāraṇa, dhyāna* and *samādhi*.

PRINCIPAL PUBLICATIONS

Mediaeval Sinhalese Art (1908).
Rajput Painting (1916).
The Dance of Śiva (1917).
History of Indian and Indonesian Art (1927).
A New Approach to the Vedas (1934).
The Transformation of Nature in Art (1934).
Articles in the *Encyclopaedia Britannica* and *National Encyclopaedia.*
Editor of Indian words in *Webster's International Dictionary* (1934).
Recent articles include a series on "Early Indian Architecture" in
 Eastern Art; "*Kha* and other words for zero, in connection
 with the metaphysics of space," in *Bulletin of the School of
 Oriental Studies*; and "The technique and theory of Indian
 Painting," in *Technical Studies*.

ĀTMA-VIDYĀ, OR THE SCIENCE OF THE SELF

by BHAGAVAN DAS

Born January 1869

E*

ĀTMA-VIDYĀ, OR THE SCIENCE OF THE SELF

PRELIMINARY

IN the year 1880 A.D. a boy was studying in the Matriculation Class of the School attached to the Queen's College of Benares. From time immemorial Benares has been and continues to be the greatest publicly known centre of Saṁskṛt learning and the religious capital of India. In that same year, 1880, when the boy was in his twelfth year, he witnessed his dearly loved and loving grandmother pass away. He followed her bier to the funeral pile, wondering deeply what it all meant. Then came into his hands casually papers which spoke of holy men, Rishis, Yogis, possessed of sacred, mystical and philosophical knowledge, as if they were still to be found. He also happened to have some conversations with benevolent Saññyāsins and spiritual-minded persons. In earliest childhood he had greedily absorbed story portions of the purànas, the Rāmāyana, and the Mahābhārata, sitting beside his grandmother, when the Pandit recited and expounded them in the afternoons; the philosophy with which they were saturated passed over his mind, leaving behind only sub-conscious traces, if any. But now some sleeping germinal tendencies (*samskāras*) awoke, though the boy of twelve understood but little of the things that he read and heard.

A curious sense of the futility of this earthly life came into his sensitive boyish mind. Mixed with the usual distractions and engagements, play and school, of boy-life, vague mystical achings, yearnings for something better, "The desire of the moth for the star, of the night for the morrow, The devotion to something afar from the sphere of our sorrow," seized him off and on. Gaining strength as he grew older, these questionings took definite shape as the ever present wish to understand the "why" of the misery within and without, the "how" of its cure. All subordinate questions were inseparably connected with the great question of the "why" and the "how" of the Universe. No part can be understood unless its articulation with the whole in the ways of co-ordination, subordination, super-ordination is worked out. Part and whole, individual and society, society and the universe, finite and infinite, can be understood and dealt with only in relation to each other. To convince Arjuna, distraught with a sudden compassion and a horror of the slaughter of cousins, that it was his duty to war against his sinful kinsmen, Krishna had to compress into seven hundred verses an explanation of the whole scheme of the Universe and the meaning of all life.

The boy took up courses of psychology, ethics, metaphysics in the College; thought, discussed with sympathetic friends, and read all he could in English and Sanskrit. The disadvantage of two unfamiliar languages ultimately proved an advantage, for the times required that the invaluable ideas enshrined in the old Sanskrit medium should be interpreted in the new counters of thought. Only so could they help towards a *rapprochement* between Eastern and Western, ancient and modern, thought and life.

The longing to find out the "why" and the "how" became a psychic fever. Consciously, subconsciously even more, this was the mood of the youth up to 1887. In that year he somehow found satisfaction; an answer arose in his mind, which summed up, in itself, answers to countless subordinate queries. The fever abated. Aspiration for a better, a holier life, remained—and remains, unfulfilled unfortunately, to this day. But his mind is more or less at peace at the centre, though there is not and cannot be peace on the surface.

That boy, that youth, is the present writer, now in his sixty-seventh year waiting patiently to cast off his nearly worn-out body, wishing well to all, praying with all his heart that other hearts may find much greater peace, at least no less, than he has found.

In humble endeavour towards this great object, by inner compulsion, and even more by the wish of kind friends, who liked his reinterpretations and presentations in fresh forms of the eternal truths recorded in the scriptures by the ancients, the writer has compiled a number of books to be of service to such readers as may be more interested in the modern ways of thinking, to express them livingly, since the old ones have become hackneyed with much use.

BRIEF CONFESSION OF FAITH

The writer may mention here at once that he is a believer in (1) infinitely countless individual selves or souls; (2) their rebirths, evolution and involution, in and through evolving and involving, integrating and disintegrating, forming and dissolving, material bodies and surroundings; the passing of each self, through all possible experiences, in infinite time, space and motion; in (3) cycles and circles of time and space on all possible scales of duration and extent, in which the processes of rhythmic evolution and involution manifest themselves; in (4) One all-including, all-pervading, ever-complete, timeless, spaceless, Universal Soul or Spirit or Self, which is Absolute and Changeless, which is also identical with and includes within It-self all the countless individual selves, and whose eternally changeless, and yet also ever-changing, Ideation the entire world-process of all souls and bodies is.

Reasons for this faith, expounded in his books, as fully as was possible for the writer's very feeble powers, may appear briefly in the course of the present paper.

THE PSYCHIC FEVER OF SPIRITUAL ADOLESCENCE

Psychic fever seems to be a normal event in the evolution of the human soul, somewhat like adolescence in that of the physical body, and frequently, though not always, coincides with it in time. A certain dissatisfaction with the ever-disappointing, fleeting, painful, deathful world seems to be the main emotional characteristic of it; and a disinclination for the apparently futile daily duties of life, the actional characteristic. If the intellectual characteristic of enquiry into causes is weak (as it is in the earlier stages of the soul's evolution), and the frustration of wish and hope and consequent fear and anger and despair are very severe, then, in extreme cases, physical

suicide may be the result. If both enquiry and distaste are
weak, the mood passes, and the individual settles down to the
routine of life quietly. But if the intellectual enquiry is keen,
persistent, invincible; if the passion of revolt against the cruelties
and injustices of life which inspires that enquiry is compassion
for fellow-sufferers; if the revolt is against the sufferings of not
only oneself but of all selves—as it is when the soul has arrived
at a certain stage, as every soul must, and is turning from
egoism to conscious altruism, on the way back to Universalism
in the great cycles of the World-process—then the result is an
Understanding, a philosophy, a theory of who am I, what am
I, whence and whither and wherefore am I; who, what, whence,
whither, wherefore, are all these other I's; what, why, how,
is all this, i.e. the world of objects and its incessant process;
what the meaning and purpose of life with all its pains as well
as all its pleasures.[1] The result of the successful passing through
this experience seems intended by Nature to be the strengthening
of the individual body, soul and spirit, in action, emotion and
intellect, for the discharge of the duties of life, physical, superphysical and metaphysical.

VAIRĀGYA AND ITS CONSEQUENCES—OF DIFFERENT KINDS

Vairāgya (dis-passion, dis-taste), if it is predominantly (*rājasa*
and *tāmasa*) inspired by "egoistic restless or clinging passions,"
leads in its extreme form to "physical" suicide, whereby the
unhappy soul destroys the outer apparatus through which it
experienced misery, under the false belief that it will thereby
destroy the real source of misery (*kleṣa*); a source which, however,
is fundamentally internal, and only superficially external; for
the outer apparatus itself is created by it and will be fashioned
by it anew, again and again, until it, the internal cause, has been
diagnosed and cured. But when the dis-affection is intelligent
(*sāttvika*), enlightened, philanthropic, accompanied by intense
intellectual seeking for cause and remedy, is guided by dis-

[1] See the opening chapters of the writer's *The Science of Peace, Tales
from the Yoga Vāsishtha*; *The Science of the Emotions*; and two pamphlets,
Psychology of Conversion and *The Fundamental Idea of Theosophy*.

crimination (*viveka*) between the permanent and the transient, the lasting True and the fleeting False, when it is combined with the "cardinal virtues" (*sādhana-shatka*) which are the opponents and vanquishers of the six "deadly sins" (*ṣadṛpu*), and is motived by poignant "yearning for freedom" (*mumukṣā*), not only for oneself but for all selves, freedom from that quint-essence of all pains, viz. the fear of pain and death, the feeling of being at the mercy of another, the doubt of Immortality and Self-dependence—then the result is Realisation of the True Universal Self (*Ātma-bodha*), Spiritual Knowledge, Theosophia, God-Wisdom, Metaphysical knowledge of "that which is beyond the physical" but yet includes the physical; conviction of the Immortality and invulnerable Self-dependence of the Self, the Universal Self with which all selves are identical; the destruction of Error, Delusion, Nescience, False Belief (*avidyā-nāśa*), the "meta-physical" "suicide" of the inner egoistic selfish self, under the compulsion of the True Knowledge (*Vidyā*) that separative egoism (*ahamkāra*) is the final internal root of all misery; then the result is the realisation, by the person, of the identity of his individual self (*jīvātmā*), personal ego, with the Supreme Self (*Paramātmā*), the Absolute Ego, and consequent freedom from all fear and sorrow, extinction of the sense of separateness, the uprising of the Bliss of the sense of non-separate-ness; the conviction that All is One-Self, that All is I, unto I, by I, for I, from I, of I, in I; that all possible relations expressible by any prepositions are ever-present between I and not-I.

The far-reaching nature of this sense of non-separateness is seen in the awful consequences of its opposite, race-separatism, nation, class, creed, colour, sex, age-separatism; consequences from which the human world has been and is suffering, in the shape of war, pestilence, social convulsions, perpetual semi-starvation in intensive and extensive forms, since the beginning of the twentieth century.

Sensitiveness to the sorrows of others, sympathy, is the sensing of the Universal Self in all selves and things, round which every atom, every orb of heaven, the breath in the lungs, the blood in the veins and arteries, every manifestation in every department of Nature, revolves in cycles, and in which all duality, all opposites, are "turned into one" (uni-versed). Such compassionate passion of dis-gust (*vairāgya*) with the heartless iniquities of life, and such indomitable faith that the secret of the universe is powerless to withstand the might of thought are indispensable for the kindling of "the Light that lighteth every man."

Buddha, in his divine madness, abandoning wife and child, takes the oath: "I will not enter these gates again until I have won the secret of life and death to help my fellow-sufferers." The secret he wins and teaches all who care to learn is that "we suffer from ourselves, none else compels"; there *is* none else to compel.

THE UNITY OF LIFE AND THEREFORE OF THE SCIENCE OF LIFE

In Indian tradition the culmination of philosophy is the same as that of pragmatic ethics, science, art, religion—in the sense of ultimate principles, or rather one final principle. Nature, God's nature, Nature's God, is a breakless continuum. The bodily-mental life of man, with all the varied organs and functions involved, is the life of an organic unity. The laws and the facts of all the sciences, arts, philosophy, the religion of God—Nature —Man are all at work simultaneously in that life, in the body and mind of man, as indeed in everything, everywhere, in varied degrees. Indian philosophy, Vedānta, the "final knowledge," is not only a theory, a body of knowledge, a set of beliefs; it is a philosophy which arises in, and in turn gives stronger rise to, philanthropic aspiration, and inspires and guides bene- ficent action. It is eminently emotional, devotional, humani- tarian also, for it sees and worships the One in all animate and seemingly inanimate Nature. It is Jñāna-bhakti-karma, knowledge —devotion—works, all in one. Its purpose is to maximise human happiness and to abolish sorrow; to satisfy not only intellectual curiosity but also emotional hunger and actional craving; to reconcile and balance and give just scope to head, heart and limbs; to give duly apportioned equal opportunity to the man of knowledge, the man of desire, the man of action, the undeveloped man, one and all. It is called darśana (insight), vision, view, because it enables us to see the heart of all things.

THE LOGION WHICH SUMS UP THE SCIENCE OF LIFE

In the exalted mood which followed the "sudden flash" of insight that lighted up the darkness and brought the answer the writer composed a little poem in the manner of the aphoristic and ecstatic utterances; the last lines were:

> Out of the storm rose calm the thought—
> I (am) This not, I (am) This not.

These words, slight though they look, enclose all the philosophy which the present writer has been able to achieve. The soul must crave to discover the true nature of God, of Self, as frantically as the suffocating man struggles for air, before it finds the Truth. The spiritual preceptor of the Upaniṣads imparts the "commonplace" knowledge by a solemn, earnest, tenderly affectionate whisper into the ear of the equally earnest and devoted listener, in psychical conditions which transmute the common lead into exceedingly uncommon gold; and a mental, a spiritual, miracle is performed; *Tat tvam asi*: *So'ham*, Thou art That which thou seekest; Thou hast been seeking thine own True Self; I am That; the I is That; "That I (which Thou and I are, that I is, and am) not this." For the requirements of the writer's mind, the Upaniṣad teaching, "That am I," was completed by the thought, "Not this." Positive and Negative together make up the Absolute, the Whole Truth, of the Relatives abolishing, neutralising, each other.[1]

THE STRUGGLE FOR THE LOGION

Failing to find satisfaction in the current philosophies of the East and the West—very likely because of his imperfect understanding of them—and having struggled on till he arrived at

[1] See the writer's *Science of Peace*.

this great word, this Logion, his quest ended, though the unending routine of duties remained. After this glimpse, the hidden
word began to shine out clearly from the pages of the Scriptures.[1]
Recapitulating the progress to the logion, the following steps
can be traced. The popular theory of causation (*ārambha-vāda*),
that an extra-cosmical personal God makes and unmakes the
world at will, fails to convince lastingly. The scientific theory
of causation (*pariṇāma-vāda* or *vikāra-vāda*), that the world-
process is a continuous transformation or creative evolution
which is the result of the interplay of two infinites, indestructible
matter and indestructible force—this is only a description, not
an explanation. Two infinites are illogical. The metaphysical
theory of causation, that the world is an unreal dream-idea
(*māyā-vāda*, *ābhāsa-vāda*), is the ideation, the willed-imagination
of My-Self (*Param-ātma, Brahma*), the Infinite Universal Self,
comes nearer home.

But some difficulties remain. Why should the Self dream at
all? And such a very painful dream! Why any change—which
means desire, incompleteness, imperfection? And what after all
is change? Every change means the passing of something, some
being, into nothing, and of non-being into some being, something; this violates the very fundamentals of ordinary logic.
How can we reconcile Change with the Changeless, Brahma
with Māyā, and Joy of Self-dependence with Misery of Life—
this is the ultimate trouble with this last theory of causation.

"I am" is the most unquestionable eternal fact. "Cogito ergo"
is superfluous. "Sum" is enough. But "This," the world of objects,
the opposite of "I" (*vivarta*), this "Other-than-I," this "Not-I,"
this "Else-than-Subject," all the mass of objects which consciousness looks at as "This"—this is also an indubitable though
utterly changeful, ever passing, fact. If we succeed in reconciling
the two in such a way that the not-I shall be at the will of the
I and not the other way round; such a way that the I, while
doing what it pleases with the not-I, shall still not lose its eternal
fulness and completeness; such a way that disorder, arbitrariness,
shall go hand in hand with law and order; then we shall have

found the consolation and the peace that we are seeking. The insistent question, why this process, why this posing and opposing, this mutual limitation, remains the crux. The incomprehensibility is admitted; the synthesis seems partial, almost superficial. But if anything remains incomprehensible, all remains such; the chain is no stronger than its weakest link. The unquestionable fact of Becoming, of change is utterly illogical and impossible to understand, so that we want to feel that there is *no* change in reality. As regards Being and Non-Being or Nothing, the only real, ultimate, permanent Being that we are aware of is "I am"; and the non-real Being, the No-thingness that we are simultaneously aware of, is that of the transient, evanescent, "This," the not-I.

We must try again. The secret lies hidden somewhere between "I" and "This." If we can discover the precise nature of the relation between these two, which are the only things that interest us, which fill our whole life and make up and exhaust the whole universe, we will surely have discovered the secret.

Instead of saying "Being is Nothing" (as Hegel said), it seems more readily intelligible to say, "Being is Not Non-Being, Not Nothing, or rather Not-any-particular-thing"; better than that, "Ego is not non-Ego"; better than that, "I is not not-I"; better than that, "I (am) Not Not-I"; and, finally, better than all else, "I (am) not-This," or in the Samskṛt order, "I-(am)-This-Not" (*Aham-Etat-Na*).

In this sentence we gain the reconciliation we sought, the all-comprehensive synthesis which includes both thesis and antithesis within itself. The contrast between "I" and "not I" is so utterly complete that any thought of mutual identification (*anyonyā-dhyāsa*), complete or partial (in the way of mutual limitation), is not possible. But if we use the word "This," the impossibility disappears. Our body is clearly "This" to us. We say: "This body is mine," as we say, "This coat is mine"; "mine," not "me" but different, only belonging to me. And we obviously feel identified also with our body when we say "I am coming," "I am going," "Here am I." Mine is not I. Yet it is an extension of "I," a part of "I."

In the awareness "I (am) Not This," or "I-This-Not," the whole of all possible not-I s is affirmed, is present here, now, all at once, and, at the same time, the being, the existence, the reality, the truth of them all is denied. Affirmation and negation, supposition and opposition, are simultaneous in it. In the Logion (*Aham-Etat-Na*) we have the Motion, the movement, of the endless, everlasting, pseudo-infinite rhythmic swing of Self-heterisation and Self-establishment, both compressed into one successionless, timeless, spaceless, motionless, Uniform Awareness of the I as Not-Not-I. Such is the transcendental view (*param-ārtha-drishti*), the view from the standpoint of the Infinite, the Whole, the Unmanifest yet Ever manifest, the Unlimited and Unconditioned I.

But from the experiential standpoint (*vyavahāra-drishti*), the point of view of the conditioned This's—to the eye of the "This," the simultaneous All-consciousness of "I" and of all possible "not-I's" affirmed and denied in the same breath appears as the Illusion of the alternating swing of to and fro, inbreathing and outbreathing, which is motion, of *first* affirmative identification and *then* negative rejection in the *succession* which is Time, amidst the *co-existence* of "here and there and side by side" of pseudo-infinite not-I's, which is Space. The successive appearance and disappearance of every "This" is its supposition and opposition by the I.

THE SIGNIFICANCE OF THE LOGION

The complete dialectic process of the full and final synthesis thus appears to be—not merely a positing or posing of the I, an opposing to itself by the I of a not-I, and then a composing of the two by mutual limitation (which can be understood only as partial identification), but—a posing of the I, an imposing, upon it-self, by the I, of an opposite of it-self, then an opposing and deposing of that imposture, and finally, a reposing, the repose, of it-Self in its own pure Infinity (*Swé mahimni sthitih*). But the perpetually recurrent, superficial, incomplete, unreal, synthesis of endless particular compositions of I and not-I's is also a fact, an illusory fact; it *appears* as the unending spiral circling of the Self in and through a pseudo-infinite number of individual selves, all recurrently first connecting and then disconnecting themselves with pseudo-infinite "this's," bodies, mineral, vegetable, animal, human, superhuman, etc., on all possible Scales of time and space and motion in an endless World-process of evolution and involution, "cycles in epicycles" all "inverterately convolved."

Because the Supreme I is one, infinite, eternal, motionless, attributeless, differenceless, conditionless, and the This is Its opposite in every respect, yet inseparable from It, and imitative of (because falsely identified with) It, therefore the This is Many, is pseudo-infinite or illimitably extensive in space, ever-lasting or pseudo-eternal in time, never-resting, full of all sorts of particular qualities, differences, conditions. The One I is individualised, personalised, particularised, into pseudo-infinitely many selves by the pseudo-infinite bodies with which it is associated and dissociated.

Because each I is the One I, therefore each soul asserts and achieves its indefeasible immortality by and in a pseudo-eternity of endless rebirths. When it becomes tired of being an actor in the drama, it becomes a silent spectator of the cinema. When it tires even of that, it can retire into deep slumber, of (*mokṣa, nirvāṇa*) freedom from all particular limitations, extinction of all distinctions, for as long as it pleases. When it is tired of slumber it can wake again, in a new world, a new system, if it so wills. Heavens and purgatories are no less and no more real than the fair and foul places of the waking world, the vivid glad-visions and nightmares of dream-life; our near and dear, as also objects of our hate and fear, are always present and close to us, according as we deeply wish and so deserve; so also is profound slumber wherein we and friend and foe all are One. All is ever-present in God's Memory, Supra-Conscious Omniscience; our memories are infinitesimal parts of That, as are our pleasures and pains and peace. We have whatever we really want. To really want is to will and deserve.

Since there is only One Self manifesting itself in all, there is no limitation of Its Will possible. Limitation is by an-Other; there is no-Other. Compulsion is by an antagonist; the adversary of the Self, viz. Not-Self, is within the Self, and ever-slain. All sorts of opponents are willed by the Self itself, in hostile pairs, and are destroyed by internecine war. The World-process, with all its loves and hates, laughs and sobs, friends and foes, weals and woes, lights and shades, is Its Will (*Līlā, Krīdā, Nāṭaka*), play, drama. The reflection in, the imitation by, all selves, of this Supreme Wilfulness, "My Will there is none to dispute," is the illusion, the fact, but illusory fact, of "Free-will" in the individual. But the Supreme Will *necessarily* wills *opposites* which abolish each other; hence the contra-illusion of "Predestination."

From the Own-Being (*Svabhāva*), the very Nature of the Supreme Self, as expressed by the Logion, it follows that all proposings and imposings of not-I s *must inevitably* be neutralised, counter-balanced, contradicted, by equivalent opposings and deposings, in rhythmic swing, on the two half-circles, the arcs, of (*Pravṛtti* and *Nivṛtti, bandha* and *mokṣa*) birth and death, growth and decay, "pursuit" and "renunciation," "bondage" and "deliverance," descent and ascent, putting on of bodies and putting off of them. All plusses, additions, multiplications, must necessarily be nullified by equal minuses, subtractions, divisions, so that, taken together, they may be always making up the Absolute Zero, the Endless Circle, Vacuum-Plenum. Thus the Absolvedness from all particularities, the Ab-solute-ness, of the Supreme remains ever undisturbed.

Because the One Self, from the transcendental standpoint, includes at once, here, now, in utterly restful peace, all space, time, motion, therefore each self, from the empirical standpoint, in order to prove the identity of the Son with the Father, the Part with the Whole, seeks to encompass all time, space, motion, and accomplish its Parent's Perfectness, by perpetual procession, on all scales of these three, in and through all sorts of bodies and all possible kinds of experiences connected with those bodies. Witness the everlasting rush of the orbs of heaven through space, and of the living beings that may be on those orbs—all seeming separate from each other, in pseudo-infinite multiplicity, yet all also perpetually interlinked with each other into a Unity of "cycle in epicycle, orb in orb," system in system, individual and species and genus within and without one another, atoms within worlds and worlds within atoms, without end. Consider also the "inveterately convolved" and limitless *spiral* traced in empty space by the *circling* and *rolling* of these globes, these dead and living planets and bright and dark stars.

If we get firm hold of and are satisfied with the distinction between the transcendental standpoint of the Infinite and the experiential standpoint of the Finite, we still realise that to the former view there is *no* change, that "all is every-where and every-when and all-ways" (*sarvam sarvatra sarvadā sarvathā*); and where there is no change there can be no questioning of why and how. If we are convinced that the five senses which "prove" the existence of material objects do not cognise and prove themselves, that the eye which sees sights does not see itself, the ear which hears sounds does not hear itself, nor the skin, tongue, nose, touch, taste, smell themselves, but that they all are cognised and "proved" by the I, that "I" feel, am aware, am conscious, that they exist and see and hear, that the I-Consciousness is the Ultimate Fact which proves all other-facts, and is not proved by any other-fact, that is the locus of all experiences, good and evil, pleasurable and painful, that it is also Universal and the *Same* wherever there is an I-Consciousness, that "there is another" is also "*my*-consciousness" and the "other" is within "my-consciousness," that "within" and "without" are both "within," "thing" and "thought" both "thought," "subjective" and "objective" both "subjective," then too, we would see that our curses and sorrows, as much as our blessings and joys, are all within us, all equally the creations of that I My-Self. It creates them all by Its own Will, of Its own pleasure. Why have you done this? "Because of so-and-so"; Why that? "Because of such-and-such other reason." Finally the answer comes, "Because it was my pleasure to do so, because it pleased me to do so, even to inflict pain upon myself"; and therewith the questioning ceases. Things are proven by their opposites. The I proves Itself by opposing an imaged, imagined, Non-ego. If we wish to taste pleasure we must feel and contra-distinguish pain also. Pain, limitation, cramping, finitising, is prime incentive to search for remedy in the Infinite, and its inseparable bliss of freedom and self-dependence. But the final answer to all possible questioning, the abrogation of all enquiry, complete satisfaction and peace, seems possible only by means of the transcendental stand-point of the Logion and the negation and abolition of change itself.

RECONCILIATION OF ALL VIEWS

In the light of these principles, we may find the means of reconciling different views if we only substitute for their "only" —"this view *only* is the true view"—the word "also" and explain in what sense and with what qualifications and reservations each and every view is true. Thus, since the grades of evolution stretch endlessly either way, "above and below," souls of very high grade and power may well occupy the places of personal Gods of planets, of suns, of systems, Brahmas, Vishnus, Shivas, and Saraswatis, Lakshmis, Gauris, Archangels, Elohim, Ilaha, of higher and higher grades, as the Puranas and the scriptures of all religions say, and rightly be objects of devotion and worship to subordinate souls; in this sense, to this extent, theism is justifiable. Again, since I and Not-I, Spirit and Matter, are inseparable, in the general metaphysical sense, it may well be said that there is no strictly inanimate matter, that "the Universe is one stupendous whole whose Body Nature is, and God the Soul"; in this sense, pantheism is justified. Similar is the case with the views of transformation, of creative evolution, ever-new, "nothing is ever repeated"; also ever-old, "there is nothing new under the sun"; also chance, fate, and so on. Absolute Monism, as expressed by the Logion, explains and synthesises them all.

TRINITY

The word-sound made of three letters, A, U, M, may be regarded as the elemental sound-continuum which can yield all the sounds of animate and inanimate nature. This sound-word reverberating through space is the prime manifestation of the Unmanifest. It represents the Primal Trinity of the Self, the Not-Self, and the affirmative-negative Relation between the two. The World-Process has been described as made up of pairs of opposites, the ultimate opposites being Self and Not-Self; these together with the Nexus between them make a triad. The Nexus is itself dual, assertion—denial. The Unity of the One in the Many gives rise to the Law of Uniformity, of "similarity in diversity," the seeing of which is science, as the culmination of such seeing, the seeing of Unity in Multiplicity, is metaphysics, completed science, completely organised or unified knowledge. The opposition of the "I" and the "not-I" generates the law of duality in its static aspect; in the dynamic aspect it engenders pairs of activities like progress and regress, evolution and involution.

The relation between the One and the Many sets the stamp of triplicity upon the Universe and its processes.[1] All triads spring from the Primal Trinity, which is an unbroken Unity or Zero. Groups of these triads form the subject matter of the several sciences, all interlinked, by the law divine embodied plainly in the Logion.

Since the whole nature of the I (*sva-bhāva*) requires and includes, for self-realisation, by contrast, a pseudo-infinity of not-I's, we have the appearance of arbitrariness, disorder, if we look at any one particular not-I from the empirical standpoint. But since that same Nature requires that every not-I *must be* contradicted by an opposite not-I, we have law and order. Desire is the element of arbitrary whim; reason is the element of law and system.

This unavoidable perpetual cyclical return of the Finite to the Infinite is the basis of all logical and mathematical necessity and world-order. All the fundamental concepts root back in

[1] See *Praṇava-Vāda or the Science of the Sacred Word*, by Bhagavan Das.

this Primal Trinity of Spirit (*Puruṣa*), Matter (*Prakṛti*) and the positive-negative Force (*Śakti*), which constitutes the Relation between them. The *facts* of every science reflect the arbitrariness of each affirmation; the *laws* the necessity of the perpetual negation.

A FEW IMPORTANT TRIADS

All these triads may be grouped into three Sciences[1] of (a) the I (*Paramātma, Puruṣa*), the Infinite Spirit; (b) the Not-I (*Anātma, Mūlaprakṛti*), Matter, the Finite, the pseudo-infinite; (c) the Nexus (*Śakti*) Energy.

I. In the Science of the Infinite Ego we may see the triad of (a) the Impersonal Absolute Ego, including (b) all limited, personal egos and individualised by (c) mind-bodies; thus we distinguish metaphysics, psychology and psycho-physics. When the Ego posits the Non-Ego, three moments or aspects develop in that single act, fact, or moment. It *knows* the non-ego; it *desires* to attach or absorb the non-ego; it *identifies* itself with the non-ego. In the individualised Ego, these three functions are known as cognition, desire and action (*jñāna, icchā, kriyā*).

The abstract universal aspects of these three concrete functions of the soul, psyche, or mind, are known in Sanskrit as Chit, Ānanda and Sat, respectively. They are the principia of Omniscience, Omnipotence and Omnipresence. The objective aspects of the Pure Ego, corresponding to these subjective potencies, are the True (*Satyam*), the Beautiful (*Priyam*), the Good (*Hitam*); or Śāntam, Sundaram, Sivam, the Restful, the Lovely, the Auspicious. The object of knowledge is the True, the one changeless fact amidst endlessly restless and changing illusions; the Self is the only such sure and constant friend that will not, cannot, ever abandon us. The object of desire is the Beautiful; the Self is the ultimate heart's desire of all hearts, the One object of all longing; all Else is dear for Its sake; It is dear for Its own sake. The Good is the object of action; self-realisation,

---

[1] A full discussion of the classification of sciences is found in *The Science of Social Organisation*, i, pp. 264–274.

in and through and by love and service of the higher Self in all selves is the *summum bonum*, greatest good (*niś-śreyasa*).

The properties in the Non-Ego (*Prakrti*) corresponding to these attributes or potencies of the Ego (*Purusha*) are cognisability, desirability, movability (*sattva, rajas, tamas*). In a concrete piece of matter they become quality, substance, movement (*guṇa, dravya, karma*). Though strictly belonging to matter, our living bodies are identified with our souls; hence these three words, sattva, rajas, tamas, are used to express functionings of the soul.[1] A sāttvika soul is the luminous soul of the man of wisdom truly cognising the qualities of things; a tāmasa soul is full of inertia and tenacity, clinging to objects; a rājasa soul is the man of action, restless, ever-moving.

When the Ego begins to turn away from the Non-Ego and wishes to de-pose it, to put it off, what it formerly regarded as True it now regards as false, what was Beautiful and Joyful as Ugly, painful; what was Good becomes ill, Evil; cognition as true becomes cognition as false, desire takes on the form of aversion, action turns into reaction.

II. In the Science of the Relation which connects the other two Sciences, we see that the Nexus has two aspects: a negative and a positive. The negative appears as the triple condition of all experience—Time, Space, Motion. The positive manifests itself as causal Energy and yields the triad, Action, Reaction, and the connecting Causation. The Mathematics of Time is Arithmetic with its triplet of one, many, connected by the rule of three, ratio and proportion. The numbers and the cipher are all metaphysical concepts never exactly reproducible and fixable in the concrete. The Mathematics of Space is Geometry, with its triplet, the point, the radii, included in the sphere; another triplet is that of definitions, axioms, postulates. Similar features may be distinguished in the Mathematics of Motion, Dynamics.

Since Time, Space and Motion constitute the triple condition of all experience of the World-Process, mathematics runs through all sciences. None can be perfectly known unless the

[1] See note to Chapter xi of *The Science of Peace*.

connected mathematics is also known. Hence to know well and fully (*samyak-khyānam*) is to know in terms of (*sankhyā*) numbers. Sānkhya, in the days of the Gītā, seems to have meant the same thing as Vedānta.

III. The Science of the Non-Ego may be said to be the History of the Universe, i.e. of a relatively complete cosmic system. Our solar system makes the unit for our purposes. In such cosmic History, the leading triad of Sciences would be (*a*) Chemistry, dealing with atoms (*aṇu-s*), super-atoms (*param-āṇu-s*), and other primal forms of matter; (*b*) Physics dealing with forces of different kinds; (*c*) Astronomy, dealing with the formation and the movements of "eggs of the Infinite" (*Brahm-āṇḍa*), the orbs of Heaven, the globes of the stars, suns, planets, their action and interaction. It has always to be borne in mind that all things and therefore all sciences intermingle, overlap, permeate one another in overt or subtle ways; that if atoms make up worlds, worlds are stored away in atoms; that infinitesimal and infinite are both equally infinite; that space, time, motion are relative illusions created by the moods of the seer.

Under Astronomy in the large sense would fall Geology, Physiography, and Biology; the last may be subdivided into Mineralogy, Botany, Zoology and Anthropology. Under the last we may distinguish Psychology, Physiology and Sociological History, corresponding broadly to the Ego, Non-Ego, and the Nexus, Mind, Matter, Life. Thus, we come back full circle to the principles noted in connection with the science of the Ego. The more our consciousness expands and our faculties extend, the more does that which was distant and appeared useless come near and become utilisable—on the Path of Pursuit and Power and self-assertive Egoism, for purposes of selfish enjoyment; and on the opposite and complementary Path of Renunciation and Peace and self-effacement in Altruistic Universalism, for purposes of philanthropic service.

In History, chronology is the time feature; Geography is the space feature; Narrative, the march of events, is the Motion-feature.

Physiology is also full of triads: (*a*) Functional Physiology, (*b*) Morphological Physiology or Anatomy, and (*c*) Medicine; the last can be distinguished into the triad of sciences of health, pathology and treatment. In the human body any number of systems are discernible, all arrangeable into triplets, traceable to the primary triplet of entoderm, mesoderm, ectoderm.

Psychology naturally divides into (*a*) the Science of Cognition, (*b*) the Science of Desire, (*c*) the Science of Action. The psycho-physics of the human body as the indispensable apparatus of all physico-mental experience has to be dealt with alongside of Psychology proper. In cognition we may discern three kinds: (*a*) of the present fact, sensation, perception; (*b*) of the past fact, memory, recognition, recollection; (*c*) of the future fact, expectation, pro-cognition, pro-gnos-tication. All processes and moods of the intellectual aspect of the mind would seem to be compounds of these three factors in various degrees.

THE SCIENCE OF COGNITION

The practical aspect of the Science of Cognition is Logic, the science or rather the Art of sifting Truth from Falsehood. The triad of the Science of Reasoning is (*a*) correct observation of facts, (*b*) correct generalisation or induction as to the relation between facts, and (*c*) correct inference as to similar relation between other things newly seen to be of the same kind. This triad takes the well-known forms of concept, judgment and inference. The inductive generalisation in the form of one of the premises represents the memory of the past; the particular new fact stands for the present cognition; the conclusion connects the two and extends them into the expectation of the future.

Indian Nyāya does not make the distinction between Deductive and Inductive Logic. In deduction, strictly speaking, there appears to be no proper inference, no expectation, no advance from the past and the present to the future, but only axiomatic self-evidence, clearer understanding of the present, as in pure mathematics. The reasoning of Nyāya proceeds by inductive generalisation (*vyāpti-graha*). All the tests of truth are ultimately based on the first, viz. direct experience (*Pratyakṣa*). A remarkable consequence follows. Inference proceeds from directly observed particulars to some other similar particulars, in a conclusion, which, by the very fact of similarity, is capable of being *verified* by direct observation, as the first particulars were. But Consciousness is always "My"-consciousness, "I"-consciousness; it is *unique*; there is nothing else, *No Other*, like it.

Na tat samaś ca abhyadhikaśca dṛṣyate. (*Sveta Upaniṣad.*)

We can never cognise an-other-consciousness. We can cognise only My-or-I-consciousness. Hence a real *inference* that others have souls, are *selves*, like mine, is not possible; because such an inference is impossible to verify by direct observation. Other *bodies* like mine by all means. They are observable, and inferrible, and verifiable. Consciousness, the Self, can be and is cognised, recognised, only directly. Hence we instinctively, intuitively, directly cognise and recognise the One and only Self in "My-" self and body, as well as in all other bodies.

The method of making sure of the generalisation is that of agreement and difference or concomitant variation (*anvaya-vyatireka*). The Nyāya explanation of generalisation from one single observation is that when we cognise any (*viśeṣa*) *particular* object and its qualities, we simultaneously cognise (the *sāmānya* or *jāti*) the *genus* included by (*samavāya*) *inherence* in it. The Vedānta explanation of this inherent genus would be that the Infinite One inheres in each particular one and gives it a pseudo-infinite generality which is expressible by the affix "ness" (*tva* or *tā*). This is the element of law. Variation is introduced by other *ones*, other particulars, the progeny of Multiplicity, which is inseparably included in the Primal Unity. Repeated observations are not necessary, though they often help to make the generalisation more precise, within the limits of given times, places and circumstances. From the standpoint of Final Knowledge (*Vedānta*), the Ultimate and Sole Truth and Reality as well as Ideality is the Absolute, and the relative or comparative truths and falsehoods distinguished by scientific logic are both Unreal, Illusory (*Mā-yā*).

THE SCIENCE OF DESIRE

The next department of Psychology is the Science of Desire. The triad of Desire may be said to be (a) simple elementary Wish, primarily for food, (b) Emotion, (c) complex Sentiment, as that of cognition is sensation, memory-expectation and reasoning. What is the nature and meaning of desire? The Infinite Self, having made itself finite, as individual self identified with a finite body, tries to recover its lost Infinity and appurtenant attributes by encompassing all experience and thereby proving itself possessed of all power, omnipotence. The feeling of its smallness, the nisus towards greatness, this "lack," this "want" appears as the state of mind which we call desire. Pain is the feeling of smallness; the feeling of the removal of such smallness, the feeling of greatness, is the feeling of pleasure.[1]

The final surcease of pain and the gain of infinite pleasure is the realisation that I am the greatest, that "I al-one am," that "there is non-else" to hinder Me, My freewill and play. But this pleasure is no longer pleasure. It is transformed into the bliss of peace which includes and abolishes both pain and pleasure into which it was broken up. Desire is the motive-power, the energy, the potency that vitalises and keeps going all living things and therefore all the World Process. This pair of pain-pleasure, which is the heart-beat of desire, is more important than any other pair. Desire subdivides into two kinds: that which causes pain causes hate, the desire to thrust away; that which causes pleasure creates love, the desire to bring near and foster. The connecting third, peace, may be said to be indifference of many forms, grades and shades. Self-preservation, self-increase, and self-multiplication are the three main forms of desire.

The simplest physical "wish to be" is hunger for food; hence the industrial arts; intellectual wish is curiosity for knowledge, the food of the "mental body," hence educational institutions; spiritual wish is longing for eternal being, by union with the

---

[1] *Nālpe sukham asti, bhūma-eva sukham:* (*Upan.*) "There is no joy in the small; greatness is happiness."

Eternal, hence religion. "Wish to be much and more" on the physical plane is ambition for wealth, whence property; on the intellectual plane it is ambition for possession of valuable things, whence art galleries, museums, libraries; on the spiritual plane, it is the desire to realise that "All is I and I am All," whence renunciation of all separative limitations. "Wish to be many" in the body is the wish for spouse, progeny, followers, power, whence the institutions of marriage, family, dynasty, inheritance; in the mind it is the wish to make discoveries, write books, create works of art; in the spirit it is the wish to love and serve all beings and identify oneself with them all, and manifest in them all.

EMOTIONS

Inclination and aversion for things which bring pleasure and pain, when they become connected with living beings, become the emotion of love and hate. Love, with consciousness of the (*a*) superiority, (*b*) equality, (*c*) inferiority of the object, respectively, becomes (*a*) respect, (*b*) affection, (*c*) compassion. So hate becomes (*a*) fear, (*b*) anger, (*c*) scorn. All other emotions are derived from these in combination with other cognitional facts. Love emotions become permanent, appear as virtues in the character; hate emotions, as vices. Of the six "internal enemies" (*ṣad-ṛpu*), lust, greed, and infatuated clinging may be regarded as excesses or perversions, by attachment to wrong objects, of love-emotions; while hatred, pride and jealousy are forms of hate-emotions. The six "enemies" running to extremes become "manias," which may be named as eroto-, avaritio-, phobo-, cido-, megalo- and zelo-manias. The social forms of these, which are making a madhouse of the world, are sensualism, mammonism, mutual terrorism, militarism, imperialism and diplomatism. All abnormal psychology, psychiatry, psycho-analysis has its origin in the perversion and unbalancing of the emotions. All health in the social life means balance in them. The changing and moving life which surrounds us is formed by the "hearts" of human beings.[1]

[1] Full treatment of these matters is given in *The Science of the Emotions*.

As the practical aspect of the science of cognition is the art of ascertaining the truth, so that of the science of desire is the art of cultivating the right desires and emotions and achieving the highest virtue of character and the ability to respond, in every situation of life, to every demand, with only the appropriate benevolent emotion.

The Rishis and prophets of the world brood over the human race, yearning that all may attain, in their turn, the majority of the soul, that higher second birth, regeneration, which will enable them to stand upon their feet and help the next generation of young souls forward on the path of evolution.

The life of the spiritual "office-bearers" (*adhikārins*) is a life of awful sadness as well as of sublime gladness. They have realised their oneness with the whole, and in their hearts the sin and sorrow of the world have to be sublimated and transmuted in the fire of ever greater self-sacrifice. The Buddha's ears ever do hear the whole world's cry, and his mouth ever speaks the words which bring the only and perfect consolation: "Ye suffer from yourselves; none else compels. Would you be free from pain? Then give up selfish pleasure, come to me, enter the glorious path of sacrifice and find the final peace." Every teacher and consoler of mankind has said the same.

THE SCIENCE OF ACTION

Life, mind, has three aspects or functions. Every civilisation has therefore the same three: (*a*) its characteristic body of knowledge, its science; (*b*) its ideals, aspirations, culture, art; (*c*) its enterprises, ways of living, social structure, external conduct towards other nations. Religion has the same three: (*a*) jnāna, basic truths; (*b*) bhakti, devotion, worship; (*c*) karma, sacraments, works.

Metaphysical and psychological "Scientific Religion" (the literal meaning of Vaidika Dharma) applies itself expressly to the administration of human affairs and enjoins a "social organisation" (*Varṇa-dharma*) interwoven with an orderly "planning of individual life" (*Āśrama-dharma*), which are to

F

philosophy as practical or applied science is to pure or theoretical science. The Individuo-Social organisation of India is Applied Metaphysic and Psychology.

"None who knows not the science of the Self can carry action to fruitful issue" (Manu). The quintessence of the Ethic of Action[1] has as its indispensable motive power the desire enshrined in the golden rule: "Love others as yourself and do as you would be done by." The cognition behind this desire is the fact that the "others" are your-self, and yourself and all other selves are *in* God and *are* God, the Universal Self.

But life and surroundings are simple only in principles; they are very complex in details because of the proliferations and convolutions of the duads and triads.

Deśa-kāla-nimittānām bhedair-dharmo vibhidyate. "Duty must perforce vary with time-place-circumstance." Hence guidance is needed. The divine law of the golden rule has to be particularised and fitted to the situations and relationships of life by human law. Dharma, law, binds together rights and duties, and by means of these mutual rights-and-duties binds together human beings into a society "wherein all individuals move forward and progress together," advance towards clearly recognised "ends of life" in co-operation, by regulated, balanced, egoism subordinated to collective altruism, not trying to outrace one another in blind suicidal competition driven by unregulated egoism.

To be made practicable, the golden rule is provided with a technique, a social structure, with well-defined temperamental vocations, rights and duties, work and renunciation, distinct means of livelihood, incentives to best egoistic as well as best altruistic work within the capacities of the different psycho-physical temperaments.

APPLIED PHILOSOPHY, i.e. ADMINISTRATION

Accordingly, philosophy and psychology are applied by Manus and Rishis, the patriarchs and lawgivers of the race, to establish a system in which the life of each individual and the life of

[1] See the writer's *The Essential Unity of All Religions* for texts.

society as a whole are both organised and interwoven as warp and woof to subserve clearly visualised "ends of life." Individualism and socialism are duly combined and balanced. Co-operation and competition are properly regulated. Class co-operation is maximised, class conflict is minimised. The means of doing all this is the clear defining and equitable partitioning of the hardships and the prizes of life in accordance with the laws and facts of human nature.

This system of Socio-Individual organisation is known as Varṇāśrama Dharma. In it each individual life is divided into four natural stages, and the total social life into four main vocations, according to natural temperaments.[1] This ancient system can be appreciated only if the relation between society and the individual is realised in its true nature. The governing principle of the arrangement is the end or final cause which the organism subserves. Organisation is practical reason, fulfilment of intelligence. To organise wisely individual and social life, it is necessary to know their meaning, purpose, origin and destiny. The purblind leaders of the blind, the statesmen, politicians, economists, who have no thought for these ultimate values, can lead themselves and their willing followers or unwilling serfs only into the bottomless pit. Metaphysic tells us of the penultimate values and the supreme value, viz. self-expression and self-realisation (a) first in and through and by identification with a body, and then (b) by separation from and negation and transcendence of that limiting body; (a) happiness here, and (b) hereafter or rather in the Eternal—happiness, the essence of which is the feeling of Self-existence and Self-dependence, i.e. Self-allness.

THE ENDS OF LIFE

The end and aim of life of the individual and therefore of society is dual: (a) the fulfilment of bodily, physical, material, sensuous desire, (b) the realisation of spiritual desire which is desire-lessness,

[1] Fuller treatment can be found in the writer's *The Science of Social Organisation* and *Ancient Versus Modern Scientific Socialism*.

the perfection of Allness. These two are known as Kāma and Mōkṣa. At the human stage of evolution, material desire has to be refined by wealth (*artha*), artistic possessions; such possessions have to be regulated by Law and Religion (*dharma*, means both human and "divine" law). Law and Religion, property and family are thus the fundamental institutions of human life in its first half. In its second half should prevail the other part of the *summum bonum* (*Brahm-ananda Mokśa*). Herein is achieved the complete transcendence of individualism and separatism and the culmination of socialism and collectivism.

Men and women at this different-sexed stage of evolution are patently incomplete, each without the other; both without the relating third, the child. God and Nature need man to embody and express both. Hence the family is the true unit of society and not the individual. For family life parity of temperament between the mates is necessary—a matter for psychophysical testing and ascertaining before marriage. Earning of sufficient livelihood, possession of sufficient property, vocations suited to temperament and ability are necessary. This is matter for wise legislation. How to harmonise and synthesise the conflicting elements of human nature, antagonistic temperaments, so as to make the social organism healthy, how to organise society for peace and obviate organisation for war on the one hand, and, on the other, to have the social organism ready for self-defence at need is told us by unsurpassable Vedic Metaphor.

INDIVIDUO-SOCIAL ORGANISATION

Society is made up of individuals; the purpose of its life can be nothing else than the attainment of the *summum bonum* by each individual life in its proper time; therefore it also should be organised like the individual. Head, trunk limbs subdivided into, arms and legs, in the body; cognition, desire, action, inchoate plasm of consciousness in the mind; nervous, nutritive, muscular, skeletal systems, in the body; intellectual, emotional, volitional, sub-conscious systems, in the mind; these give us the principles of social organisation and the four main organs thereof, the four natural psycho-physical types or classes of human beings, viz. the man of knowledge, the man of desire, the man of action, the man of unskilled or little-skilled labour and of undifferentiated, unspecialised, comparatively un-educable child-like mind, who has no initiative of his own and can do mostly only what he is told by others of the other three types.

(a) The first quarter of life, devoted to the stage of education, discipline, (b) the second given to the stage of householder, family life, and the earning of income, (c) the third quarter given to the stage of retirement from busy competitive life, practising renunciation of possessions, doing honorary public service, engaged in study of the deeper sciences of the spirit; (d) the last quarter set apart for laying aside all worldly things, immersed in spiritual exercise and prayer for the well-being of others—these four stages correspond with the two halves of growth and the two halves of decay and indicate the principles which govern the organisation of the individual life. The first two show decreasing egoism and the last two increasing altruism. The new-born baby is one lump of pure selfishness; the grand-father, ready to give up his body, should be the acme of un-selfishness. In the moment the baby appears as essence of selfishness, the parent becomes the "mother," unselfishness incarnate. Thus, in the individual life, in family life, in social life, God's nature, if reverently understood and obeyed by man, balances and gives due scope to both egoistic individualism and altruistic socialism.

This socio-individual organisation has four main departments: (a) Educational organisation by means of the wise men of knowledge, "the learned professions" (brāhmaṇas); (b) Protective, defensive (political), organisation by means of the valorous men of action (kshattriyas), "the executive professions" who protect the weak and enforce the law; (c) Economic organisation by the settler on the land, the supplier and nourisher, the manager of wealth, production and distribution, "the business professions" (vaishyas); (d) Industrial or labour organisation by means of the worker, the man of helpful unspecialised labour, "the labouring professions" (shūdras).

These four vocational classes are constituted into Guilds (Śreṇis),
each elastically self-governing but inter-dependent with the
others, all presided over by the Presidium (Dharma-pariṣad) of
"holy" men and women, chosen from all the four, after their
retirement from family life, who possess special knowledge and
experience. Such holy persons would have no personal ambitions
to gratify; they would be patriarchs chosen to legislate by
universal acclaim, because they are philanthropic; they would
not represent antagonistic interests and would have no need
to fight with each other in the legislative hall, as in a gladiatorial
arena with tongues for weapons; they would represent different
and mutually supplementary departments of knowledge and
experience in harmony with one another as organic parts of a
whole; they would disinterestedly wish well to all just interests
and would make good and wise laws for the promotion of all
such equally. The form of government is a comparatively minor
matter; the right structure and organisation of society is all-
important. The four-fold social organisation has remained the
ideal, and the undisputed duty of all political forms of (Hindu)
government has been, by tradition, throughout Indian history,
simply to maintain it. The chief executive head should be a
heroic man of action ever ready to risk his own life to protect
every one in the exercise of his proper rights and duties. The
sole duty of the Guild of Executors (which in most countries
now has become the "State" and the "Government") is to see
that none encroaches upon the rights of others, that no person
belonging to one profession is allowed to usurp the functions
of others. By this arrangement the always disastrous consequences
of concentration, in the same bureaucratic or autocratic hands,
of all the four main kinds of power, science-power, arms-power,
bread-power, labour-power, is avoided; balance of power and
peace between the four main vocational classes can be maintained
within each nation and therefore between all nations. The marvellous pencil of the Puranic artist limns forth in permanent
colours for all time in a few great broad strokes the type of the
all-grasping autocrat in the description of such imperial despots
as Nahuṣa and Rāvaṇa.

The two main functions of the State, (a) prevention of evil (*dushta-nigraha*), (b) promotion of good (*shishta-sangraha*), would be discharged separately yet interdependently by the four guilds. The preventive or constituent function is discharged by the Guild of Executors. The promotive or ministrant function sub-divides into (a) education, (b) provision of necessaries and comforts, (c) supply of unskilled assistance by and through the other three Guilds, viz. of Educators, of Suppliers, of Helpers. Each Guild has its own special means of earning livelihood prescribed. This way equitable distribution is promoted.

Necessaries would thus be ensured to all; comforts and luxuries would have to be won by special competitive achievement; special honour, as heart-nourishment and incentive, to the man of science and art; special power of authority to the man of valorous action; more private possessions, property, wealth, to the man of desire; extra dose of amusement to the man of labour. The Guild of Educators (*brāhmaṇas*) would see to it that all members of society received appropriate cultural and vocational education; the Guild of Defenders (*kshaṭṭriyas*) would see to it that none offended by commission or omission, would redress wrongs, ensure enjoyment of rights and duties; the Guild of Feeders and Suppliers (*vaishyas*) would ensure that all are supplied with necessaries; the Guild of Workers (*shūḍras*) would supply all the unskilled help needed by the other guilds.

Thus, the Book guides the Sword, the Sword guards the Granary, the Granary feeds the Plough, the Plough supports the weight of all. Without the Plough all the others would crash down, as head, arms, trunk must all fall from their respective positions in the standing body, and roll in the mud and mire, without legs. This in the waking condition; in sleep, head, trunk, arms, legs are all on the same level, without difference of function. It must be reiterated and carefully noted that all are always inter-dependent, always balanced in power, within each nation, and therefore making peace between all nations. No swelled-head, no muscle-bound-arm, no pot-belly, no all-calves are permitted. All the parts of the social organism, as of the family organism, are equally loved and nourished; the junior are more carefully loved and looked after and not despised. Such "moral equivalent of war" as is necessary for the satisfaction of the ineradicable "aggressive" instincts is amply provided by the difficulties, the hardships, the risks to limb and life, that have to be perpetually contended against in even the most normal discharge of the duties of each guild.

CONCLUSION

Thus may each individual of all human society, generation after generation, in country after country, life after life, progress steadily to the goal, along the two paths of (*Pravṛtti* and *Nivṛtti*) pursuit and renunciation, connected and unified by (*Anuvṛtti*) cyclic revolution, casting off his body eagerly when it is worn out, triumphing over death by realisation of the deathlessness of the Spirit. At the turning-point between the two paths, the two arcs, God who had forgotten Himself into man, begins to remember again that He is God, in the body-temple of the soul that has arrived at that stage. In this sense is true man's instinctive feeling that "the crown of creation is man," the western philosopher's belief that "the Absolute becomes conscious of itself in man."[1]

In the stages and the conditions of the "forest-dweller" and the "renouncer" are the possibilities of developing (*Yoga-siddhis*) superphysical powers, extensions of faculty (*Ātma-vibhūtis*), spiritual perfections. One of these is the power to concentrate the consciousness in the (sūkshma-sharira, the mano-maya and higher koshas) "subtle-body," "mind-body," made up of subtler

[1]
> *Sṛiṣṭvā parāṇi vividhāny-ajay-āṭma-śaktyā,*
> *Vṛikṣān, sarisṛipa-paśūn, khaga-ḍamsa-maṭsyān,*
> *Ṭais-ṭair-atuṣṭa-hṛidayo, Manujam vidhāya,*
> *Brahm-āvaloka-ḍhiśaṇam mudam āpa Ḍevah.*
> > (*Bhāgavata*)

House after house did God make for Himself,
Mineral, plant, insect, fish, reptile and bird,
And mammal too. But yet was He not pleased.
At last He made Himself the shape of Man,
Wherein He knew Himself the Infinite.
And then the Lord of All was satisfied.

"mental" matter, and leave and re-enter the (*sthūla sharira*)
"dense physical body" at will, as a person his clothes.

Ṭam swāṭ sharīrāṭ prabrihén-munjāḍ-ishikām iva dhairyéṇa.
                                        (*Katha Upaniṣad*)

"Let him draw the subtle soul from out of the physical body
by patient, persistent, and undaunted endeavour, as the core
is drawn out from the sheaths of the thatching-grass," as the
butterfly draws itself out from the chrysalis.

He who has attained this power becomes literally, technically,
"super-physically" (*jivan-mukta*) "free while living," free from
terror of death of the physical body, for he has experienced and
mastered the death of this body while yet alive;[1] but not necessarily free from fear of death of all bodies, fear of annihilation.
He who has attained to the conviction, in thought, of the Universality of the Self, is "spiritually" "meta-physically" "free,"
free from all fear of annihilation. The former freedom is the
(*kāryā vimukti*) "to be achieved" by difficult processes of psycho-
physical yoga-concentration, and has higher and lower grades;
the latter is the (*citta-vimukti*) "freedom of the consciousness"
from the sense of separatist limitation, which is gained by steady
unflinching labour of persistent thought and the yoga of introspection; and it also has higher and higher degrees. The two
kinds, it is so indicated, are not necessarily inseparable.

Thus does the Science of the Self, metaphysical psychology,
help the orderly conduct of the individual life within the social
life, and bring material as well as spiritual happiness within
the reach of all.

Within this well-proportioned and well-balanced system of
(*Śāstra* and *Vyavahāra*), Theory and Practice, this (*Ātmavidyā*
and *Varṇāsramadharma*), scientific code of individuo-social and
materio-spiritual life, given to mankind by the eternal spiritual
wisdom (embodied more or less fully in the Scriptures of all
the races) through its exponents, the primal patriarchs, out
of their love for their progeny—within this scheme, degenerations

---

[1] The Prophet Muhammad gives the same advice to his advanced
disciples, in a Hadis-saying: Muṭo qablun ṭamūṭo, "Die before you die."

F*

set in and deformities grow, from time to time, because of the Law of Decay. Then regenerators and reformers arise, whenever and wherever there is need, to re-proclaim the self-same ancient truth in its purity, but in new words and forms and ways. Avatāras, Messiahs, Messengers, Prophets, Saintly Sages, have come in the past and will come again in the future, whose grand figures loom and names of might echo through the haze of the ages. They have come, and will come, to close effete epochs and open fresh ones, to call to birth new civilisations out of the ashes of that self-same Phoenix, the Human Race. One lays greater stress on some one aspect of the total (*Brahma* and *Dharma*) Truth and Duty, another on some other, and thus gives to the religion and civilisation which he founds a distinctive predominant characteristic, though all other features must be present also in subordination. All the glories of the Infinite cannot be equally manifested in one time and place. Also, when any one function of human nature runs to excess and so breeds evil of a special type, an opposite quality has to be emphasised by the Guardian—Lovers of Humanity to restore the balance which means health and happiness.

But the one burden of the teaching of all, the innermost truth and the principal purpose and duty of all life, has ever been and evermore shall be, by ever deeper Yoga-Vedānta to realise ever more fully the Infinite Glory of the Eternal Self.

> Sarvéshām api chaitéshām Ātmā-jnānam param smritam;
> Tad hy-agryam sarva-vidyānām prāpyatē hy-amritam tatah.
> (*Manu*)

> Ijyā-chāra-dam-āhimsā-dāna-swādhyāya-karmaṇām
> Ayam tu paramo Dharmo yad-yogén-ātma-darsanam.
> (*Yājñavalkya*)

> Étaḍh-hy-evĀksharam Brahma, étad-hy-ev-Āksharam Param,
> Étad-éva viditvā ṭu yo yad-ichchhati ṭasya tat.
> (*Katha Upaniṣad*)

> Sarvas-taratu durgāṇi, sarvo bhadrāṇi paśyatu,
> Sarvah sad-buddhim āpnotu, sarvah sarvatra nandatu.

"Greater than all other truths and duties is the truth and duty of Self-realisation, for it bringeth the certainty of immortality. The essence, the final purpose of all rites and ceremonies, all virtuous conduct and sacrifice, all self-control and harmlessness, all charity and all study, is to achieve, by Yoga, the Vision of the Self, Knowing It, whatsoever one desireth, that is his."

"May all cross safely beyond the places that are difficult to cross; may all see happy days; may all achieve Right Knowledge; may all attain the Peace."

Aum—Āmīn—Amen.

PHILOSOPHY OF DEPENDENT EMERGENCE

by SURENDRANATH DASGUPTA

Born October, 1887.   Principal Sanskrit College, Calcutta.

PHILOSOPHY OF DEPENDENT
EMERGENCE

I COME from a family of Eastern Bengal where Sanskritic study especially in literature and medicine continued for upwards of one hundred and fifty years without any break. The family is known by the illustrious title "Kavīndra" of one of my ancestors. My father was the only person who broke away from the traditional pursuits of the family, acquired a working knowledge of English and became a surveyor. There were certain occurrences in my childhood which deserve mention in order to throw some light upon my temperamental background. During the ages of five to eight, when I had a very elementary vernacular education and no knowledge of Sanskrit or English, I could, in some intuitive manner, explain the purport of the Sanskrit verses of the Gītā. I could also demonstrate the various Yogic postures (āsanas) and also give practical instruction to people regarding the complicated processes of internal and external washings technically known as the *dhouti* by the Yogins. I could also give pretty satisfactory answers in a simple manner to most questions on Indian philosophy and religion. As a result therefore my house was crowded from morning till night with ardent enquirers seeking instruction on Indian religion and philosophy. English and vernacular papers at the time in Calcutta were always busy in narrating many episodes about me, whom they branded as "the wonderful boy." Three saintly persons then living in Calcutta, Bijoy Krishna Goswāmi, Sibnārāyan Paramahamsa and Jagadbandhu of Faridpur, were my special friends and associates. At the age of seven I also delivered a lecture before a large gathering in the Theosophical Society Hall in Calcutta. My occupation at the time was the answering of questions from early morning till late at night, excluding the intervals for meals.[1] I also often spontaneously entered into a

---

[1] The sorts of questions that I used to answer are as follows. These questions and answers are collected from a daily newspaper of 1894, a

meditative trance condition as I gazed on the Ganges from one of the ghats (landings) or when I sat in front of the temple-deity at Kalighat.

I was employed as the senior professor of Sanskrit in the Chittagong College in 1911, and since then I have worked on Indian philosophy devotedly and also carried on my studies in European philosophy. As I conceived the plan for writing a comprehensive history of Indian philosophy and worked assiduously, it occurred to me that the outlook of Indian philosophy was obstructed in some directions by certain fundamental limitations. The impressions of a super-conscious trance-state which I had in my childhood never left me, and as they were being continually revived in me in my maturer years, it was impossible for me to deny the existence of the mystical state of self-absorption so much referred to in the Upaniṣads. When I went to Cambridge and worked for a thesis on *Contemporary Idealists and Their Critics* under the illustrious Dr. McTaggart and came in contact with personalities like Moore and Ward, my mind became more critical not only towards European philosophy but also towards Indian philosophy as a whole. I had thrown off the shackles of Hegel long before I went to England, but Einstein's theory of relativity, the *anekānta* relativism of the Jains, and the realists with whom I came in contact in England, finally drew my mind away from all sorts of Absolutism in philosophy. I was getting sick of Absolutism for a long time but lacked the initiative to make an open revolt. My life in Cambridge invigorated me, and the main fruit that I reaped there was courage.

Indian philosophy is like a tropical forest, where almost all types of thought, that have been current in the West since

copy of which I have been able to preserve. *Q*. What is the relation between knowledge and devotion? *A*. It is through knowledge that devotion springs. *Q*. What is the nature of God? *A*. He is a spiritual illumination which cannot be compared with any physical illumination. *Q*. What is the relation between *Prakriti* (primordial-nature-cause) and *Puruṣa* (the soul)? *A*. The creation happens spontaneously from the Prakriti under the direction of the Puruṣa and both are intimately associated with each other, like a lame man sitting on the shoulder of a blind man and directing him.

the days of the Greeks, can be found. The writings of the commentators through successive generations abound in logical precision of thought and true philosophical acumen, which are almost unparalleled. The note of ethical purity, religious contentment and inwardness of mind, with which Indian philosophy rings, and the practical harmony between life and philosophy that forms the central theme of almost all systems of Indian philosophy, mark them out from systems of European philosophy, where philosophy is looked upon more as a theoretic science than as a science of practice. The chief concern of the philosophers of India in the past was not to conceive a philosophical scheme like a toy-machine to play with, but to make it a real chariot on which they could ride. But life here on the earth was sorrowful and was only a life of probation. The real life consisted in the ushering in of a life of emancipation, which would absolutely extinguish this life. Philosophy should be brought into practice for conducting this life to that end. Philosophy was never blended in harmony with the present life as we experience it without subordinating the latter to some other higher forms of existence. In this view, philosophy was the guide for the attainment of a permanent state of being from which there is no fall, no change.

Indian philosophy, in spite of its magnificent outlook, thoroughness of logical dialectic, its high appreciation of moral and religious values, is closed all round by four walls of unproved dogmas: (1) the dogma of the infallibility of the Vedic wisdom, (2) the dogma of emancipation and bondage, (3) the dogma of the law of Karma, (4) the dogma of rebirth. Of these, the first is the primary dogma which is associated with the corollary that reason is unable to discover the truth—a creed which is almost suicidal to any philosophy in the modern sense of the term. According to this view, reason is only useful for biological or sociological purposes, but is impotent to give us any glimpse of the nature of truth. Reason must always be a hand-maid to scriptural testimony and must always, therefore, be used for discovering the import of such testimony and for persuading us to believe it. A student of Indian philosophy knows well how reason entered into the Vedic circle like the camel in the fable and ultimately practically dislodged the Vedic dogma professing only a lip-loyalty to it. Different interpreters of the Upaniṣads have always treated the Vedic texts like noses of wax and twisted them differently to suit the convenience of each specific type of reasoning. If reason is the interpreter, the infallibility of the Vedic wisdom becomes only nominal.

An ineffable super-conscious state is often described in the Upaniṣads, and in some passages there is a tendency to regard it as an unchangeable condition or state from which there is no fall. This has often been interpreted as the doctrine of emancipation. It has been argued that, if there be an unconditional state, that must be no state but the pure self as pure consciousness. If that is the only reality, its associations with appearances of diverse contents must be in some sense false or illusory. Relation of identity, or rather the identity itself, is the only reality. The act of relationing implied in identity, which is responsible for the notion of difference, is the nescience (avidyā) somehow subsistent in the identity. So long as the identity remains in the ineffable state, there is no relationing; but as soon as it descends into the knowable, it can only do so through the extraneous association of a relationing implied in its very nature. Relying on the unrelational ineffable state as the ultimate reality, the relationing factor implied in it is regarded as false. Others, however, such as the Sāṁkhyists, while admitting the existence of the unconditioned as the ineffable super-consciousness (the puruṣas), could not restrict the concept of reality to it alone, and were obliged to admit another order of reality as an indefinite complex (the prakriti), which somehow evolved from itself, varied forms of mutual relations, and through them, qualities and their appearances. They thus admitted the concept of identity-in-difference as determining reality. In the realm of world-phenomena, they admitted a spontaneous evolution of difference and change and the emergence of new categories of existence at different levels. The emergents are not regarded there as mere additive resultants, but as emanations somehow coming into being from the structural complexes. But in the field of knowledge they admitted a different order of causality, that certain mental complexes being there in co-presence with the unconditioned—the self—there was the phenomenon of knowledge. This was a contradiction of the doctrine *ex nihilo nihil fit*, for if knowledge was not already there, it could not have come into being. It is further unable to explain why in spite of the same co-presence with the unconditioned, the phenomenon of knowledge should cease at emancipation. Thus the assumption of the unconditioned either as the only reality or as a parallel reality made it difficult either to explain change or the return from the change to the changelessness. Had it not been for the dogma of emancipation, the systems would not have been fettered in this way, and a more rational explanation might have been effected.

On the moral side, the assumption of the unconditioned as emancipation led to the view that all our experiential states are states of bondage. Bondage, thus considered, has to be regarded as the natural tendency of some mental states to flow towards other mental states (which in the moral terminology is called "*tṛṣṇā*" or desire), and the actual flow of it and its resultants are called Karma. But as the hypothetical emancipation is never experienced by any one of us and as its reality cannot be denied on account of the scriptural testimony, the only way left was its indefinite postponement. Such a postponement necessitated the postulation of a practically endless series of succeeding lives, through which the relational mental structure persisted. The cause of this rebirth is *tṛṣṇā* or Karma, which represents the relational tendency and the actualisation of it, which is inherent in the very structure of the mind. The possibility of emancipation necessitated the postulation of the possibility of the destruction of mind and this implied the assumption of an inherent contradiction in mind, such that, while at certain stages in co-presence with the unconditioned it would produce relational groups, at other stages it would cease to produce them. This is the so-called "teleology" which appears explicitly in the Sāṃkhya and implicitly in the Vedānta.

Without going into an examination of other systems of Indian philosophy, I can say that the principal lesson that I derived from my study of it is that extraneous assumptions of any kind, which do not directly explain experience, but which are brought in from outside, are bound to hamper the progress of philosophical speculations and blur the philosophical outlook. Philosophy, if it is to grow, has to be founded on experience, either direct or indirect. The word experience is very difficult to define. Definition implies that the term to be defined has to be explained by a reference to the underlying relations subsisting between simpler but yet constitutive notions. I do not mean that the constitutive notions are in themselves sufficient for the purposes of definition. But at least the relations subsisting between the constitutive notions should be sufficient to indicate the nature of the emergent idea to be defined. The word experience covers for us all possible mental facts. Facts, again, are not necessarily expressible in propositions. They are the possession of one or more qualities or relations by an appearance or by an existent. By a mental fact, again, I do not mean the mere inward occurrence in the mind, but I mean by it anything that is revealed in the mind either through the inward workings of the mind or by the outward relationing that it may have with the objective world or the minds of others. All sense-occurrences, feelings, desires, willing, the logical and the reflective phenomena, images or the imaginings, *a priori* faiths, all stock of ideas derived from social intercourse, all promptings of value, hopes and aspirations of men (civilised or uncivilised), psychological experiences of all descriptions, the inheritance of knowledge that we have through the works of other people, are all included within experience. Experience also includes the mystical experiences of religious men, the aesthetic experiences of the artists, the emotional experiences of the devotees and the supernormal trance experiences of the Yogins. Science, in the ordinary acceptance of the word, restricts itself to the study of facts in an inter-related system in special departments of the workings of Nature. As soon as discoveries are made or anticipations achieved, they become parts of human experience. When the poet, the dreamer or the

lover fills his mind with his mental creations, throbbing
and pulsating with emotions, with the vague and indefinite
wanderings of his mind and with conflicting oscillations of pangs
and happiness, we have a field of human experience which has
its law and order as much as the experience of an insane person.
The fanatic, the contemplating Yogin on the banks of the
Ganges at Hardwar, the ecstatic devotee forgetting himself in
the divine communion, have all their experiences; and the non-
relational or the supra-relational state into which a man slowly
passes inward far beyond the threshold of consciousness—a
state which is inexpressible by any logical propositions, but
can be felt in its uniqueness—is also experience. But all these
experiences are concrete occurrences in the human mind,
howsoever they may or may not be related with the objective
world. But if any philosopher imagines that there is an ultimate
experience in which all the special experiences have commingled
together indistinguishably like the rivers in the ocean, then
since it exists as a philosophical supposition, but is not directly
the content of any apperceived concrete human realisation, I
would not call it direct experience because it is not a human fact.
The Absolute of Bradley, which he describes as "Experience,"
is no experience at all, as it is never felt or realised. The conception of such an Experience, however, is an experience inasmuch
as it is a mental fact. If, however, a hypothetical metaphysical
entity, such as Bradley thought he discovered, can explain our
various concrete experiences in their varied relations, I should
admit it as an indirect experience. All that is felt, perceived or
realised, forms the content of our individual experience, whereas
all that is gathered or learnt from the direct experiences of
other people forms the content of human experience in one.
The totality of this human experience must always remain
unknown to us to a large extent. In acquiring all individual
concrete experiences also we are helped in an indirect manner
by the experiences of others. For, though an experience may
be concretely realised in us, it may appear like a fleeting phantom
on which we are slow to put our reliance, unless its existence
in others is somehow demonstrated to us. It is only in the case

of experiences, relating to biological self-preservation and race-preservation, that we are primarily sure; but in these cases also the surety of our convictions arises through a long process of other experiences associated with our physical activity and the achievement of the end. This idea appealed to some Indian philosophers to such an extent that they defined right knowledge as that which leads to the fulfilment of objective ends. The cognitive operation is described by them as beginning with an awareness, impelling the person to action and ultimately leading him to the attainment of the object signified or presented by the awareness. Such a definition of experience can only be true to some extent regarding our experiences in relation to the biological satisfaction of ends. The word "biological" is of course used here in a very wide sense. It proves, however, that an experience, appearing in the mind, has to be rehabilitated by a reference to other sets of experiences which cannot be so rehabilitated by a reference to the fulfilment of objective ends. In a major portion of such cases through social intercourse with our fellow-beings, through mutual communication with those around us, by putting ourselves in touch with other minds far removed from us in time and space through the medium of books and through the observation of the behaviour of persons around us, we are always comparing notes about what we feel with the similar ideas and feelings of others, and thereby gravitate towards a common level of experience. In such operations our minds behave more as automatic machines than as free agents responding and reacting in the environment. Language itself is a great machine with which we must work for getting ourselves levelled down to the experiences of our compatriots. In every turn of expression that we use or hear we are forced to adapt ourselves to the thoughts and feelings of others. This forced adaptation, on the one hand, quickly draws us up to the high level of the experience of civilised man, and on the other, looked at from a different angle, it curbs free spontaneity of the mind which has to create anew by reacting on the environment of the mind. The natural result of this process is that we are habituated to take as valid only those experiences of ours which are found in consonance with the experiences of others. Moreover, there grows a tendency in us to shut out and discourage all such experiences as are not likely to be compatible with the experiences of others. Ordinarily the validity that we ascribe to the experiences which we hold in common with others arises out of a sense of a relation of consonance that we feel with regard to our own experiences. The doctrine of self-validity of knowledge that each cognitive state carries with it a sense of its own validity, as preached by some Indian philosophers, is false. Such philosophers draw a distinction between validity and invalidity, and suppose that invalidity arises out of incompatibility, whereas validity is a natural character of all cognitions. This is a misconception of the whole situation. Validity means the consonance of an awareness with what it professes to be. Whenever an awareness refers to a field of experience, related to the objective world or to the objective experience that we have in common with our fellow-beings around us, such awareness carries with it implicitly a history of previous references by virtue of which it automatically asserts its right. This history of references is the average resultant of previous experiences with a predilection towards validity or invalidity, as the case may be. Thus, when on an April noon a motorist perceives water flooding in the Red Road at the maidan of Calcutta, such knowledge does not carry with it any sense of validity. Moreover, it is a matter of common knowledge that an element of doubt is often associated with our sense-experiences regarding the objective world, unless the history of previous experiences associated with it renders them indubitable. Such doubts are more largely associated with the experiences that we have in social or psychological intercourse with other minds. Our notion of validity in such field of experience is merely the appearance of the apex of a triangle of which the base is at the moment hidden from our view, but is apparent on closer analytic inspection.

Regarding the experiences of feelings and emotions, it is only those which proceed from compatible or incompatible inner biological relations of the brute man, that may be said to be somewhat independent of common human experience, woven through mutual intercourse. But most of the other feelings and emotions of a civilised man proceed from the compatibility or the incompatibility of the relations that individual mental states have with the bigger human experience from which they have bubbled up. Our experiences of value, moral, aesthetic or religious, are also largely dependent on this social intercourse. As the horizon of this intercourse gets larger and larger the parochial and the limited characteristics of the experiences, the associated joys and sorrows and the sphere of the value-sense get broader and broader, which may bring a man in conflict with his immediate social surroundings and yet make him confident of the validity of his experiences. Yet we are not entirely bound to the experiences of our immediate social surroundings or to the most distant human horizon of thought; for there is always a scope, in at least some minds, for the creation of new relations and new experiences as newly emergent forms with which they particularly identify their personalities. There they may be absolutely lonely and may come in such a conflict with their immediate social surroundings that they may be smashed into pieces as it were, but still they maintain their confidence in their newly emergent forms of knowledge, feeling or belief. In such cases the validity of their beliefs does not depend upon a previous history of reference, but upon the new forms that have emerged out of such a reference and in their uniqueness possess special history. Their history is dominated by the creative process of their own thought.

It will now be seen that there are two forms of validity: (1) that which establishes its right by an implicit or an explicit history of reference to the structure of our experience woven out in association with the experiences of others, (2) that which emerges out by itself borne on the shoulders, as it were, of a previous mental history of a different order. This second form of validity attaches to experiences, which appear in this or that mind for the first time, but later may, through communication, become the common property of human experiences as a whole. Even if they are incommunicable for their uniqueness, they may yet by sufficient description serve as light-posts for the guidance of others having similar experiences. This applies to various kinds of religious and ecstatic experiences which are often unique and the history of which can only be traced to the temperamental background of the individual.

At this point a relevant question may be raised as to whether there is any such concrete reality as the social mind, German mind, English mind or the mind of humanity. To this our answer is at once yes and no. I do not believe in the existence of any experiential whole, the parts of which are not directly amenable to any individual experience. In this sense the word "social mind" or any other like expression is merely a convenient phrase to denote the idea of numerous experiencing individuals working towards a common purpose. But we shall see later on that different relational groups, when they co-operate together in the same direction, may behave like an individual. In that sense it would not be unwise to admit the existence of a separate social mind. Even parts of the social mind may, in this sense, be taken out separately and regarded as an individual having its growth and career towards a particular goal. Thus we may speak of the growth and development of the political mind, or of the religious mind of India. I wish to make it clear that I do not use the word in a figurative sense. I wish to lay stress on the fact that particular relational groups co-operating together behave as an individual. Converting the proposition, in another way, I may say that an individual manifests itself wheresoever the relational groups of one or more different orders co-operate for a harmonious end.

It is unfortunate that language should practically be the only mode by which we can express our experiences to others or in a very large measure deal with them ourselves. Experiences are dynamic, concrete and showing themselves in different shades of tone and colour in association with other experiences, whereas language is static, abstract, definite and lacking in the wealth of reality. The growth of language has hardly been able to keep pace with the ever-growing experiences. In the very structure of language there is a false logic which has to be wedded to experiences of all descriptions, in order to keep going their currency either with us or with others. Even the Mathematicians, who deal with merely abstract ideas, had to invent a language of their own for giving precision and perspicuity to their investigations. If this is so in the case of Mathematics, how much more should the difficulty be felt in giving expression to experiences or in pinning them down in our minds with a few inadequate terms. Joy, bliss, happiness, gladness, pleasure are some of the terms to denote the mental sense of elation which occurs in myriads of forms, each one of which has its own specific uniqueness. This difficulty of expression reserves for us to a very great extent the privacy of our individual experiences. It limits the sphere of general communicability to such an extent that in a large measure communication in a proper sense is only possible between individuals having similar kinds of experiences. This makes possible the formation of such new relational groups among like minds, that what is real to them may be false to others. Closely allied with the language difficulty there is a difficulty, associated with the general structural relation of our mental states, which may be designated as the *a priori* logical mode. It is by no means certain that the facts, which our experience denotes and which our language expresses, obey in all respects the peculiar structures or relations of our experiences. We must, therefore, have to rest satisfied with the anticipation that our experience may not be able to denote facts and relations of all orders. There may be facts and relations of all orders. There may be facts and relations which would for ever remain undiscoverable by human experiences.

It has been said above that experiences may be direct and indirect. What we mean by direct experience is similar to what Bertrand Russell means by "knowledge by acquaintance." Our indirect experience seems to have a wider scope. It means, firstly, knowledge attained by descriptive communication or by inference. Secondly, it also implies the knowledge by implication or of any hypothetical fact or entity which, though not directly perceivable, may be regarded as explaining the phenomena of nature and of mind denoted by our experiences. All scientific theories, and laws of nature explaining the attested facts, and also almost the whole of pure Mathematics and a very large portion of mixed Mathematics, are examples of this indirect experience. The assumption of more dimensions of space than what are directly perceived by us, so necessary for explaining the truths of Mathematics and Physics, may also be regarded as examples of indirect experience. So also metaphysical assumptions that may serve to explain a philosophical system may be regarded as matters of indirect experience. The validity of indirect experiences is to be tested by their logical cogency in explaining facts or by attestation by direct acquaintance.

The aim and purpose of philosophy is to give a connected and systematic explanation of all our experiences in their mutual connection and relatedness and, through them, of the phenomena which they denote. Philosophers must, therefore, gather all possible facts in different departments of nature and also the various kinds of relevant human experiences. New facts are being discovered every day, and the discovery of one little fact which may not fit in with a particular philosophical scheme may upset it or endanger its existence. A philosophy which starts from certain *a priori* notions and seeks to deduce or distort all phenomena according to them, or which merely occupies itself with dealing with one or a few special kinds of experience, does not deserve the name of philosophy in our sense of the word. As an illustration of the former, we can refer to the philosophy of Hegel or of Spinoza, and as an illustration of the latter we can take the philosophy of the Vedānta. But philosophers should not claim to be omniscient, and it will be a training for them in humility if, instead of twisting facts for a supposed explanation, they would simply confess their ignorance where they fail to know, or where the nature of things is such that no knowledge of the situation is possible. By the very nature of our definition of philosophy it would appear that philosophy is a growing science. It is not correct, however, to think that philosophical systems worked out by the great masters of the past are mere fanciful creations. They are genuine attempts to discover the truth, and even though they may have failed in the entirety of their conceptions, they have always made some discoveries, and even in their failures have demonstrated the hollowness of philosophical investigations in particular lines, and have thus forewarned the future traveller. Thus both in their positive and negative results they have aided humanity in paving its way towards its destined goal of progress. The history of science is also a history of errors and misconceptions, and also a history of the discovery of truth which had to be purged of its impurities by the untiring work of later investigators. Both in science and in philosophy, each important investigator has put in a brick by which the temple of knowledge is being constructed. But, while science collects facts only in a particular department of study, philosophy, in its most comprehensive sense, has to collect facts from all possible departments of knowledge, not only of nature but also of mind. All sciences and human experiences—moral, religious, aesthetic, social, psychological, mystic and the like—form the data for the constructive work of philosophy. The data of philosophy increase with the growth of human knowledge and attempts at systematisation may fail at the most crucial points in failing to explain facts. Both philosophy and science have thus to move forward together. It has been the belief of the past philosophers that the purpose of philosophy is to discover the nature of reality, though the term has been used in very different senses by the different writers. With me reality means all that can be experienced directly or indirectly, all that appears and the immediate pre-suppositions of such appearances. Philosophy must remain silent about bare dreamy possibilities. With the growth of knowledge new realities may dawn upon our vision which it would be the business of future philosophers to deal with. A dream, a mirage, a hallucination are also reality so far as they are experienced. A dream may be called unreal in the sense that it has no connected relation with other dreams of other days or with the experiences of the waking life. It is this break of connection, the impossibility of relating it with other experiences at other times, that makes us call it unreal.

So far as it is an occurrence as an experience at a particular time, it has a definite aetiology and is in that way connectible with other facts and experiences, and is thus within the scope of philosophical investigation. Freudian attempts in this direction are an illustration to the point. The older idea that reality can be equated with the non-relational has so well been challenged by many other philosophers, that it is needless to attempt a fresh refutation of it. The belief that reality is something behind the phenomena, behind the experience and behind the relational out-look of things, seems to me to be a positive superstition. If there are facts, entities or relations behind the phenomena as determinants of them, they are no doubt real. But that does not take away the reality of what is experienced; since we shall have to deal only with what is experienced, that alone has supreme importance for us. It is only through what is experienced that what is not experienced will gradually come in our view in an indirect manner. The view that, because experiences are real and are related, only the relational whole of experiences is the real, is also a gratuitous assumption. Such a totality is never given in experience, and in attempting to affirm the whole as the real the philosopher denies the reality of parts and brands them as illusory. Such a point of view also ignores the most fundamental part of reality and of knowledge consisting in the passage of experience to experience through relations which is the very structure of knowledge. It, therefore, ends in denying the reality of knowledge, feeling and willing which constitute our concrete experience.

The method of philosophy is that of science. It analyses experiences and the facts denoted by them, collects them, and arranges them in order, forms hypotheses and theories to explain them in relation to other experiences. It thus uses both the de-ductive and inductive methods of science and attempts a systema-tisation of all known facts and experiences. Its difference from other sciences consists in the fact that while other sciences are busy at the work of systematisation and the discovery of new facts and relations in their own specific departments, philosophy takes the results of those sciences and other facts arising out of human relations and tries to bring them together in such a system of relations that it may discover a common ground-plan which holds them all; or if facts in a special universe cannot be harmonised with facts of other universes, philosophy would show the extent to which explanation is possible and what are its natural limits. Thus Physics, Chemistry, Biology, History, Sociology, Anthropology, Aesthetics, moral experiences, psychological experiences, mystic experiences, are all the feeders of the science of philosophy. Philosophy deals with all the objective, the subjective, and the supra-subjective facts in their broad outline of relationships, leaving the study in the specific and special relationships and facts in charge of special departments of science.

I cannot leave off here without saying a word about what I mean by explanation. The word explanation is used in a variety of senses. When a fact is subsumed under a general law, or when it is deduced from one or more axiomatic principles, or when the various relevant conditions which invariably precede an occurrence are enumerated, it is said to be explained. When universal laws cannot be discovered, a reference to occurrences of a similar nature may also serve as an explanation. A man gets influenza in October and it is explained by saying that such fevers are very common in October. Again the explanation of an occurrence of a complicated fact of nature, such as the formation of dew-drops, is to be found by a close analysis of the occurrence itself in various fields. Thus we have not only dew-drops in the early morning on the leaves of grass, but on the sides of a glass pane also. It requires also a knowledge regarding the presence of moisture in the air and the conditions under which such moisture is retained or given up. By piecing together the various bits of information and by comparing the different occurrences on analogical grounds, an explanation of the occurrences may be available. Explanation of the origin of the biological species is sought in different ways, e.g. the climate, the locality, the environment, the conditions of life, the comparative anatomy and modes of life of analogous animals. Explanation of historical events is sought in the socio-political and the economical con-

ditions of the country, the socio-political and economical history
of the people, traditions, customs, religions and other kinds of
beliefs, temperamental and the general psychological characteristics of the people together with the exciting events that
led to a crisis, such as those of the French Revolution. All these
events, which are facts of entirely different orders, are connected
up in our minds as co-operating towards one final result. Analogies
in history fail to be instructive when any of the relevant conditions
or facts, positive or negative, is omitted. Explanation of a literary
passage has first to clear up the anticipations or allusions which
are implicitly contained in it, but, even then, the peculiar charm
and emotional suggestions may be entirely missed unless the
person to whom the explanation is offered is already initiated
in those kinds of experiences. It is needless to multiply examples
in such a short paper; but from what has been said, it will be
evident that explanation consists in relating a particular fact
or occurrence either with kindred other occurrences or with other
previous occurrences which more or less invariably precede it
or with the component events or facts which give it its structure.
When a fact is subsumed under a general law, we also follow
the same process, for a law is only a symbolic statement of
certain similar occurrences under similar conditions, and, as
such, all deductions imply the relating of a particular fact or
occurrence with similar other occurrences in a particular and
definite manner. Explanation by reference to axioms or *a priori*
principles also refers to the fact in question as being an instance
of the axiomatic statements. Analogy plays a great part in
explanations, and the enumeration of causal conditions serves
as the vehicle of explanation by a backward reference to history
and also by implicitly relating the fact in question to similar
other facts limited by similar causal history. The demand for
explanation is the most natural demand of the mind which
reveals its very nature.

The word "mind" is a symbolic term for what is in reality a
process of weaving experiences together in a definite and systematic order, which transforms a denotation of objective presentation into an experience, by associating it with meaning. In one

sense, therefore, mind is not an entity, it is a series of relation-ing processes, not in a lineal order but in a structural order. When anything is presented to the mind it is not introduced at a particular point (using a spatial imagery) but in inter-connected waves and processes of inter-relationing. That being so, anything that cannot fit itself with these inter-relationing processes has virtually to be rejected by the mind. Truth consists in the subsistence or non-subsistence or the affirmation and denial of one or more relationships between determinants and relational complexes or between them and relations or qualitative emergents to the extent or in the order or manner in which such relationships subsist or do not subsist or exist or do not exist (restricting the word "existence" to objects of non-denotative experience and "subsistence" to objects of denotative experience or their pre-suppositions). Error, however, may be defined as a subject-object polar occurrence which, though denotable in a particular character under proper relations by any dimension or dimensions of knowledge, is not denoted by it or them as such, under the said conditions, though it is denoted by one or more other dimensions of knowledge. Such errors are rejected by the mind, because they could not have a place in the mind. So also the dream-experiences are rejected. It is for this reason that wise instructions or scientific truths may be rejected by a wrongly-bent or prejudiced mind. This relationing activity of the mind may be called the economic activity by which the mind refuses to entertain lonely individuals in their separatedness; these must be bound together in family-ties of relationships and be taken together along with other similar or dissimilar members, in order that they may have a place in the mind. By the expression "economic activity" I mean that activity which is pertinent to the mind as a relational complex by which it integrates separate facts into the wave-structure of other facts, and makes them co-operate in unison with them. When facts of the same order are integrated, we have universals; when facts of the same or different orders are integrated in the same time-instant in a specific relation, we have the inter-pretation of facts as propositions of a factual order; and when different time-instants are involved in an invariable relation, we have what is called causality. When such integration is implicitly mediated by other facts, we have what is called conditions. The super-vention of such a condition modifies the relation of causality. When facts or events that are qualitatively different are integrated together in universal time-relation of occurrence or non-occurrence, we have what may be called laws. The notion of law is, thus, closely related with the notion of causality. In our ordinary notion of causality we apprehend that the cause somehow impels or necessitates the effect. But, as many philosophers have pointed out, there is no such notion of necessitation involved in causality. It may well be asserted that a causal proposition has no idea of force in it. The application of the idea of universality is also not correct in any scientific sense. The idea of universality is only present in deductions where what was implicit is made explicit, and no new element is introduced. The relation that the whole state of the universe bears to the next instant cannot be definitely predicted even if we could know the whole state of the universe at any particular instant. Causation, thus, is only an approximation of anticipation from a large number of individual instances of the sequence of partial states of the universe with regard to another individual instance, where such a sequence is expected to turn out. If under certain conditions an eclipse is predicted in 1937, it is because under similar conditions eclipses have occurred in all observed cases of the past. It is, thus, merely an anticipation or expectation of one particular event from innumerable series of sequential events that occurred in the past. This expectation may turn out to be true or false, but the affirmation of its probability in all such future cases would be hazardous and unscientific. There is, thus, no causality in a universal sense. Causality, thus viewed, is a relational integration from individuals to individuals. Excepting the case of assertion of causation regarding pure mathematical quantities, where the word "causality" is used in a sense of deduction, making explicit what was implicit, probably no case of cause explains the structural quality of the so-called effect as a mere resultant of it. Causality, thus, is a study in history which explains the aetiology of an occurrence by noting down its fairly large number of invariable antecedents. When causality is used in the sense of analysing the structural components of a qualitative complex, then also it cannot explain the concrete qualitative fact which is more than a resultant of the components. Where the complex is merely a resultant of the components, we have a case of deduction and not causation. No true case of causation, therefore, explains the "why" of a situation; it merely records the "what" in temporal order. In some Indian systems it has been assumed that the emergence of qualities through a causal process is an inexplicable extraneous affair and emphasis has been laid on the identity of the causal entity with the effect, and the process as such has been denied, whereas in others causal process has been regarded as making explicit what was implicit, and thus causality has been treated as a case of deduction. Others, such as the Nyāya and the Buddhist, however, have regarded the effect as a new emergence. The concept of the emergence of new qualities or relational complexes does not involve as a necessary pre-condition that the causal elements or the processes leading to emergence should persist as an integral part of the emergents. The function of the causal conditions in a causal process consists in the fact that they co-operate together towards the appearance of emergent qualities or relations. When causal elements or the diverse relations involved in a causal process lead up to an emergent quality or relation or relational complexes, they may be called, for the sake of convenience, the "basis" of the emergents. The use of this term does not imply that any part of it is a constituent of the emergent qualities or the emergent relational complexes. In a certain class of such emergents the "basis" may, however, be a constituent of them, but that is not necessarily so. But even when the basis is not a constituent, it may remain as co-operative factor in inducing the emergent qualities or complexes such that the modes of the modification of the basis should have its counterpart in the emergent quality or complex. The relation between the basis and the emergent qualities or the complex may be designated as an emergent relation as distinguished from the analogous resultant or the deductive relations. This emergent relation being a unique and inscrutable relation, the converse relation subsisting between the emergents and the basis should also be regarded as unique and inscrutable, and may be designated as a converse emergent relation. The relation between an emergent and other relational complexes through the medium of the basis may be designated as the translated emergent relation. A basis may also itself be an emergent of other causal complexes. Two emergents may also come in direct relation as two original relational complexes and produce further emergent qualities or relational complexes.

The concept of mind and of the ego or the perceiver is indeed a difficult one. Idealists in India and in the West have sometimes maintained that the object of awareness, being given in awareness, is nothing but awareness, and, therefore, that there cannot be an object unless there is the awareness of it. The fallacy of this position was shown by Moore in a brilliant paper in which he showed that awareness and its object are two different things. The Buddhists argued that the two are one since they are given simultaneously. They regarded it as a deduction from a supposed general truth that things realised at the same instant of time are identical in nature. The fallacy is obvious. The image of orange is co-present with the word "orange," and no one would think for a moment that the word "orange" is identical with the round yellow object. Again, it has been held that the subject and the object are given in and through knowledge. The term in-and-through is ambiguous; for if it means a relation, two terms S and O must be present before the relation can occur; and if it means that knowledge alone exists and the subject and object are both its modes and a sort of extraneous imposition on it, then also the reality of knowledge as such, independent of such bi-polar modification, must be demonstrable to us in experience, and some justification ought to be available as to why such bi-polar modification should occur. It is a peculiar situation that nothing can be denoted or referred to except through knowledge, but yet it is unfortunate that the situation be so exploited that knowledge should be regarded as the only reality. The word "knowledge" is used in a variety of senses. The knowledge of a blue patch of colour in front of me is very different from the knowledge that I suppose I have of the n-dimensions of space, or the knowledge that I may have of a tense pain, or an ecstatic state which is more or less unrelational. The use of the word "I" is also very ambiguous when used as a subject of the verb "to know." Had it not been for the crude conditions of grammar, the situation might just as well have been described as "there is a knowledge of such and such." One may as well say "there is knowledge of such and such at such a centre at such an instant." The spatio-temporal limits are just as much necessary for knowledge as for any other event in the world, though on account of the peculiarity of the phenomenon of knowledge its spatial location is not possible. Again, it is said that both the subject and object are revealed in and through knowledge. In that case the subject, being revealed in knowledge, is as much an object of knowledge as any other object. Unless the existence of pure objectless knowledge is demonstrable, it seems irresistible that there is only knowledge, and object or objects are denoted by it. The existence of subjects as such cannot be proved. The existence of knowledge as such cannot also be proved. Furthermore, there is no characteristic appearance of the subject with which I can directly be acquainted. The knowledge of the subject, if we have it at all, is only a knowledge by description or a fiction of linguistic construction. It is difficult to discover if there is a special content of "I," the knower, as a mere perceiver, what the Vedāntists would call the "Sākṣi." If there were such an unchangeable perceiver, this entity would have a character and would be perceived as such. On the other hand, we know that in the consciousness of a new-born babe, who is unaware of a linguistic construction, there is hardly any apperception of "I," and it is extremely doubtful whether his knowledge ever takes the subject-object form. As the individual grows through experience, there are special associations of meaning attached to the "I." He not only says " 'I' perceive" but he also says "I am good," "I am powerful," "I am the hero in battle-fields," "I am unconquerable." All these expressions point to a growing association of meaning with the "I" which not only characterises the subject but also the nature of the perceived object. A common man perceives certain symmetries in a picture and a master artist also perceives them, and even others; the perception is common to them both, but yet the two apperceptions are poles asunder. The apperception of the master artist is associated with the whole history of the "I" as the perceiver, as the creator of many beautiful pictures appreciated by his fellow-beings throughout the world. This shows that though we cannot refer to any particular unchanging entity as the "ātman" or the "self" as the perceiver, we find that in each case of adult perception the apperception of any particular fact or object refers to a history which it modifies and by which it also is modified. According to our theory (the details of which cannot properly be elaborated and justified in this brief paper), there is no sensation, no image, no appearance, no apperception which appears as a singular unitary atomic fact. It appears in a background of a mental complex which has as its counter-part a pretty large area of physiological happenings and processes. Using a physical imagery, I may say that as we grow in experience, the area that is determined by and determines an apperception also enlarges, and the relational processes involved therein also become more and more complicated. This complex area is structurally intimately connected with the entirety of the mental complex; but at any particular time-instant the excitation involved in the mental complex on the occasion of an apperception is in a comparatively limited field. It is these processes excited in a limited field which, being in themselves relational complexes, behave as an individual that is referred to as "I" in "I perceive." The "I" is thus referred to not through indirect acquaintance as such but through implication. This implication involves the operation of a part of the mental whole in relation to the apperceived object. Such a self is neither a bundle of perceptions nor an entity which has perceptions as its body, but is an integrated whole, as a part of the bigger mental whole. It, therefore, not only grows but may change its nature at different times as a result of the mental history, as also on account of environmental influences, and on the occasion of diverse kinds of apperceptions. The mental history is composed of four elements: (1) the original tendency of mutual operations of the mind-complex which is an emergent from the physiological complex, which determines its emergent relations, (2) the environmental history, (3) the history of the manner in which emergent qualities and facts are integrated in the mind-complex, (4) the integrations that have actually been effected. Though the mind-complex is described as a co-relation of diverse relational processes, and though it has been said that there may be groups of relational areas, which may appear to be separable from the rest of the mind-complex and may behave as individuals at different time-instants, yet such a separation takes place only in the interest of the practical activity of the mind, as it is impossible that all relational processes should show themselves at any particular time-instant. But this should not, on any account, be interpreted to mean that any mental field is not connected and integrated with the whole history of the mind complex, or that an individual mind-complex, which has grown in association with other mind-complexes, should be wholly or even largely separable from them. Just as an individual human body can tend to move in one direction at one instant of time, though it has the capacity to move in various directions, so the fulfilment of practical activity requires that the mental history should converge towards a particular area in consonance with the environmental requirements, which would oppose its movements in other directions. The more the mind-complex liberates itself from the environmental conditions and creates for itself more and more stable psychical environments, the more is it possible to have the activities fulfilled more freely and spontaneously in consonance with such an environment. Under proper conditions it may be possible to have glimpses of the mind-complex, as if it were an apperceivable unit separate from the body. Though the mind-complex has been described as a relational complex, such a relational complex must be

viewed as one of free and spontaneous activity and, though
the activity of any separable field of it may be determined by
the operation of the continually evolving mental history, yet
it is possible under proper conditions that the activities of any
such field should grow so intense that it would not merely be
a function of mental history, but, behaving as an individual,
it would largely modify the mental history itself. This spontaneous activity may be designated as free-will. It is as much
determined by history, as it may itself determine the history.
History is not a static fact but a fact of continual mutations—
history determining spontaneity, and spontaneity determining
history. The history on its cognitive side is the meaning which
is the soul, as it were, of any conscious state. No state is conscious
which is not referent at least to some history. The greater the
reference to history, the greater the meaning and depth of
consciousness.

Kant conceived a theory in which it was supposed that there
were unknown things-in-themselves, the influences of which
were interpreted by the minds in spatio-temporal and logical
relations for the construction of experiences. Criticisms of such
a theory are too well known to be repeated here. But one
question naturally arises. Are the spatio-temporal and logical
relationings entirely arbitrarily given by the mind or are they
determined by the very nature of things-in-themselves? In the
case of the latter supposition, the things-in-themselves would
not be unknown, but would be entirely of a determinate character. On the former supposition, the orderliness of experience
would be merely accidental, a supposition quite impossible
to accept. Without the relationing activity of the mind ascribing
meaning to every mental occurrence and thereby rendering it
a fact of experience, it would be difficult to compute the contribution or modification that is effected by physiological
processes, through which a fact of objective nature can be
presented in a newly emergent form to the mind-complex.
It is, therefore, extremely difficult to believe that knowledge
is a relation such that the objective sense-data are present at
the same time both in the external world and in the mind,

and that the mind is only like a door of ingress. For, in that case, we have to ignore the modificatory contributions of the physiological medium, as also the historical contribution of the mind-complex. We know that there are different avenues of experience which I have elsewhere designated as dimensions of knowledge. There are the five senses and also the sixth sense, the muscular; in addition to these, there are the different kinds of inferential processes, the emotional, the ecstatic, the mystic and the trance-states, omitting the other super-normal processes, such as are found in hypnotism, thought-reading and the like, regarding which there are many differences of opinion. Our first start in mental life is in association with the six senses of which, again, the ocular dimension is regarded as the most important. If we take into consideration the modificatory contributions, through which the external something is presented to us, say, through our eyes, we see first of all that there is no contact between the eye and the external something. We know that the external something by itself cannot be presented to the eye. What is presented to the eye are certain reflected rays of light, which have been distorted in various manners (inter-molecular or physical) by various objects. Thus, instead of saying that the external something—the object—is presented to us, we may as well say that the external something, commonly called the rays of light, impinge on the eye in a distorted manner, yet holding a special order among them. Both this order and distortion have an orderliness imposed on them by the nature of the object, which leads to the affirmation of ocular phenomena, and the objects denoted by them. At the apex of all these processes (which are known only by scientific investigations of recent times and of which we are not directly aware) there is an emergent quality of colour-sensation, at the basis of which there are sundry physiological processes. This colour, again, in order that we may be explicitly conscious of it, must be integrated in the mental history and be subordinated to the principles of working of the mind-complex. Under the circumstances, we cannot say that the blue patch of colour, that is implicitly projected in the mind or explicitly perceived as such, exists outside of us

in the self-same quality. It is an emergent quality which has
as its basis the physiological processes acting in unison with
certain other physical facts. But it has a certain co-variant
relation, firstly, directly with the physiological processes
which form its basis, and, secondly, with the physical stimulus
which roused the physiological processes. This co-variant
relation is a determinate relation of an unalterable nature.
Even when the colour-image passes through the fourth order
of transformation by its integration with mental history, the
co-variant relation remains true to a pretty definite extent.
The exact nature of the relationship cannot be determined on
account of the fact of new emergence at each of the stages. But,
though the nature of the relationship cannot be estimated, the
co-variant relation has such definiteness that, howsoever the
nature of the external world may vary as related to our experience
of it, our awarenesses of it stand in a definite co-variant relation
with it, such that our awarenesses may be said to denote real
objective facts, and this is the basis of our commerce or intercourse with the external world. This is what I may call the
denotative theory of knowledge. Our knowledge does not
correspond with the object, nor is it a fact of such a nature
that it means a modification of the entire state of the universe,
nor is it a mystic history-less illumination or a mere product
of co-operating collections, but it is such that we have one to
one relation with the so-called external object and also with
our mental history. It is a function of them both. The word
"orange" has no similarity with the round yellow object, though
it denotes it by a specified type of relationship; so our knowledge
is related to the so-called objects which have no nature in themselves except in relationship with other relational complexes.
Relation is a word the connotation of which is ultimate
and indefinable. The relations may be of different orders and
types. One of the distinctions that are observed regarding
relations is that they are either symmetrical or asymmetrical;
with reference to the relation that holds between the sensory
acquaintance and the external fact denoted by it, it may be
said that it is asymmetrical, that is, the relation between the

external fact and the internal acquaintance is different from the relation between the sensory acquaintance and the fact. It is on account of this fact that while a sensory acquaintance projects itself as an external fact, the external fact co-operates with other data towards the emergence of the sensory acquaintance. The contention of the ultra-idealist that there need not be an external fact but that the mind has the ideas impressed on it, or evolves them by its own activity, would render community of experiences impossible of explanation. If we were to suppose that such a community is possible on a theory of accidental harmony of illusions, it would be merely running the philosophy to bankruptcy. Thus, the external fact has to be admitted. It has also to be admitted that we cannot know it just as it is. But not to know it, just as it is, is not to have no knowledge of it. So long as the co-variant relation between the external facts, which may be regarded as the determinant at the one pole, continues through other determinants in the chain, with the determined at the other pole as the sensory acquaintance, we may say that we know the external fact. When we say that we know the number "2," all that we mean by it is that we know a number of relations that it has with other real or imaginary numbers. An object is said to be known when we know some of its relations in a variable or invariable order with other relational complexes. It is not given to us that we should know any entity whatsoever in all possible relations, and we should have to be content if any entity or complex is given to us in at least some definite relations with other entities or relational complexes. Knowledge implies the knowledge of relations. Even a sensory impression may be said to be known only so far as its relations with other things are known. A thing is nothing but a complex of relations. The question about the possible relatum will be taken up in due course. According to the explanation of knowledge given here, it will be seen that even what is called a direct acquaintance and direct experience is in fact only a mediated experience where the terms in the middle are merely jumped over and we have a direct passage from the determinants to the awareness, and *vice versa*. Awareness of relations may be regarded as the particular mode of the passage of the mind from one term to another or from one item of experience to another.

But are awareness of relation and the relation the same? Or do relations exist externally outside the mind? If they do exist, what must be their nature? The position that I have to take is that relations exist as ultimate facts, but their knowledge as imparted to us is through a relation of translated emergence. Since relations are admitted and relation of relations also admitted, and it is also admitted that we have knowledge only of relations, it will be absurd to ask if we can know any relation as it may exist outside of us without any further relation. Knowledge is possible only in the possibility of relational structures emergent from the mind-complex. No single relation *per se* can yield an acquaintance of it, for acquaintance itself consists in the emergence of certain relations as a qualitative fact in and through a relational structure, which may remain implicitly as the basis of it, but which can be made more and more explicit by a process which can be designated as deliberation. The traditional classification of logical propositions shows that the structure of knowledge consists in relations. When a particular relation is said to be known between A and B, the relation becomes explicit and the terms remain implicit; but all the same, the terms are relational complexes, out of which a particular relation emerges as a qualitative fact, which is commonly designated as acquaintance. The qualitative nature of a fact is nothing but the emergence of one or more relations from relational complexes. When the relational complexes become extremely implicit, we have an instance of abstract logic or Mathematics where direct experience is at its minimum. Since only relational emergents arising in and through relational complexes which are constituents of mind-complex can reveal themselves in acquaintance, knowledge of relational determinants in the external order or in the other mind-complexes can only be through a co-variant order of emergence. Relational complexes or relations existing in external order are designated as relational determinants, as distinguished from our awareness of relations. If we remember that relations can only be known when they become emergent in the mind-complex, the fear of the vicious infinite vanishes. Relations may become emergent through successive series of other relations or of relational determinants of different orders, and the whole process of such a connected series of mediation may be there without being emergent, in which case we can have no direct acquaintance of them, though we may be indirectly aware of them only as co-variant terms of determinants. Relational emergents of the mind-complex may thus be regarded as the function of other relational determinants of one or more different orders. Relational determinants may in their turn be emergents from other determinant complexes; but they cannot be known since only relational emergents of the mind-complex show themselves in acquaintance. The so-called revelation in knowledge is nothing but the emergence of relations in and through relational complexes.

A question here naturally arises whether there are any relata. This is a difficult question. Since relations can only arise in and through relational complexes, we have no experience of relations without there being any relata. But what may be the ultimate nature of relational determinants as apart from all relational emergents must remain for us doubtful. If there are such ultimate relata or terms of reference, relations must be interwoven in their very nature and structure. Thus there is no position where we can get to ultimate terms without involving relations. Even the assertion of the identity of any ultimate term involves the relation of identity; and without asserting the proposition that an ultimate term is what it is, we cannot refer to it even in the most indirect manner. From an analysis of our experience we know that relations may behave as emergent qualities and may thus behave as relata to other relations. The question, therefore, regarding relata and relations becomes only a relative one; and it may be admissible to think that there are ultimate relational determinants which behave among themselves both as the relata and relations. Our ultimate starting-point must therefore be with relations that are determinants. An analysis of our awareness of relation also shows that it consists in the passage of the mind from certain relational complexes to certain others. Such a passage may be designated as a movement of determination. Determination thus is the very nature of relations and is nothing extraneous to it. The world as such is a big mathematical equation in which most of the relations have not taken an emergent form in the mind-complex. The world that we can know is by its very nature only a small fraction of the world that is. Howsoever our knowledge may advance, it has to be admitted that there is always a limit both as regards scope and extent and as regards the ultimate levels, beyond which relational determinants must remain wholly unknown. The limit is the limit of the emergent mind-complex. Relations, in our view, are both external and internal. When they contribute to the projection of an emergent they are internal, and when they do not they are external.

In some systems of modern philosophy, space-time has been regarded as the ultimate original in nature. But, in our view, since space-time also is a relational whole, having definite properties of its own, there must be some level of which it is a product. That level is the level of our ultimate relational terms. I have intentionally used the term "product" in this connection, as I do not at the present time feel sure whether the space-time has for its component or constituent the ultimate relational terms. When a product is a resultant of some elements, such elements may be said to be components of the latter. But when the product is an emergent fact, the elements that led to its projection may be said to be its constituents. But it seems to me quite possible that it will be gratuitous to suppose that all the determinants in the space-time structure should be emergible in the mind-complex. The mind-complex acts in harmony with our sense-organs and, as such, with the so-called matter. If there is any definite type of space-time structure which is not co-terminous with mass or matter, it is quite possible that we may not have any knowledge of it. Since space-time structure is a relational whole and since mass and force are ultimately reducible to it, the existence of force as a separate determinant cannot be admitted. The force that appears to our mind is only an emergent fact, the datum of which has to be sought in the relational field. Space-time structure being a relational whole, slices taken from it for any consideration must be of a purely relative nature. The space-time structure being the ultimate experiential basis of all emergents, at least some of its characters continue through the series of emergents up to the mind-complex. This explains the fact why mind starts with some vague notions of space-time, which get more and more explicit with training and the history of experiences.

When a relational complex leads to the projection of another relational complex, such that only some of its constituent characters are manifest in the latter and the latter has some new characters associated with it, we would call the latter an emergent of the former. It thus appears that in all cases of emergents there is, on the one hand, some loss of old characters, and, on the other, some gain in the formation of new ones; and the new ones are not explainable in terms of the old ones as a resultant of them. Thus the protons, neutrons, electrons and the ions are some of the fairly ultimate facts of the order of matter, the phenomena of which as protons are emergents in the mind-complex and the nature of the determinants of which is being discovered by the mind through complex spatio-temporal relationships of waves, corpuscles and the like. The protons, electrons and the ions are the constituents of all inorganic and organic substances—in fact, of the entire material world. The properties of different inorganic substances are due to the different spatio-temporal structure and the proton-electronic fields in them. These properties, which entitle them to their special existence as different elements, are emergent facts in consonance with our general principle of emergence. But the relational fields of these relational complexes are such that there is no specification and division of functions in them, so that the only ways of their working are in inter-molecular and inter-atomic directions. There is no selective action in them and no effort to retain their persistency or recover damages wrought on them by environmental conflict by any functional modes. They are thus not true individuals, though in a general sense electrons or protons—though constituted as a commingling point of various relational fields—may, for explanatory purposes, be taken as individual wholes.

It is only when we come to life that we come to the peculiar situation where a piece of structural matter distinguishes itself from the rest of the material world by its selective action, effort to persist, attempts at repairing damages and by a peculiar phenomenon, technically called behaviour, and reproduction. In the field of matter, some distant resemblance to selective action in living organisms can be traced in the peculiar responsive action of coloids to ions. Life, whatever it may be, manufactures the material stuff suited for its manifestation by itself from other organic and inorganic substances in a manner and to the extent that no laboratory chemist can ever hope to do. As life advances from the vegetable to the animal and from the lower animals to the highest, the human, we have a gradual advance of a multifold differentiation of functions and activities which all work in a selective harmonious manner leading to the development of the body and the reproduction of similar bodies in it in endless series. In multi-cellular animals, each cell possesses the characteristic of an independent living being and yet merely in the presence and association with other fellow-cells an entirely different individual, the animal, is projected as an emergent. Here we have a relational complex which is of an entirely different order from the relational complexes in the material order. Here we have two emergents, the life-process-complex, and the body-complex, and though body-complex is the basis of the emergent life, the body-complex is itself also an emergent of the life-process-complex. Neither of them can be said to be prior to the other. We have here a peculiar instance of two relational complexes of a different order, mutually determining each other, just as we have in man the mind-complex, determining the life-process-complex and the body-complex. No instance of this order is available in any of the lower levels. It may well be supposed that the crude beginnings of mind-complex must have begun at least with the unicellular animals. The inter-relation of the relational processes subsisting between the relational complexes, mind, the structure of the body, life-functions and the environment, cannot be considered separately except as an abstraction. They are all in one, and one in all. The different constituents that compose the living man are such that each co-operates towards the emergence of other forms in definite directions. We have already noted that in the case of man the presence of other mind-complexes is an important factor towards the development of the mental life in various grades of social life uniting the past, the present and the future. It is impossible for me now to do justice to the many problems that are associated with a study of the biological field, which are not only extremely interesting but which could have thrown a flood of light on the elucidation of the above view. One or two points may be cursorily touched.

The distinguishing feature of life is that here the relational modes are of a dynamic nature, such that the reality or existence of any particular mode is dependent on other modes of a different order and *vice versa*. We have here a situation in which a particular relation-mode or function does not exist *per se* but through others, and there is thus a mutual dependence of such a nature that it is impossible to start with any one of them as being prior to the other. We have here a circle of revolutions in which any point can be regarded either as the first or as the last. Yet the first is in the last and the last is in the first. If this relationship is such in life, it is still more so with regard to the flowing activity of the mind-complex, which is absolutely unrepresentable by any terms of physical notation, which behaves as an integrated growing whole and yet keeps its co-variant relations with life-processes, the body and the environment. Another point is that even the cellular membrane has a special selective action which attains its highest evolution and development in instinct and human intelligence. The selective action in the case of all animals beginning with the uni-cellular is to be found in the peculiar phenomenon called behaviour, which is the registration in an unknown manner of past experiences. This peculiar phenomenon of behaviour serves to destroy the barrier of time and makes the past, present and the future coalesce at any given instant, and thus starts the history of the individual as personality. In the lower grades of life where the behaviour of the individual animal is largely under the control of the body-complex, the term personality may not suitably be used. But as the mind emerges out of the body and begins to assert itself in its spontaneous existence though carrying with it the peculiar body-emergents as appetitive functions, begins to show itself as a true individual, the integrated history of which, having risen above the appetitive functions, begins to reveal itself in accordance with a selective purpose, which is its own emergent as value. The appetitive functions here do not lose their existence but have a transmuted modification in consonance with the value-sense. Here the biological tendencies are not destroyed but their potency, and indeed the potency of the whole life-history, converges towards the achievement of the self-emergent purpose, the value. There is thus here a new ordering of the old existent states of previous history producing by their harmony, contentment and blissfulness associated with the progressive march of the higher man. In the lower order the conflicts between the animal and the environment are annulled by the life-process itself in a very naturalistic manner. With the evolution of mind, mental conflicts of different orders arise through our intercourse with other minds. Such conflicts are natural and obvious; and the life-process instead of annulling them often increases them. But as a new selective purpose as value emerges in man, he sets his house in order. The integrated history behaves as a person and the conflicts are annulled and the whole history becomes a history of self-realisation in the light of the value. Where the emergent value cannot exert itself as the real and constant selective purpose of the man but is in conflict with the biological selective purpose and only inconstantly shows its supremacy from time to time, we have the picture of the ordinary struggling man.

The selective action associated with life introduces us to a relational complex, which deals with purpose. The idea of purpose must be conceived as a relational order that makes for the persistence of itself by introducing only such relations into itself as are contributory to its existence and growth. When we say that the world has a purpose, we only mean that it is contributory to our being and development. To say that the entire universe is purposive is probably an exaggeration. Only those relational orders and complexes which are contributory to life may be regarded as fulfilling the purpose of life. There may exist many types of relational complexes which originate in their own law, but which are not contributory to the purpose of life. Thus, if a fragment of the world is purposeful, there is probably another fragment of it which is purposeless. When the mind emerges from the biological basis and feels itself in its integrated history as a self-subsisting unity of relational complexes in commerce with other minds, which being contributory to its development may be felt as its constituent, a new non-biological purpose arises, the whole field of vision of which is raised above the biological level. Minds separately chained to bodies can be held together as constituents only through love. Love is thus the fundamental non-biological relationship which can cement together in a common goal of higher relationship all minds of the past, present and the future. Such a possibility cannot happen unless and until the apperception of value as a self-emergent purpose of the mind-life is enthroned in the dominating position of a queen.

The one important fact is that the mind-complex should have such an independent existence that it may transmute the biological tendencies (used in a very wide sense) to its own order under the guidance of the emergent value-forms. When there is a beginning of it we have the beginning of saintliness. Our process, therefore, is not a process of mental annihilation but a richer process of mental growth, where mind assumes its true role of an emergent reality linked to the body as its basis but leading a life which is entirely its own. The emergent forms of value may appear as the beautiful, the good, the realisation in knowledge, the realisation in will, the realisation in higher non-biological emotions turning towards an apex as God or in any other form. The treatment of the emergent forms of value is a very wide subject by itself, and cannot be treated in the present paper. The true God is not the God as the architect of the universe, nor the God who tides over our economic difficulties or panders to our vanity by fulfilling our wishes, but it is the God who emerges within in and through our value-sense, pulling us up in and through the emergent ideals and with whom I may feel myself to be united in the deepest bonds of love. The dominance of value in all its forms pre-supposes love, for it is the love for the ideal that leads us to forget our biological encumbrances. Love is to be distinguished from passion by the fact that while the latter is initiated biologically, the former is initiated from a devotedness to the ideal. When a consuming love of this description is once generated, man is raised to Godhood and God to man.

PRINCIPAL PUBLICATIONS

A Study of Patanjali. Calcutta University Press.

Yoga Philosophy and its Relation to other Systems of Thought. Calcutta University Press.

Yoga as Philosophy and Religion. Kegan Paul (London).

Hindu Mysticism. Open Court (Chicago).

Indian Idealism. Cambridge University Press.

History of Indian Philosophy. Five volumes, two of which are already published by the Cambridge University Press.

REALISTIC IDEALISM

by HIRALAL HALDAR

Born 1865; M.A., Ph.D., Calcutta University
Late Professor of Philosophy in the University of Calcutta
Sometime George V Professor of Philosophy

REALISTIC IDEALISM

MORE than fifty years ago, when I entered Calcutta University as an Undergraduate, there was very little of what can rightly be called philosophical teaching in the University. Certain text-books, mainly on psychology and ethics, were prescribed and all that the Professors generally did was to expound them and to dictate to the students short summaries of them. Very often the exposition was wanting and the dictation of notes everything. One conspicuous exception to this method of teaching was that of Dr. William Hastie, who was Principal of the General Assembly's Institution affiliated to Calcutta University when I became a student of the College in 1882. But I was a freshman, and as Dr. Hastie's lectures were delivered to the higher classes only, I had not the opportunity of being benefited by his stimulating teaching. Dr. Hastie was one of the few real teachers of philosophy that ever came out to this country. But by the time I reached the B.A. Classes he had quarrelled with his home authorities and resigned. The usual sort of teaching did not suit me at all. I had a perfect horror of taking down dictated notes. I longed for instructive and inspiring lectures but none was available. Under such circumstances I was forced to ignore college teaching altogether and to acquire such knowledge of philosophy as I could by means of private study only. This reliance on my own efforts probably did me a great deal of good by compelling me to think a little on my own account. At first I had not much taste for philosophy. But fortunately my attention was drawn to a series of short articles in a weekly journal of Calcutta inculcating an idealistic doctrine of the Berkeleian type. These articles awakened my interest in Berkeley and I turned to his writings. I read his *Principles of Human Knowledge* and *Three Dialogues between Hylas and Philonous* and was very much impressed by them. But I was enabled to avoid a subjectivist bias by reading almost simultaneously expositions of Kant by Stirling, Green, Caird and Adamson. The *Critique of Pure Reason* I studied a little later. Hegel I tried to read but without success. Such expositions of him as came into my hands were perfectly useless. I remember spending hours one evening over Ueberweg's account of Hegel in his *History of Philosophy*. Not a single line was intelligible and I closed the book in despair. This, I suppose, is the usual experience of those who first approach Hegel. The book which first enabled me to comprehend something of the meaning of Hegel was Edward Caird's *Hegel* in Blackwood's Philosophical Classics Series, a book which is justly described by Professor Watson as "small but golden." William Wallace's Prolegomena to his translation of the *Encyclopaedia of the Philosophical Sciences* was also of immense help. By and by I managed to read the *Encyclopaedia* itself. The philosophical movement known as Neo-Hegelianism was in my student days gathering strength in Great Britain and I was one of the very few, not improbably the only one, who then felt its power in India. I eagerly studied everything that appeared from the pens of J. H. Stirling, the two Cairds, Green, G. S. Morris, R. Adamson, J. Watson, A. Seth, afterwards Pringle Pattison, D. G. Ritchie, F. H. Bradley, B. Bosanquet, R. B. Haldane, afterwards Viscount Haldane, Henry Jones and others. I was very powerfully influenced by these writings, particularly by those of Green and Caird. Bradley's *Ethical Studies* also very deeply impressed me. A new heaven and a new earth seemed to be disclosed to my eyes. In later years Hegel was studied with much difficulty and slowly.

I should add that in the Proceedings of the Society for Psychical Research and Myers's *Human Personality and its Survival of Bodily Death* I have found much that is informing and suggestive.

I have seen myself described as a Hegelian. The basis of my thought is undoubtedly Hegelian, but in the course of years, as this sketch may show, I have been led to modify in many ways what I have learned from Hegel. No man, however poor a thinker he may be, can exactly reproduce the views of another. The very essence of individuality is its uniqueness and therefore the angle of vision of one man is bound to be somewhat different from that of another. In the process of making my own the ideas acquired from Hegel and others, I have inevitably transformed them more or less.

Alexander Bain was perfectly right when he said that the ingenuity of a century and half had failed to see a way out of the contradiction exposed by Berkeley. The contradiction is that of supposing that the objects all around us, the things which we see, smell, taste, hear and touch exist on their own account independently of their being perceived. To be, argues Berkeley, is to be perceived. Take away from things the relations in which they stand to the perceiving mind and they lose all meaning, simply cease to be. The objective world can no more exist apart from mind than can the outside of a thing exist in isolation from its inside. The self is the very centre of being of whatever can be called real, the life and soul of all that is. The experienced world has its support in mind. This argument is by no means of modern origin and Berkeley was not the first to use it. It was well known to the sages of the Upaniṣads nearly three thousand years ago. In the *Bṛhadāraṇyaka Upaniṣad*, for example, probably the oldest of the Upaniṣads, Yājñavalkya tells his wife Maitreyi that all things forsake him who supposes that they are separate from mind. As the sound of a musical instrument cannot be taken hold of apart from that instrument, as the sound of a conch-shell cannot be apprehended separately from the conch-shell, but if the musical instrument and the conch-shell are cognised the sounds emanating from them are necessarily cognised along with them, so none of these things issuing forth from the self can be known independently of the self. It may be said that the plausibility of the idealistic argument is due to a confusion between a thing and the thing as known. A man with whom I am shaking hands is necessarily related to the act of handshaking but this does not mean that his very existence depends on it. The food I am eating implies the act of eating, but eating is not the necessary condition of the existence of the food. So a thing *as perceived* is dependent upon perceiving, but the thing as perceived is not identical with the thing. The latter has no necessary relation to knowledge. The contention of the idealist is that no such distinction can be made between object and object of knowledge. The very essence of an object is its being known. As Yājñavalkya says all things flee from him who attempts to separate them from the self. Food which is not eaten is possible, a man with whom no one is shaking hands is possible, but a thing which no mind knows is impossible. It is the outcome of false abstraction.

But however sound and unassailable Berkeley's fundamental principle, in its essence, may be, the conclusions he draws from it are not all tenable. In the first place, he gives a too restricted meaning to it. Perception is not the only mode of knowledge and it is therefore not possible to say that what is perceived is alone real. It would have been better if he had said that the *esse* of a thing is its *intelligi*. In his earlier writings he ignores almost completely the universal forms of knowledge and takes cognisance of its contents only consisting of particular sensations and ideas. In the *Siris* this view is to some extent corrected and the importance of universality in knowledge realised. Even in the *Principles* he admits that the self is an object of thought, not of perception. In the second place, from the right premiss that nothing is real apart from mind the wrong conclusion is drawn that everything is reducible to ideas of the mind. So far from it being true that things are only ideas, ideas have no meaning, as Reid urged, without their reference to things. The *opposition* of mind to its object is the very basis of knowledge and without this duality no sort of cognition can take place. If to be is to be perceived it is equally true that to be perceived is to be. In all knowledge the distinguishable but inseparable factors opposed and irreducible to each other are the mind that knows, the object that is known and the act or process of knowing. Imagination also has this three-fold character. The imagined world is as much opposed to the imagining mind and its activity as the solid world of perception in time and space. This being so it is the images of the mind, the ideas that are to be brought into line with things and not the latter with the former. The imagined world is quite as objective as the physical world of perception to which we belong. Things therefore are not mental ideas, they are objects of mind. Instead of things being ideas, it is ideas which have the status of things. This truth is clearly realised by the idealist philosophers of India. Śaṁkara, for example, who is commonly but wrongly supposed to be an illusionist, a thinker who denies the reality of the world, lays the utmost stress on the opposition of what is known to the mind that knows. In the absence of something distinguished from mind and opposed to it knowledge is no more possible than it is possible for a dancer to dance on his own shoulders. Epistemologically, Śaṁkara is a thorough-going realist. He does not say that the empirical world is in any way dependent for its being on the finite mind. All that he maintains is that ultimately, from the highest point of view, it has no independent existence apart from Brahman. Both Śaṁkara and Rāmānuja maintain that even illusions are not unreal and merely subjective. They are as objective as the things of ordinary perception, the only difference being that they are not common to all, but individual and last only as long as they are experienced.

The objective world then is wider and more comprehensive than the world of common cognition and contains numberless extensions in the shape of the products of the imaginative activity of the mind. What is imagined is not one whit less objective and opposed to the mind than what is perceived. It is not more mental than the latter and has no specially intimate connection with the subjective process of knowing. It is on the same footing with sensible realities and differs from them not in essence but in respect of detailed characteristics only. Imagined things are not of common experience and are peculiar only to those who conceive them. Unlike perceived substances they have no tangible qualities and do not offer any resistance to movement. They are not enduring and are in being only as long as the activity of imagination continues. The error of the subjective idealist is to suppose that images, ideas, representations are purely mental and to maintain that perceived objects are like them. The subjective processes of cognition alone are mental. The contents of the mind to which they refer, no matter whether they are perceived or only imagined, are all equally objective and antithetical to mind and constitute ingredients of

CONTEMPORARY INDIAN PHILOSOPHY

different kinds of what is called the external world. It is not
things that are to be reduced to ideas but ideas are to be assimilated to things. There is nothing that belongs specially to the
knowing mind except its own activities.

In what has been said above stress has been laid on the
opposition of the experienced world to the mind that knows it.
It stands over against the subject on its own legs and is in no
way reducible to it. Its existence is not dependent upon the
finite minds which are included within it except those portions
of it that are the products of their imaginative activities. On
the opposition of subject and object all knowledge is founded.
There is no such thing as an insulated mind contemplating
only its own internal states. The whole content of mind, percepts
as well as ideas, belongs to objective experience. What are
specifically mental are its own activities of knowing and willing.
But the opposition of subject and object does not mean that
they are separable from each other. The error of realism is to
make this opposition absolute, just as the error of subjective
idealism is to ignore or minimise it. There the opposition is
undeniably, fundamentally and glaringly, but it presupposes an
ultimate unity from which it arises and of which it is the other
side. In the realisation of this truth consists the strength of idealism. Berkeley's doctrine is an inadequate and misleading
expression of it. The South Pole is not the North Pole or a
locality within it; it is diametrically opposite to it. Nevertheless
the being of the one pole is implicated with that of the other
and they exist only as two necessarily connected sides of the
earth. Similarly the front and the back of my body do not look
at each other. They are not on speaking terms with each other,
but in spite of this they are the inseparable parts of my entire
organism. Just in the same way mind and its object are the
two opposed aspects of the one all-embracing unity which also
is mind. The term "mind" has two meanings. It is the knower
opposed to the object of which it is conscious. Further, it is
the unity presupposed in the distinction of subject and object
and manifested in that distinction. This all-inclusive spirit
within which distinctions of every kind arise, which is bifurcated

into subject and object is the ultimate reality—the universe in
its last interpretation. It is not mere mind nor abstract matter
but the source and presupposition, the truth of both.

To superficial observation nature seems to be but a vast
aggregate of independent entities existing side by side with
one another in space and time without being in any way essentially connected. It is by pure chance that a thing is what and
where it is. Remove it from its place and there is no change
whatever anywhere in the world except in itself. What necessary
connection is there between the individual bricks heaped together
there on the ground? May not the earth vanish into nothing
to-morrow owing to some catastrophe and the rest of the universe
remain exactly as it is? What modest man does not think that
his coming into being and passing into nothing makes no difference
whatever to the world to which he happens to belong unaccountably for a few years? Self-subsistent realities are somehow put
together and to the totality thus formed we give the name of
nature. This view seems to be plausible at first sight but on reflection it turns out to be quite erroneous. According to Spinoza
it is imagination, not knowledge. Things exist in virtue of the
relations in which they stand to one another. These relations
are not external to the things. They constitute their very nature,
make them possible, sustain them and are inseparable from
them. Lotze has shown that if things were isolated no interaction between them would be possible. How could one thing
affect another if there were a breach of continuity between
them? A influences B. What is this influence? If it emanates
from A then in being detached from A and passing on to B, it
momentarily at least enjoys independent existence and becomes
a third thing C giving rise to the problem of its relation to A
and B. Bradley's argument against external relations is in
spirit the same. If a relation be outside the related terms how
does it get itself connected with them? The truth is that things
are not self-subsistent and independent. They have being only
in so far as they are essentially related to one another. It is
not that things first exist separately and then casually enter
into relations. Apart from the relations they are mere abstractions

as unreal as the top of a thing separated from its bottom. Relations are the very pith and marrow of the related entities, their foundation and support. Science brings this truth to light. It regards the universe as a unitary system of which individual objects are constituent elements. Everything is real only in its own place necessarily connected with other things by means of definitely ascertainable relations. Everywhere in the Cosmos isolation means death.

> Nothing in this world is single,
> All things by a law divine in each other's being mingle.

Objects are continuous with one another and because of this continuity they are also different. They are one because they are many, many because they are one. Unity finds expression in difference and difference has its presupposition in unity. Undifferentiated unity and mere difference are the products of abstract thinking. In the concrete world unity and difference go together. They are complementary aspects of the whole—the universe. If things ceased to be different they would coalesce with each other and vanish into a geometrical point. On the other hand if they absolutely flew apart from each other they would be dissipated into nothing. It is because they attract and also repel each other, are one as well as many, that they exist as integral parts of a single spatio-temporal world. The world undoubtedly looks like an aggregate of independent units. But this is superficial appearance only. In its true nature it is an organic whole realised in the difference of its members. It is the concrete reality of which finite beings and the so-called things are only fragments kept apart by false abstraction. These fragments scientific reflection shows to have being only as elements of the whole—the Cosmos.

But what is the ultimate nature of the unity of all things? Is it some form of the universe itself or some supra-cosmic essence into which the world is absorbed and from which it emanates alternately? The latter view, in spite of the support it has received in the history of thought, is untenable. The unity of the world is the world itself in its ideality, the world regarded as the spirit in which it is centred and of which it is the expression. Inter-connected things which exist in virtue of the influence which they reciprocally exert upon one another are one, not as this or that thing is one but as the universal principle that pervades them, connects them and at the same time maintains their difference. Their unity, in short, is not a numerical unity, for a numerical unity presupposes other similar unities from which it is excluded. It is ideal unity, the unity of a principle common to them, realised completely and indivisibly in each of them but limited to none of them. It is the universal mind at the root of things manifested in them and their mutual relations. In the words of the *Bhagavad Gītā* it is the supreme Brahman that "exists in the world pervading all things and having hands and feet everywhere, eyes, heads and faces in all directions and ears on all sides." It is "without and within all things and beings, the unmoving and also the moving. Though undivided it yet exists as if divided in them."

We thus see that from the highest point of view the universe is spirit self-distinguished into the knower and the known, the cognising mind and its own other, namely the object-world that is cognised. The distinction of self and not-self, mind and matter, is fundamental and inescapable. It is not by obliterating but by maintaining and transcending this distinction that the Absolute is what it is. Neither can matter be evaporated into subjective impressions nor can mind be regarded as a by-product of matter. They are opposed to each other as correlated aspects of the one ultimate reality.

The mind in which the universe finds its truth and explanation is not foreign to it. It is the mind of the universe itself, its own highest form. What at a lower level of interpretation is a system of mutually determining things in space and time is at a higher level of interpretation mind—mind that does not exclude the physical world but takes it up into itself. The material world is inwardised in mind and mind is externalised in matter. They are the correlated phases of the one all-inclusive spirit. In preaching this truth idealism is in no way inconsistent with realism. It does not make it its business to deny the reality of the world. On the contrary, it strongly affirms it. It goes as far as realism does but goes farther, maintaining that the world is indeed real, even what are called ideas are component parts of it, but that in order to know that it is real it has got to have mind. What is the use of being real if mind, without which consciousness of reality cannot be, is wanting? It is not enough that you or I are aware of it. The real world ought to have its own mind so that it may enjoy the abundance of its wealth which is never completely known to any finite being. Surely the idealist who says that the objective world is spiritual without ceasing to be physical is a better realist than he who denies mind to it and thereby makes its reality worth nothing.

The spiritual whole is internally divided into subject and object, self and not-self. The object-world again as related to intelligence involves the distinction and inseparable union of the universal and the particular, the forms of thought and the contents of experience. The relation between the universal and the particular has always been a subject of controversy among philosophers. It was Plato who first realised the importance of the universals, ideas as he called them, and saw that without them neither knowing nor being is possible. But he separated the ideas from sensible phenomena and thought that they were imposed upon the latter *ab extra*. The empiricists, on the other hand, think that they consist of the common features of experienced facts obtained by means of abstraction. Kant's great achievement was to show that experience is richer than what the empiricists take it to be and involves both the categories of thought and the particulars of sense. Like Plato he separates the universal from the particular but perceives that so separated they are names only, the one empty and the other blind. The empiricists suppose that experience consists of particular phenomena only. Kant does not deny that they have independent being, but argues that they are as good as nothing unless they are subjected to the categories. He undertakes the impossible task of showing how the forms of thought and the matter of sense are brought into relationship with each other and of course fails. But the solid result of his philosophical thinking was to demonstrate that apart from the principles of the understanding experience is not possible. In actual knowledge the universal and the particular are never found cut loose from each other. Sensible phenomena are never merely discrete and disconnected but are always pervaded and sustained by universal forms of thought as connected members of the intelligible and orderly cosmos. Nature is not made by the understanding but is the outer expression of reason. A firm grasp of this truth is the merit of Hegel. In his eye, the material universe, always involving the duality but not the dualism of the universal principles of reason and the particular facts of experience, is the embodiment of the Infinite mind. It is this mind "that is the ultimate nature of life, the soul of the world, the universal life-blood which courses everywhere, and whose flow is neither disturbed nor checked by any obstructing distinction, but is itself every distinction that arises, as well as that into which all distinctions are dissolved; pulsating within itself, but ever motionless, shaken to its depths, but still at rest."[1]

Kant regards the categories only as instruments used by the self for the purpose of producing knowledge out of the data of sense. In themselves they are but empty forms not essentially related to one another and to the self. Hegel, on the contrary, views them as at once forms of thought and modes of being, subjective as well as objective. They are not airy abstractions but comprehensive systems implying particularity. They are all essentially related to one another as vital parts of the whole of reality. The organised whole of which they are members is the Absolute. Each of them is implicated with and has no being apart from the rest. They form a graded system and the business of philosophy is to show how thought necessarily passes from the lowest of them step by step through the intermediate stages to the highest. Each category incorporates the immediately lower one into itself and is taken up into the immediately higher, and the highest, the Absolute Idea, therefore contains them all as necessary elements of itself. It is to them what the living body is to its members. For Hegel this view implies that the

[1] *Phenomenology of Mind*, Baillie's Tr., George Allen & Unwin, vol. i, p. 157.

226 CONTEMPORARY INDIAN PHILOSOPHY

Absolute Idea is a completed and closed system and that human knowledge is co-extensive with reality. There cannot in his view be anything in thought or reality which has not a definitely ascertainable place in the system of the Absolute Idea.

Now it is not easy to avoid being overpowered by the persuasiveness of Hegel's argument. The methodical procession of the categories produces an immense effect on the reader's mind. But in the end few are able to accept the view that the Logic exhaustively discloses the contents of reality. The really valuable work which Hegel does is to demonstrate that the universe is an orderly and intelligible system with mind at its centre, but this does not mean that we know in detail what its constitution and contents are. If the categories specified by him were the only elements of this system, if human intelligence penetrated reality to the very core, omniscience would be the necessary consequence and there would be no room for doubt and hesitation of any kind. It sometimes looks as though Hegel actually claimed omniscience. But the revisions to which he himself subjected the arrangement of his categories, the alterations he made in their list from time to time, show that he by no means knew all that there is to be known and that reality after all very largely eluded the grasp of his intellect. The truth, of course, is that human knowledge is not co-extensive with reality and the categories of Hegel's Logic do not furnish a complete exposition of it. They are only a section of the contents of Absolute thought detached from the whole. The fragmentary character of our knowledge is obvious. It bears unmistakable marks of its narrowness and incompleteness. The breach of continuity which is everywhere apparent in the world, the abrupt manner in which facts of one order are marked off from those of another order, the immense blanks between the bright spots of knowledge, the failure of the universals of thought and the particulars of sense to fit in with each other smoothly and without hitch, the inability of time and space to attain the completeness at which they aim, the antinomies and contradictions of which experience is full, the unreason obtruding upon us on all sides in a world which theory forces us to regard as rational through and through, the evils that mar the beauty and orderliness of the cosmos, the angularities and rough sides of things, the trials and tragedies of life, all plainly indicate that the world to which we belong is not the whole, but only a fragment of the real universe the major part of which is beyond our ken. It is in Kant's words but an island in the vast ocean of reality, only the ocean is not something unintelligible but the rational whole of existents.

The categories of human knowledge do indeed express the nature of reality but only partially. They are valid so far as they go, but in the Absolute they must be supplemented by others not at present known to us. Of them organised into a complete whole the objective world, both seen and unseen, is the expression. What we call nature is only a tiny fragment of this greater universe, if we may call it so, and in it alone the Absolute mind finds its full content. The unseen world or worlds, it must be remembered, is not psychical. There is nothing purely psychical or purely physical. All the *contents* of the mind are objective and opposed to the self that knows. The unseen universe, therefore, although not material, is of a piece with what is material. It is spiritual exactly as *this* world, the material world, is spiritual. Whatever is, is the expression of mind. There is nothing which is out of relation to intelligence. As Bradley says, "Outside of spirit there is not and there cannot be any reality." All the worlds, the visible material world and the invisible immaterial but objective worlds, are parts of one stupendous whole and in this whole the Absolute mind is completely embodied. A purely spiritual or psychical world is as much a fiction as a purely material world. What is real is also ideal and the genuinely ideal must be real.

The Absolute mind is one but it is not a monadic unity. In it the minds of the things that constitute the world are fused into a single whole or, what is the same thing viewed from the other end, it is pluralised in them. The universal mind is immanent in all things. This means that it is present in each of them undivided and as a whole, which cannot be unless it is in it as its inner soul. To be a self-complete whole, to be in all parts of it equally and yet to remain a whole in each part is the prerogative of the universal. The mind for which the universe is, is not apart from it; it is its own central principle. Its relation to things, therefore, is not an external relation like that of one thing to another. It is the ideality of each of the things themselves, the very core of its being. In being externalised in the multifarious objects of the world, the Absolute mind goes forth to them and dwells in them as their own individual minds. It becomes manifold and yet remains one. Were it not so it would be external to them and being limited by them would be just like one of them. The self of the world is one and yet many. In it many minds, the minds of the myriads of objects that are comprised within the world, are gathered up and, on its part, it is diversified in them. There is nothing unintelligible in this notion of minds being many and yet one. The self of every one of us is such. A is a distinguished statesman, a great metaphysician and an expert player of cricket. These are distinct personalities with different characters and yet they are fused into a single whole in the self of A. Pathological cases of multiple personality prove this. In them the process of disintegration goes so far as to give rise to distinct personalities sometimes of opposite characters and very hostile to one another. The case of Sally Beauchamp is an example. We speak of the conflict of the better self and the worse self in us. Why should this be regarded as only a metaphor and not literal truth? What every man is that the Absolute itself is. Is not man made in the image of God? The self is our ultimate principle of explanation. In analogy with it we think of the Absolute. But our self is never a solitary unit. It is not only composite in itself but is always a member of the social whole. The concrete actuality is the social mind. If therefore the Absolute is spirit, its nature must be analogous to the composite mind of society. It is on one side mind consisting of many minds and on another the physical world consisting of inter-related objects. There are thirty-three millions of Gods in the Hindu pantheon. This need not be denied; only it must be remembered that they are all integral parts of the supreme Brahman. An infinite number of selves, the selves of the constituent members of the objective world, go to form the Absolute mind. This is what Arjuna sees in *Viśvarūpa* (the cosmic form of the Lord) in the *Bhagavad Gītā*: "O Lord of the Universe, O thou whose form the Universe is, I behold thee of countless forms everywhere with many arms, bellies, mouths and eyes. I do not see thy end, nor thy middle, nor yet thy beginning."

Things existing in time and space and excluding each other are limited, but in their ideality, as minds, they are all-pervading and omniscient. A finite object is marked off from others, repels them, but this is possible because it is also continuous with them and includes them in its own being. Such inclusion takes the form of the consciousness of them. What is distinguished from others is in the very process of distinction joined with them. That is to say, it transcends the distinction between them and itself as inclusive mind. Nothing, therefore, as ideal can be limited to the place where it is as a reality. It encompasses all being, is everywhere. A strong point of the pluralistic systems of Indian philosophy, Jainism, the Sāṁkhya and the Nyāya Vaiśeṣika, is their conception of the many selves as omnipresent and eternal. These, however, cannot be regarded as independent and self-subsistent but must be viewed as component factors of the one Absolute mind. The many are one and the one is many. Each of the particular selves into which the Infinite mind is differentiated represents, because of its all-inclusiveness and omniscience, the whole world. But it does so in its own unique way, from its own special point of view. It is the merit of Leibniz to emphasise this truth. But unfortunately he distinguishes the ideation of the world from the world and isolates the monads from each other, thereby making the unity of the world inexplicable. The Jain doctrine of Syādvāda has a clearer perception of the truth. The one world is known by many minds, the minds of the things that constitute it, in various ways like different triangles standing upon the same base. Their world-pictures are different. The universe presents itself in different perspectives to them, but they are all fused into a composite whole. Different views of things obtained from different standpoints become complementary to one another in the final synthesis. What is seen with the right eye is also seen with the left eye in a slightly different way but the two visions are merged in one and do not remain apart from each other. See a word consisting, say, of five letters with attention mainly focused on each of the five letters successively and you will get five somewhat different appearances, but they are all amalgamated with each other in the ordinary appearance of the word. Nothing is as simple as it seems to be. A lump of sugar is no doubt sweet, but who will undertake to prove that it is sweet to me in precisely the same way as it is to you? Its real sweetness may be the synopsis of the sweetnesses felt by all those who taste it. As no two faces are alike, so it may be that no two perceptions, no two ideas of the same thing are alike. The vulture finds enjoyable repast in a rotten carcass, but to men it is noxious. This ought to give us food for reflection. The truth is that relatively things are different from different standpoints, but absolutely they combine in them all these variations. There is no contradiction in this, for the essence of contradiction is the confusion of standpoints. The Absolute cognises the world in an infinite number of ways from the standpoints of the countless things the minds of which are confluent in it without detriment to their distinctness. Its knowledge therefore is infinitely rich and complex. The universe is not only diverse in composition but knows itself in diverse ways.

Finite beings belong to nature; they are rooted in it and arise out of it. They in no sense create it. By means of their cognitive processes, they merely select certain elements of reality which go to constitute the world we experience and live in. They have been regarded as partial reproductions of the Infinite mind, emanations from it conditioned by organic processes. But as the Absolute mind is a unity of many minds, finite selves can only be fragmentary expressions of these constituent minds and not of the Absolute as a whole. Except the contents of their experiences there is nothing additional in the Absolute. Human bodies are among the things whose minds enter into the composition of the Absolute. Each of it is the objective side, the outer expression of an omniscient mind having its abode in the Absolute as one of its members. Consisting of millions of cells it is itself highly composite. In one body, consequently, there are many bodies and many minds. One self has not many bodies, and many selves, as is sometimes supposed, do not belong to a single body. The many cells that compose the body are the many bodies of the many selves unified in the one mind of the whole body which is the ideality of the body itself. It is a constituent element of the Absolute mind. Finite selves are detachments from these deeper selves, assuming new forms, relatively independent and setting up their own households. They are sustained by the Absolute but not swayed by it from outside. They participate in its being, share in its freedom and are not mere excrescences upon it. Finite selves no doubt derive the materials of their life and experience from the Absolute but are not useless repetitions of what already exists. They give rise to novelties in being limited and in the course of the changes they undergo as they grow and seek to realise their purposes, to work out the ideals of their lives. They do not revolve round and round the same point but move on from freshness to freshness, from one stage of life to another and newer. They do not stagnate but alter and progress, do not perpetuate the existing but create the non-existing. In them the Absolute attains new modes of being, new outlooks on existence. In their knowledge they carve out only a small section of the whole of reality. The things we experience are not the things as they are in the knowledge of the Absolute but selections made from them for the purposes of life. Only so much of them is known as our organs of sense are fitted to take in and the sense-organs as they are at present are constructed not to reveal to us the total wealth of existence but to enable us to adapt ourselves to our existing environment and thereby to live. The table before me is not the table as it is in Absolute knowledge possessing an infinite number of properties but only the sum of a few of its characteristics that come within the range of my knowledge. Even of these characteristics a very small part only is perceived at any particular moment. What *we* perceive may therefore be said in one sense to depend on us for its existence, but as it is an ingredient of the true reality, it is in another sense independent of our cognition. Besides the features selected from the whole the perceived object may in virtue of its relation to our knowledge have new elements added to it. These, of course, exist as percepts only as long as they are perceived. But even here their support is not the human mind by itself but that mind in commerce with the object.

Finite minds necessarily seek to be the infinite that they potentially are. The Infinite immanent in them goads them on and does not allow them to rest. Even the shoemaker wants sovereignty over the whole universe. But self-realisation is not possible in isolation. Only in fellowship and co-operation with one another can human beings move forward towards the goal of life. In their ordinary lives and achievements as finite beings in time they are seldom aware of their greatness, but sooner or later they are bound to be conscious of their true nature, to be united with the source of their being in knowledge and love. God is not without man and man is not without God. The Divine spirit manifested in the community of men and the community of men rooted in the Divine spirit, God in man and man in God—this whole is the Absolute Spirit.

PRINCIPAL PUBLICATION

Neo-Hegelianism, Heath Cranton (1927).

THE PROBLEM OF TRUTH

by M. HIRIYANNA

Born 1871; Educated at the Maharaja's College, Mysore,
and the Madras Christian College
Professor of Sanskrit, Maharaja's College, Mysore (1917–27)

H*

THE PROBLEM OF TRUTH

THE logical aspect of knowledge is now commonly discussed with exclusive reference to the nature of ultimate truth. There is no doubt that this is the question with which epistemology is finally concerned, but it may be asked whether we cannot advantageously begin by having before us a less ambitious aim. Irrespective of the final solution we may arrive at about the nature of truth, there is knowledge which is distinguished as either true or false from the common-sense point of view; and we may start by asking what this distinction means. Our answer to this question may not satisfy the ultimate epistemological test, but we need not occupy ourselves with that consideration from the beginning. "Confusion often results," it has been said, "from proceeding at once to large and complex cases." If we thus restrict the scope of the enquiry, we shall be simplifying the problem to be solved; and its solution, though it may not furnish the complete explanation of the nature of ultimate truth, may be expected to throw considerable light upon it. We propose to adopt this plan of treatment in the sequel.

Let us begin by analysing an act of perception. When a person opens his eyes (say) and sees a table before him, there are, as ordinarily supposed, three elements that can be distinguished in the situation: First, the percipient who sees; secondly the object, viz. the table; and lastly the sense-data or sensa, as they are described—a certain shape, colour, etc., which he associates with the table and regards as its actual characteristics. These sensa he takes as revealing the nature of the table but partly, for, while he may be seeing only its shape and colour, he believes that it has also other qualities like hardness and weight. It may appear that the common man does not distinguish between the last two of the three elements just referred to; the fact, however, is that he only does not attend to the distinction between them particularly but passes over swiftly from the sensa to the object which is what practically interests him. The process has been compared to our overlooking the peculiarities of the print in reading, because it is the meaning of what is printed that interests us.[1] This is the popular notion of the perceptual situation; and it implies belief in (1) the presence of the self, (2) the givenness and the direct apprehension of the object and (3) the partial revelation of its character by the sensa, which are likewise given and directly known. Of these, the ultimate nature of the self or the knowing subject is not relevant to our present purpose. It is a problem for metaphysics. All that we have to remember is that it is a factor which enters into the cognitive situation. The same observation holds true in the case of the final nature of the object also. The points that chiefly matter for us now are the nature of sense-data, their relation to the object and the manner in which they both, viz. the sense-data and the object, come to be known.

I

According to the above analysis, the sensa are actual features or "literal aspects" of objects; and they both are directly apprehended by the self. We should now ask to what extent this analysis stands the test of reflection. If it be correct, it should apply to all perceptual knowledge; but it seems that, though it may be right as an analysis of perception that is true, it does not apply to illusion and error[2] where we apprehend an object or some aspect of it which is not there. Without pre-judging the question, however, we shall try to find out whether errors can be at all explained by assuming that even they do not involve a reference to anything that is not actually given. Such a view was maintained not only in respect of perception but also all knowledge (excepting only memory) by certain thinkers in ancient India,[3] and it will serve as a convenient starting-point for our enquiry. The illustrations usually given

[1] *Mind* (1921), p. 389.
[2] We shall, in what follows, overlook the distinction between errors of perception and illusions, as the only difference between them is that while the judgment is explicit in the former, it is implicit in the latter. Illusions have been described as "errors in the germ."
[3] Prābhākaras.

in explaining their theory are those of a white crystal which is mistaken for red when placed by the side of a red flower, and of a conch which is seen yellow by a jaundiced person. We shall select the latter for consideration, but with a slight alteration. We shall suppose that the conch is seen through a sheet of yellow glass instead of by the jaundiced eye, and that the fact of the existence of the glass is for some reason or other lost sight of. Here we have, according to this theory, the perception of the conch *minus* its true colour, viz. white, and the sensation of the yellowness alone of the glass. They are two acts of knowing, but they quickly succeed each other; and we therefore miss the fact that they are two. Each of them is valid so far as it goes, for neither the yellowness nor the conch as such is negated afterwards when we discover the error. But we overlook at first that they stand apart; and it is only this deficiency in our knowledge that is made good later when we find out our mistake. Thus discovery of error only means a further step in advancing knowledge. It confirms the previous knowledge and does not cancel any part of it as false, so that to talk of "rectification" with reference to error is a misnomer. In admitting that error is incomplete knowledge which needs to be supplemented, the theory grants that ignorance is involved in it; but the ignorance, it maintains, is purely of a negative character and does not import into erroneous knowledge any element which is positively wrong. In other words, it holds that the mind may fail to apprehend one or more aspects of what is presented, but that it never *mis*apprehends it and that all errors are therefore only errors of omission.

There is no need, on this view, to verify any knowledge. All knowledge is true in the sense that no portion of what it reveals is contradicted afterwards; and to question whether it agrees with reality in any particular instance is therefore to question its very nature. But truth being commonly distinguished from error, it is necessary to give some explanation of the distinction. The so-called error may be partial knowledge; but we cannot characterise it as such, for human knowledge is always partial in one sense or another. So another explanation is given, and

it is indirect. Though all knowledge is alike incomplete, error
is more so than truth. It is *relatively* incomplete, and its relative
incompleteness is determined by reference to an extrinsic
standard, viz. a pragmatic one. All knowledge, according to
this school, leads to action; and the success or failure of the
activity prompted by any particular knowledge is regarded as
constituting its truth or error. In other words, that knowledge
is true which works; and that which does not, is erroneous.
Though this school upholds a pragmatic view of truth, it should
be noticed that it is essentially unlike modern Pragmatism.
Epistemologically speaking, the latter amounts to a sceptical
attitude, for it teaches that absolute truth in any matter is
unattainable because it does not exist. Every truth is provisional
—true only so long as it furthers human purposes. But here
knowledge is admitted to have a logical, apart from a practical
or guiding, value. Though it may be false on its purposive side,
it is theoretically quite true and never fails to agree with the
outside reality which it reveals. If we still speak of knowledge
as sometimes false, we mean that it is not useful—thus trans-
ferring to it a feature which is significant only in reference to
the practical consequences that follow from it. All knowledge
in itself being thus regarded here as true, we may say that
while current Pragmatism denies truth in the sense in which
it is ordinarily understood, the present theory denies error.

This theory merits commendation for its simplicity as well
as for its complete consistency in explaining the logical character
of knowledge. It may be said to represent the extreme form of
realism, for it not only upholds that external objects are independent of the knowing mind and are directly apprehended; it
even denies error. But it is far from convincing. The indirect
manner, for instance, in which it explains the familiar terms
"true" and "false" is hardly satisfactory. But even waiving this
consideration, it must be said that a purely negative explanation
cannot account for error which, as a judgment, presents the
two elements in it as synthesised though they may be actually
unrelated. Its distinction from "doubt," which lacks such synthesis as shown by its alternative suppositions, and is not a

judgment but a suspension of it, points to the same fact. In our illustration, the knowledge of the conch cannot accordingly be assumed to arise separately from that of yellowness; there is only a single psychical process, and the resulting knowledge includes a reference to a positive element which is false. Error is therefore misapprehension and not mere lack of apprehension. Such a view, we may add, is implied even in the explanation given by the school of thinkers mentioned above. It will be remembered that, according to that explanation, discovery of error means only an advance from less complete to more complete knowledge. But there may be incomplete knowledge which we do or do not know to be so at the time; and it is only the latter that can be regarded as an error, for surely nobody that *knows* that his knowledge is incomplete can be said to make a mistake when that knowledge, so far as it goes, is admitted to be right. It will be wrong only when there is an implicit, if not an explicit, identification of it with truth or adequate knowledge. That is, if our knowledge is to be viewed as erroneous, it is not enough for us to be merely unaware of one or more aspects of the presented object; we should also take the knowledge as complete or adequate. And in so far as what is incomplete is taken for the complete or the less adequate for the more adequate, there is misapprehension. Thus the mind may not only misapprehend presented objects, but it invariably does so in error; and all errors are, therefore, errors of commission. Errors of *mere* omission in the sphere of knowledge are strictly not errors at all. There is, however, this much of truth in the previous view when it insists on the validity of all knowledge, that, so far as its perceptual form at least is concerned (to which we are now confining our attention), it always points to some reality or other, and that there can, therefore, be no complete error. That is, though a part of the content of knowledge may be false, the whole of it can never be so.

The outcome of the above reasoning is that there is always in error some element which needs to be recanted later, although it may be only the element of relation as in the above example; and, so far, the contention that no portion of what knowledge

reveals is ever negated afterwards has to be given up. Before
we enquire into the precise status of this element, it will be
desirable to consider another type of error. We have hitherto
spoken of errors in which, even after they are detected, the two
elements involved, taken separately—or, to state the same in
a different manner, the subject and the predicate of the propositions expressing the corresponding judgments—continue to be
presented as before. Even the false localisation of the predicate
("yellow") persists, though it no longer misleads the person
who has seen through the error. But there are other instances
in which the predicate is contradicted—and necessarily the relation also along with it—the moment the error is discovered.
This happens, for example, when we find out that we mistook
a block of crystal for ice on seeing at some distance a certain
shape and colour which are common to both.[1] The difference
between the two cases is that in the one the predicative element
("yellow") is actually within the field of visual sensation, while
in the other it ("ice") is not so. What we come to know as
false in the latter case, when we fail to find that the given
object is neither cool nor moist (say) as we expected, is not,
therefore, merely the element of relation but also the predicate.
Our perception of "ice" here, as if it were bodily present, when
it does not form part of the given situation needs a satisfactory
explanation. All that we know for certain is that there is *something* given, and that the sensa actually apprehended—a certain
shape and colour as we have assumed—are of that something,[2]
and not of the object to which they seem to pertain. Two
explanations of this "presence in absence" are possible:

(1) It may be argued that the object in question, though
not present in the given situation, is still to be reckoned as a
physical existent because it is found elsewhere and should have
been actually experienced at some other time. While the force

[1] The Prābhākara school, mentioned above, explained this class of errors
also on the same principle, the two consecutive mental acts here being
the perception of the subject and the recollection of the predicate.

[2] This statement requires modification as, for example, in the case of
the moon which looks vastly smaller than it actually is. But it will be
better to postpone the consideration of this point for the present.

of this argument may be admitted so far as it means that only
things resembling those experienced before can be seen in such
errors, it has to be observed that the question here is not merely
about the *being* of the object but also about its presence at a particular place and at a particular time. In error, it is experienced
as here and now; and the experience in this determinate form
is contradicted later. The reality of the object *in itself* may be
conceded, but it has no bearing upon this fact; and the contradiction, therefore, remains wholly unexplained by it. It may be
said that what is meant by the above contention is not that
the object is merely external and real but also that it somehow
comes to be actually presented, though remote in time and
place.[1] That would be to credit physical objects with what has
been described as "a somewhat surprising mobility." But even
granting the supposition, there is the difficulty of explaining
how, if the object be given, its givenness comes to be negated
later. The other element, for instance, in the error, viz. the one
represented by the subject ("this")[2] in the judgment—"This is
ice"—is also given; but it is not contradicted later. Its presence,
on the other hand, at the place where it appears is reaffirmed
when we replace the wrong judgment by the correct one—"*This*
is a crystal.*" The distinction in the way in which the correcting
judgment affects the two elements indicates that, although
what is predicated may be taken as out there, it cannot be
regarded as real *in the same sense* in which the subject is. The
fact is that those who give such explanations confound likeness
with identity. They forget that, while the erroneous object may
be similar to what has once been experienced, it need not be
the same. They are right in urging that knowledge is self-transcendent and always implies a content that is known—something
beyond or other than itself, and that error forms no exception to this rule. But if the reasoning should be free from all

[1] As is maintained, for example, in the Indian Nyāya-Vaiśeṣika system
and, in a somewhat different form, by Professor Alexander (see *Space,
Time and Deity*, vol. ii, p. 254).

[2] As we have already seen, the "this" in such cases signifies not merely
present time and proximate place, but also some sensa like shape and
colour.

prepossession, the only conclusion we can draw from it is that that content here is a mere presentation, and not that it is also physically real.

(2) If the erroneous content is merely a presentation and not a physical reality, it may be thought that it is either a memory-image or an ideal construction. But this conclusion again clashes with experience. If it were a memory-image, it would involve a reference to past time and to a distant place, and would not, therefore, be apprehended as immediately given. In other words, if the presentation were an ideal revival, one would realise it as such at the time. There being no such realisation here, it cannot be explained as a memory-image. It is not denied, we should add, that the false "ice" would not have been presented at all, had not real ice been experienced before. The mental disposition left behind by past experience is, indeed, an indispensable condition of the occurrence of such errors; but it only helps to determine the nature of the presentation, and does not, for the reason just stated, make it a memory-image. A similar kind of reasoning applies to the second alternative of an ideal construction. The "ice" in that case would be experienced as related to the future, or it would appear without any special reference to time at all. In either case, the apprehension of it as a *present* existence would be inexplicable. The mental attitude, besides, would then be one of supposal and not of belief, as it is here.

The considerations which singly or in combination prevent us from accepting the above explanations in regard to the status of the object in error are its felt immediacy, its determinate position in the objective sphere, and its later sublation. Both the explanations possible being thus ruled out, we are obliged to regard it as a presentation which is quite unique. Its uniqueness consists in this, viz. that its nature cannot be fully expressed in terms known to logic or to psychology. A necessary condition of its emergence is that a real object should be apprehended, but only in its general aspects, and that the percipient, while being ignorant of its specific features, should be unaware of his ignorance. A sense of ignorance would perforce prevent the occurrence of error. In the case of "doubt," for instance, only the general features of the object presented are grasped; and yet there is no error, for one is *conscious* at the time that one does not know its distinctive features, as is clear from the wavering of the mind between two alternative possibilities. It is this dependence of the wrong object for its appearance upon a defect characterising an individual percipient[1] that explains why it is private to him and is not public or open to the view of others. Similarly, it is the position in the outside world of the thing mistaken, or the source from which the sensory stimulus comes, that determines the position of the wrong presentation there. The "ice" appears where the crystal is; and a change in the location of the thing mistaken would, other conditions remaining the same, result in a corresponding change in the external location of the wrong object. Ignorance, however, is not by itself sufficient to account for error; and it is always found associated in producing it with some fortuitous circumstance or other like the flash of similarity between the given thing and another. But it is difficult to detail these circumstances, for they vary so much from one instance to another. We can only characterise them generally by saying that, in the matter of giving rise to error, they are altogether subsidiary to ignorance and that their nature is such that the removal of the latter simultaneously renders them inoperative. Thus in the present case, the resemblance between the crystal and the ice is a necessary factor in producing the error; but the removal of ignorance, which means a knowledge of the specific features of the crystal, at once makes it ineffective. The resemblance, of course, continues thereafter, and may remind one of real ice; but it cannot aid the false presentation of it as before. It means that ignorance, as characterised above, is what sustains error; and we shall refer to it alone hereafter, disregarding additional causes like the one just mentioned.

Thus in all errors of the kind we are now considering, the

[1] Ignorance also might be general or common to all; but the resulting misapprehension would not, in that case, be ordinarily recognised as an error by any one.

244 CONTEMPORARY INDIAN PHILOSOPHY

subject ("this") and some of the sensa that characterise it are actually given; but the predicate ("ice") and the relation between it and the subject are unique presentations. The content of erroneous knowledge is, therefore, a medley of the true and the false. According to the principle on which we have explained the wrong presentation here, the element of relation in the case of the "yellow conch" also should be reckoned as unique. It is experienced immediately and as actually obtaining between two external objects; it is also later discovered to be false. Thus in both classes of error there is complete correspondence between knowledge and content. This does not imply the acceptance of the view that knowing involves a psychic medium which is *like* its object. Knowledge, on the other hand, reveals reality directly; and by its correspondence with content, we here mean that no part of what it reveals is ever sheer non-being. There may be disparity in the nature of the elements included within its content, for, while some of them are real, others may be unique in the sense explained above. But the latter, though not physically real, are felt as confronting the mind and cannot therefore be absolute nothing. There is resemblance between the two kinds of error[1] in other respects also. Both are forms of misapprehension traceable to ignorance of the actual character of the given objects, and both are private to the erring observer. To an important difference which they exhibit, we have already had occasion to allude. In the case of the crystal mistaken for "ice," the discovery of error or the knowledge that the given reality is not ice, means the total disappearance of the wrong presentation.[2] The presentation is due to ignorance and the removal of the cause removes the effect. But in the other case, the knowledge that the conch is not yellow has no such effect, and the relation *appears* to persist even after it is contradicted. This appearance should consequently be traced to a circumstance other than ignorance which is the source of the error, viz. a

---

[1] Other forms of error, like dreams and hallucinations, fall under one or other of these two; or they partake of the character of both.

[2] The "ice" may appear there again, but it only shows that a man may fall twice into the same error.

particular disposition of the conch and the yellow glass relative to the point of space occupied by the observer. It is a conclusion which is corroborated by the fact that the apparent relation vanishes as soon as the disposition of the objects in question is changed.

II

True knowledge, by contrast, is that whose content is free from such unique presentations. Here also we may, and ordinarily do, go beyond the given as in error; but, on account of the apprehension of the sensa constituting the specific features of the object presented and not its general ones only, our knowledge does not become erroneous. Since sensa, according to what we have stated, are the very basis of our knowledge of the external world, they should be regarded as directly known; and it seems to follow from this that the object, of which they are the actual aspects, is also known directly. But this latter point cannot be properly argued without reference to the question of the ultimate nature of objects, which we are not considering here.

According to the description just given, knowledge is true when no part of its content has to be discarded as false. That is, it does not come in conflict with the rest of our experience, but harmonises with it.[1] This signifies that it is coherence with other experience, and not correspondence with reality, that makes it true. The rejection of the correspondence hypothesis does not mean the denial of the self-transcendent character of knowledge. It only means that since *all* knowledge, as we have pointed out, equally satisfies the condition of agreement with an objective counterpart, correspondence cannot be regarded as a distinguishing feature of truth. The conclusion that truth is coherence may be reached somewhat differently by considering the manner in which error comes to be known. Error, as we have seen, is a judgment that is self-discrepant; but its self-discrepancy remains unknown until it is revealed by another judgment which contradicts it. Now while one judgment may confirm or supple-

---

[1] Old truths may need to be modified in the light of new experience. But we are not taking such details into consideration here.

ment another, it is difficult to see how it can correct or annul it, for there is no reason to prefer either of them to the other. The only circumstance in which it may do so is when it forms part of a body of knowledge which, as a whole, is, for some reason or other, regarded as well established. That is, a judgment can correct another or claim to be true, not by itself, but as belonging to or as implicated in a system of judgments. Since without the evidence of such a system, no one can know reality from unique presentations, we may say that error also, like a judgment which is true, becomes intelligible only in connection with a body of coherent knowledge which is taken as the standard of reference. The standard is ordinarily furnished in the case of each individual by the totality of his experience. When, however, any doubt arises and the individual's experience, even at its widest, is inadequate for settling it, an appeal to the experience of others becomes necessary. It is this collective experience or the common sense of mankind that, in the end, serves as the standard. That knowledge is true which fits into it perfectly; and that which does not, is false. Herein consists the social or general character of truth, as distinguished from error. We share truth with others; and it is therefore public, while error is private. The elements constituting the content of a true judgment are mutually compatible, since all of them are alike public. Error differs from truth in this respect, for it involves a reference not only to an object of common experience but also to unique presentations which are private and are not therefore endorsed by that experience.

We have so far assumed that all sensa correctly reveal the character of the object given, if only partially, and are never false. But it does not seem to be always so, for we know from experience that the precise form in which they appear depends, for instance, upon the point of space occupied by the percipient with reference to the object in question. It shows that sensa are not only partial in their bearing upon the nature of the object given, but that they may also vary though the object remains the same. A coin, for example, presents a round or an oval shape according to the position from which it is viewed.

Similarly, a change in the position of an object may affect the sensa. A ship, which is seen as but a speck on the horizon, seems to increase in size as it approaches the shore, although there may be no change in the standpoint of the observer or in the objective situation as a whole. It may therefore appear that sensa also, like objects and relations, may be false. These altered sensa, it should be admitted, are not verifiable. A coin, to take one of our examples, cannot be both oval and round. But yet such appearances are not to be regarded as false; for, unlike erroneous presentations, they can be deduced from the actual sensa according to well-known physical laws. These secondary or derivative phenomena, as we may call them, may not literally qualify the object; but, owing to the fact that their altered form is determined by strict laws, they indicate correctly, though only indirectly, the nature of the object to which they refer. It is in this indirect, and not in a literal, sense that we characterise the data in such cases as true. The fact is that they are the result solely of the physical conditions under which normal human perception takes place, and do not in any manner depend upon the idiosyncrasies of the percipient mind to make them erroneous. Hence we should place these presentations on a footing which is quite different from those in error. Seeing a tree stump, which is at a distance, to be smaller than it actually is, is very much different from taking it to be something else (say), a human being. Besides, these phenomena do not commonly deceive us like erroneous presentations. A ship is not understood to undergo actual increase of bulk as it approaches the shore from a point on the horizon. All of them, no doubt, contain the seeds of error, and may therefore prove deceptive. A child may believe that the moon is really only as small as it appears, or that railway tracks actually converge towards a point in the distance. But then the essential condition of error, viz. ignorance of the true character of the objects in question, is also present; and its removal, though it shows the beliefs to be erroneous, does not lead to the removal of the presentations. In other words, they disappear as errors but persist as appearances of the real. These appearances may not, in themselves, be real; yet they are not false in the sense in which erroneous presentations, like the "ice" in our former example, are. For the same reason, the *apparent* relation also, noticed before in connection with errors of the first type like the "yellow conch," is not to be regarded as false.

We may designate these secondary phenomena as "perspectives of the real" or, briefly, "perspectives."[1] The distinction between them and erroneous presentations, as already indicated, is that the latter are rooted in ignorance which is a defect of the knowing subject, while the former are purely the result of certain physical conditions under which an object happens to be apprehended. The term "perspective," no doubt, implies relation to the standpoint of a particular observer; and, so far, the presentations are personal. The point here, however, is not that the phenomena in question are unrelated to the individual, but that they are in no way due to his oddities. In this latter respect, they are like sensa proper; but, unlike them, they do not directly belong to the objects to which they seem to belong. Hence in determining the true character of any perceived object or objects from such phenomena, we should apply a suitable correction taking into account the nature of the physical context in which they appear. In simple cases we make such corrections ourselves, as, for instance, when we see a coin as oval but interpret it as circular; in more intricate ones, however, the aid of science is necessary as in ascertaining the true magnitude of the moon from its apparent size. The truths so determined are impersonal because they reveal objects as they are in themselves, not as they appear, and are therefore independent of the point of view of the person or persons asserting them. While a part of empirical knowledge may be impersonal, the whole of science is so, for the one aim of the scientist is to find out the actual features or normal aspects of things. The extent to which this difference affects the correctness of common knowledge, where the pheno-

---

[1] This term, which is used by more than one modern philosopher (e.g. Professor Alexander), is intended here to stand, though not in every detail, for the phenomena underlying what is described as *sopādhika-bhrama* in the philosophy of Śaṁkara.

mena concerned are of a complicated nature, may be very great; and what are only "perspectives" and, as such, are not literally true, may often be mistaken by us for sensa or actual features of the external world. Hence empirical knowledge, as a whole, stands far lower, in point of accuracy, than the scientific. Its primary function is to subserve the purposes of everyday life, and it does not therefore ordinarily aim at greater accuracy than is needed for their fulfilment. Its value lies in its practical utility, not in its theoretical certainty; and the saying that "thought is the slave of life" is therefore essentially true here.

III

The conclusion thus far reached is that the common-sense analysis of knowledge, with which we started, requires to be modified in two important respects. There are some instances, viz. "perspectives" which only indirectly disclose the character of external objects; and there are others, viz. errors which, while they may reveal reality, also include presentations that are not genuine parts or aspects of it at all. Objects and relations may thus be erroneously presented, but never sensa. It may seem that, if proper allowance be made for these two kinds of discrepancies, the system of common knowledge, taken as a whole, will give us the final or absolute truth sought after in epistemology; but it does not, because it has other limitations. In the first place, it obviously refers only to a small portion of the whole of reality, and is therefore fragmentary. In the second place, it leaves out even from this portion a great deal as not relevant to the carrying out of common human purposes which is its pre-eminent function. Scientific knowledge is without this latter limitation, since it aims at expounding phenomena in terms of the non-human; but even that cannot be regarded as giving us the final epistemological solution, for it also is selective, though in a different way. No science treats of the whole of reality, but each is concerned only with particular aspects of it; and, since it studies these aspects apart from their concrete accompaniments, it may be said to deal more with abstractions than with reality. Moreover science, in spite of the indefinite expansion possible for it, will never arrive at an exhaustive knowledge of reality because its selective method will always leave for it a field which is still to be explored. Although the view of truth formulated above cannot therefore be regarded as final, it will yield the solution which epistemology seeks when its implications are fully worked out. We shall now point out how it does so; but, within the limits of this paper, we can do so only very briefly.

The possibility of its furnishing the final solution is contained in the conception of knowledge as a system, and of truth as coherence with it. A strict adherence to this view may seem to lead one to the conclusion that truth is relative. For there may be two or more coherent systems of knowledge which are at variance with one another, and what is true from one standpoint may not be so from another. All our so-called truths may thus turn out to be equally false relatively, not excluding the results of scientific investigation. We have explained the common notions of truth and error, it will be remembered, by reference to the body of knowledge that bears the stamp of social sanction. But it is really only one of the standards by which truth may be distinguished from error; and we should take into account the possibility of there being also other types or systems of knowledge, relatively to each of which a similar distinction can be made. These systems may be many; and every one of them, according to the view taken of knowledge here, corresponds to a self-consistent whole of objective existence—the sphere of reference, which is common to all the judgments making up that system. Hence it is not only the world in the ordinary sense that exists; there may be others also, so long as they are systematic or are wholes con- stituted of inter-related parts, making it possible to distinguish the true from the false in statements relating to them. The world of Shakespeare's *Othello*, for example, is such a system, since it admits of right as well as wrong statements being made about it. It would be false, for instance, to represent Desdemona in it as in love with Cassio. As a consequence of such an enlarged view of objective existence, there will be not one type of truth only, but several—each order of existence, constituting the basis for a distinct type of it. "Our beds are not stained," it has been said, "by the wounds of dream scimitars"; but our dream beds may well be.

It may, on such considerations, be held that there is no absolute truth at all and that we may regard any truth as relatively false, if we choose to do so. But it appears that the very notion of *relative* truth suggests the recognition of an absolute standard by which all knowledge is judged; and we have to accept such a standard, giving up "relativist epistemology," if we are to avoid universal scepticism. Only it is necessary to further define truth, if it should be absolute. This can be done by bringing in the idea of comprehensiveness, when the systematic coherence which is our definition of truth will be perfect. The fulfilment of this new condition means the possibility of conceiving absolute truth as the expansion or development of one of the above truths such that it will, in some sense or other, include within its sphere of reference the whole of existence—not merely objective worlds but also conscious subjects. To leave out any portion of it would be to admit two or more truths, none of which, on account of their mutual exclusion, can be taken as absolute. But it may appear that there is no means of determining which of the relative truths is to be elevated to this rank. If, however, the sceptical position is to be avoided, a choice has to be made; and there is every consideration, short of logical certitude, to recommend common truth for the purpose. We may now divide all the subsidiary truths into two groups— one consisting of those that relate to the everyday world, though they may not all refer necessarily to the same aspects of it; and the other consisting of the rest which relate to the world of fiction or even to the region of dreams and illusions, so far as they are self-consistent. Of these, the former may be viewed as lying on the way to absolute truth; and since they may approximate to it more or less, we may speak of them as representing degrees of truth, a higher degree of it meaning greater completeness in the view it gives of reality. The truth of science as well as that of empirical life is of this kind. They mark relatively higher and lower stages on the path leading to ultimate truth. All such truths are integrated in the absolute one which is self-complete. The others cannot thus be integrated, owing to the divergence in their objective reference. But when we remember that, whether they refer to ideal constructions or to unique presentations, they are dependent for their subject-matter upon the reality which forms the content of the first group of truths, we find that they have their ultimate explanation, through them, in the absolute truth, even though they cannot be said to actually endure in it. They may be described as lower kinds of truth to distinguish them from the degrees of it already referred to. These two groups or classes of truth correspond to two orders of existence, one less real than the other. The world of morals implied by ethical truth, for example, belongs to the common order of existence, because of its direct bearing on actual life. But the world of art, though the truth at which it finally aims may be the very highest, stands lower than that. This is evident, for instance, from the fact that, as observed by A. C. Bradley,[1] "we dismiss the agony of Lear in a moment if the kitten goes and burns his nose."[2]

It is this absolute truth that is the goal of epistemology; and it yields a unified view of the whole of reality. All the elements of the universe—whether they be knowable objects or knowing subjects—appear in it as internally related; and each of them reveals itself there as occupying the place that rightly belongs to it within the whole. That is, the ultimate truth is entirely impersonal. Further, these elements are seen in it not merely as they are at any particular moment, but in the perspective of their entire history—as what they were in the past and as what they will be in the future. Or rather there can be no distinctions of time in it—"no future rushing to the past," but one eternal now. A temporal world when viewed in its wholeness, it has been remarked, must be an eternal one. In

---

[1] The Uses of Poetry, p. 12.

[2] This preference, however, implies that we realise at the time the relative status of the two realities. There is such realisation generally in the case of art, but not in illusions.

this concreteness and completeness it differs from scientific truth, though impersonal like it. It also differs from truth as commonly understood by us which is neither comprehensive nor wholly impersonal. There is one important point to which it is necessary to draw attention before we conclude. If the absolute truth should really comprehend all, it cannot exclude the self of the person that contemplates it. It will not therefore do if he stands apart, regarding himself as a mere knower and therefore distinct from what it points to. He should, on the other hand, view himself as inseparably one with it. The subject and the object would still be distinguished in his view, but there would not be that opposition or disaccord which we commonly feel between them. It means a profound transformation in the ordinary conception of the knowing self and of the objects known. Here naturally arises the question of the precise nature of the transformation in each case; but, as our present concern is with truth rather than with reality, we shall not attempt to discuss the possible answers to it. We shall only make one observation: though we left undetermined at the start the ultimate character of the self and of the object, we assumed that they were distinct. This initial dualism has to be abandoned now, for, according to the final conception of truth at which we have arrived, the knower and the known, though distinguish-able, are not separable. Knowledge begins by assuming that they are different, but it culminates in the discovery of a latent harmony between them in which the difference is resolved. It is not merely the notions of the subject and object that are thus transmuted; the knowledge also which relates them must be of a higher order than any we are familiar with—whether perceptual or conceptual. But this higher experience, which may be described as insight or intuition, is not altogether alien to us, for we get a glimpse of it whenever for any reason we rise above the distractions of personal living. Only it is too faint and fitful to enable us to understand what the exact character of the experience will be when the absolute truth is realised. All that we can say is that for one who attains to such experience, through a proper development of this intuitive power, there will be nothing that is not immediately known and that no part of what is so known will appear as external. What the means of developing intuition are, and whether the ideal of absolute truth can be completely realised, are questions whose consideration lies outside the scope of the present paper.

PRINCIPAL PUBLICATIONS

Outlines of Indian Philosophy. George Allen & Unwin (London, 1932).

Naiṣkarmya-siddhi of Sureśvara. Published in the Bombay Sanskrit Series (1925).

Iṣṭa-siddhi of Vimuktātman. Published in the Gaekwad's Oriental Series (1933).

THE SPIRIT IN MAN

by S. RADHAKRISHNAN

Born 1888; Vice-Chancellor and Professor of Philosophy,
Andhra University, Waltair
Educated at the Madras Christian College

THE SPIRIT IN MAN

I. PHILOSOPHY AND RELIGION IN INDIA

In the history of thought the problem of philosophy is approached in two different ways. There are some who take up particular groups of phenomena for investigation and leave the links to take care of themselves. Others view the world as a whole and seek to give general syntheses which comprehend the vast variety of the universe. The two ways of approach cannot be sharply separated. The universe is an interrelated changing process. When we study its parts, by separating out in thought certain aspects, we cannot help raising the question of the nature of the universe as a whole and man's place in it. In India philosophy has been interpreted as an enquiry into the nature of man, his origin and destiny. It is not a mere putting together or an assemblage of the results obtained by the investigation of different specialised problems, not a mere logical generalisation intended to satisfy the demand for all-inclusiveness. Such abstract views will have formal coherence, if any, and little organic relationship with the concrete problems of life. To the Indian mind, philosophy is essentially practical, dealing as it does with the fundamental anxieties of human beings, which are more insistent than abstract speculations. We are not contemplating the world from outside but are in it.

The practical bearing of philosophy on life became my central interest from the time I took up the study of the subject. My training in philosophy which began in the years 1905 to 1909 in the Madras Christian College, with its atmosphere of Christian thought, aspiration and endeavour, led me to take a special interest in the religious implications of metaphysics. I was strongly persuaded of the inefficiency of the Hindu religion to which I attributed the political downfall of India. The criticisms levelled against the Hindu religion were of a twofold character. It is intellectually incoherent and ethically unsound. The theoretical foundations as well as the practical fruits of the religion

CONTEMPORARY INDIAN PHILOSOPHY

were challenged. I remember the cold sense of reality, the depressing feeling of defeat that crept over me, as a causal relation between the anaemic Hindu religion and our political failure forced itself on my mind during those years. What is wrong with Hindu religion? How can we make it somewhat more relevant to the intellectual climate and social environment of our time? Such were the questions which roused my interest.

Religion expresses itself in and discloses its quality by the morality which it demands. While there is a good deal in Hindu religion and practice which merits just criticism, dark aspects of brutality, cruelty, violence, ignorance of nature, superstition and fear, in its essence the religion seemed to me to be quite sound. Its followers are carried along by a longing for the vision of God which has brought some of them to the verge of a holy perfection in which the perplexing dichotomy between the flesh and the spirit which men for ever feel but never understand is overcome. Hindu culture is directed towards that which is transcendent and beyond. Its great achievements in times past were due to a high tension of the spirit to which our age has no parallel. The purpose of religion is spritual awakening and those who are awakened are delivered from base delusions of caste and creed, of wealth and power.

There is, however, a tragic divergence between this exalted ideal and the actual life. In the first place in our anxiety to have no temporal possessions and spend our days in communion with spirit, the essential duty of service to man has been neglected. Religion may start with the individual but it must end in a fellowship. The essential interpenetration of God and the world, ideals and facts, is the cardinal principle of Hinduism and it requires us to bring salvation to the world. In the great days, the burning religious spirit expressed itself in a secular culture and a well-established civilisation. The religious soul returned from the contemplation of ultimate reality to the care of practical life. This fact is illustrated in the lives of the great teachers like Buddha and Śaṁkara who shared in the social and civilising function of religion. Hinduism strove victoriously against the corruption of the ancient world, civilised backward people, transformed and purified the new elements and preserved the tradition of the spiritual and the profane sciences. Proceeding on the assumption that all are of the same divine essence and therefore of equal worth and entitled to the same fundamental rights, Hinduism yet hesitated to take the bold steps essential for realising this end. Exalted ideals propounded by the founders of a religion meet with obstacles imposed by social inertia and corporate selfishness and those imbued with its true spirit must get back to the ideals and by effort and example break down the obstacles. Secondly, the kingdom of spirit is an elusive thing where one is deceived by shams and illusions. There are sinister people in every land who practise a kind of sorcery and bewitch the uneducated emotional into a sort of magic sleep. Much harm is done by spiritualistic and necromantic practices in which spirit and sense, religion and the powerful seductions of life get confused. It is essential to liberate not only bodies from starvation but minds from slavery. Saintliness, when genuine, is marked by true humility and love. Religion is a search for truth and peace, not power and plenty. Thirdly, in the name of religion we are often taught that the prevailing conditions are ordained by God. Thus it had been, was now and ever would be. Rightly interpreted, religion means courage and adventure, not resignation and fatalism. The customs and institutions of a community in which moral obligations are ingrained require to be reformulated in a dynamic social order. As these give their moral education to the members comprising a community, they should not lag far behind the conscience of the community. There is such a thing as the degeneration of accepted ideas. Many of them are kept going artificially, even after life has left them. The contemplative thinkers who transmit to their generation the delicacy of old forms, reverence for the past, the breath of history, the power to feel and understand the secure and the self-contained, as well as the visions of new things and vistas of a transformed age, men who know how to look upon tradition as something fluid and mobile, constantly modified and changed by the demands of life, are not among those who belong to the priestly profession to-day. The present class of priests, with rare exceptions, have lost their good breeding, kindliness and polish and have not gained in sureness of intellect, learning or adaptability. They know only that the discipline of tradition erects a barrier against radicalism and excessive individualism. They think that they are safeguarding the community against revolutionary change but are only fomenting it. If we pull off their masks, doubters stand revealed in many cases. They are not sure of what they preach and are mere opportunists by reason of a dumb gnawing despair whose nature they themselves do not understand. They are to some extent responsible for the prevalent spiritual sluggishness. They thrust formulas into our heads which we repeat mechanically, without any real knowledge of what they mean. A few ceremonies are observed more out of regard for our reputation or our relatives or as a matter of habit than out of any inward urge or sense of community. We are Hindus simply because of the legal framework of life and the individual feeling of security within which we live and have our being. Many of us have not the slightest idea of the true nature of religion, that hidden flame, which is more active among the young whose minds are in ferment. We can hear the call and the challenge of the youth for a new emphasis in religion, a new mankind. It is of the spirit of youth that it can never entirely despair of human nature. It will debase itself rather than cease to believe in its dream visions. It is convinced that the affliction that is visited on us is the return for our common failure.

Our present political condition is the sign of an inward crisis, a loss of faith, a weakening of our moral fibre. Events happen in the mind of man before they are made manifest in the course of history. It is essential for us to get back to the old spirit which requires us to overcome the passions of greed and avarice, to free ourselves from the tyranny of a dark past, from the oppression by spectres and ghosts, from the reign of falsehood and deceit. If we do not undertake this task, the sufferings of our day would be without meaning and justification.

II. THE NEED FOR A SPIRITUAL RENEWAL

A veritable renewal is what the world and not merely India stands in need of. To those who have lost their anchorage, to our age itself which is in a great transition, the way of the spirit is the only hope.

The present chaos in the world can be traced directly to the chaos in our minds. There is division in man's soul. We assume that the intellectual and the moral exhaust the nature of man and that the world can be rebuilt on the basis of scientific or secular humanism. Man tears himself from the religious centre, discovers his own powers and possibilities and through their impetuous play tries to create a new society. The modern intellectual whose mind has been moulded to a degree seldom recognised by the method and concepts of modern science, has great faith in verifiable facts and tangible results. Whatever cannot be measured and calculated is unreal. Whispers that come from the secret depths of the soul are rejected as unscientific fancies. Since men began to think, there have always been sceptics. "The wise man," said Arcesilaus, "should withhold his assent from all opinions and should suspend his judgment." This admirable attitude for the scientific investigator is now turned to one of dogmatic denial which offers but an inadequate guide to life and action.

What are these seemingly indisputable facts on which the new world is to be built? Human life is an infinitesimal speck on a tiny planet, in a system of planets revolving round an insignificant star, itself lost in a wilderness of other stars. Life is an accident arising in some unknown fashion from inert matter. It is wholly explicable, though not yet explained by mechanical laws. It has assumed various forms through the operation of chance (variation and environment). Even the mind of man is a chance product evolved to help man to overcome in the struggle for existence. The world of nature is indifferent to man's dreams and desires. Many strange creatures, products of millions of years of evolution, have passed away and man need not be so presumptuous as to think that he alone is fated to go on for all time. He is but an episode in terrestrial evolution and his existence on earth will come to an end.

The science of anthropology tells us how relative all moral systems are, especially those relating to sexual life. To the intellectuals who were in any case gradually shaking off the traditional moral restraints and rehabilitating the rights of the flesh, Freud, without intending in the least such a result, made licence respectable. The science of psycho-analysis is said to justify the consecration of all desires and a complete liberation from all restraints.

Social groups are formed in the interests of survival. They have no other purpose than furthering their own material good, by force and fraud, if necessary. Economic welfare is the end of all existence. The principles of evolution offer a scientific basis for militaristic imperialism. When powerful groups exploit the weaker races of the earth, they are but instruments for furthering the evolution of higher biological forms which has brought us from amoeba to man and will now complete the journey from Neanderthal man to the scientific barbarians of the modern world. The great powers constitute themselves into God's policemen for preserving law and order in all parts of the globe, into missionaries for civilising the weaker races, who are treated as creatures of a lower order, annoying intruders with a different mental cast and moral constitution. The Jews are not the only people who called themselves the Chosen Race. Others also have faith in their mission, though this faith is based not on revelation but on historic or legendary destiny. To fulfil their destinies nations are converted into military machines and human beings are made into tools. The leaders are not content with governing men's bodies, they must subjugate their minds. They must transmit faith in their messianic mission to the community at large. Without much effort they gain the goodwill of the decadent and the discontented, the poor and the unemployed, the adventurous and the opportunist and the young and the eager who have neither ideal nor guiding star but only erring minds and quivering hearts. The seeds of rampant nationalism find fertile soil in the unpledged allegiance of emancipated

minds. An abnormal state of moral and mental tension results
where free thinking is replaced by dull obedience, moral development by moral quietism, feeling of humanity by arrogance and
self-righteousness.

Religion needs certainty, complete assurance, but this is just
the quality which scientific naturalism has pretty thoroughly
discredited. Our need to believe, we are told, cannot be a sufficient
foundation for faith. Religion, as a matter of history, has crippled
the free flight of intelligence and stifled glad devotion to human
values. It has fostered superstition and prescribed crime. It has
comforted millions of suffering humanity with illusions of extra-
terrestrial solace to compensate for the barrenness of their earthly
lives. Religion is only a species of poetry (Santayana), mythology
(Croce), sociological phenomenon (Durkheim), or a narcotic for
a decadent society (Lenin). Spiritual life is a deception and a
dream. At best we can use religion as a code of ethics. It can
be reduced to a few rules of morality. When Kant defined religion
as the knowledge of our duties as divine commands and made
God not a present help but a future judge rewarding the good
and punishing the wicked, he very nearly ousted God from
human life. In his *Religion within the Limits of Reason*, Kant
views moral life as a life of individual self-determination in
which neither God nor man can assist but in which each
individual must carry on his separate struggle by his own
unaided strength. Such a view leaves little room for anything
like true religious worship or for the investment of life with
purpose. The men of talent, without any binding ties or true
affinities, disastrously isolated, thrown entirely on their own
resources, their own solitary egos, with no foothold either in
heaven or on earth, but completely uprooted are the free men
who have emerged from the narrow frames of creeds and sects,
from the fear of popes and priests; these are the ideal heroes,
the beacons for all the ages. Each man is a prophet and the
result is a regular Tower of Babel where no one understands
the other. Each of them understands in his own way his own
ideal for the world. Confusion of tongues in the Tower will
and must end in catastrophe.

"This may well be called the age of criticism," said Kant, "a criticism from which nothing need hope to escape. When religion seeks to shelter itself behind its sanctity, and law behind its majesty, they justly awaken suspicion against themselves and lose all claim to the sincere respect which reason yields only to that which has been able to bear the test of its free and open scrutiny." But what has criticism achieved? It has banished absolute truth from thought and life. In aesthetics, beauty is treated as subjective. In jurisprudence, law is declared to be an expression of social convention, not of justice. In morality a full and varied life is said to be inconsistent with a rigid moral code. Even theologians have dropped the Absolute and taken to finite, "self-educating" gods.

What is the result of this new positivist criticism on life? We have a world of rationalist prophets, of selfish individualists, of a monstrous economic system compounded out of industrialism and capitalism, of vast technical achievements and external conquests, of continual craving for creature comforts and love of luxury, of unbridled and endless covetousness in public life, of dictatorships of blood and brutality, anxious to make the world a shambles dripping with human blood, of atheism and disdain for the soul, a world in which nothing is certain and men have lost assurance. In the great cities in the East as well as in the West we meet with young men, cold and cynical, with a swagger and a soldierly bearing, energetic and determined to get on, waiting for a chance to get into a place in the front rank, men who esteem themselves masters of life and makers of the future, who think, as Byron said, they lead the world because they go to bed late. Their self-assertive, off-hand manner, their vulgarity and violence, their confident insolence and cocksureness, their debasing of the law and derisive disregard of justice show the utter demoralisation through which the world is passing. They are not merely the thin crust of the social pyramid. They lead and control the masses who in the new democracies are gifted with a capacity for reading which is out of all proportion to their capacity for thinking. Life has become a carnival or a large circus in progress, without structure, without law, without rhythm.

Let us look closer for the other side to the picture. The denial of the divine in man has resulted in a sickness of soul. To suspend our will and thought and drift whither we do not know is not satisfying. Man can never be at rest, even if his physical needs are amply met. Bitterness will continue to disturb his mind and spoil his peace. Nature cannot be completely tamed to do man's bidding. Her caprices, her storms and tempests, her cyclones and earthquakes, will continue to shatter his work and dash his hopes. The great human relationships cannot be easily freed from interference by pride and jealousy, selfishness and disloyalty. Fortune's vagaries and the fickleness of man will continue to operate. Peace of mind is a remote hope until and unless we have a vision of perfection, a glimpse of eternity to prevail against the perspective of time. Security without which no happiness is possible cannot come from the mastery of things. Mastery of self is the essential prerequisite.

The world is passing through a period of uncertainty, of wordless longing. It wants to get out of its present mood of spiritual chaos, moral aimlessness and intellectual vagrancy. Burdened and tired to death by his loneliness, man is ready to lean on any kind of authority, if it only saves him from hopeless isolation and the wild search for peace. The perils of spiritual questioning are taking us to the opposite extreme of revivals and fundamentalism in religion. These are only half-way houses to a radical reconstruction of the mind. The uncertainty between dogmatic faith and blatant unbelief is due to the non-existence of a philosophic tradition or habit of mind. The mental suffering of the thinking, when the great inheritance of mankind is concealed by the first views of science, the suffering which is due to the conflict between the old and the new values, which are both accepted, though without reconciliation, is the sign that no upheaval, no crude passion can put out the light of spirit in man. However dense the surrounding darkness may be, the light will shine though that darkness may not comprehend it. Only when the life of spirit transfigures and irradiates the life of man from within will it be possible for him to renew the face of the earth. The need of the world to-day is for a

I*

religion of the spirit, which will give a purpose to life, which will not demand any evasion or ambiguity, which will reconcile the ideal and the real, the poetry and the prose of life, which will speak to the profound realities of our nature and satisfy the whole of our being, our critical intelligence and our active desire.

III. INTUITION AND INTELLECT

My attempt to answer the question stated in the previous section is largely influenced by the thought of Plato and Śaṁkara. They are not concerned so much with particular religious dogmas as with the central problem of religion. To-day, our trouble is not so much with the infallibility of the Pope or the inerrancy of the Bible, not even with whether Christ or Krishna is God or whether there is a revelation. All these problems have changed their meaning and are dependent on the one and only problem, whether there is or is not behind the phenomena of nature and the drama of history an unseen spiritual power, whether the universe is meaningful or meaningless, whether it is God or chance. Plato and Śaṁkara appeal to me for the other reason that they are masters in the art of tempering the rigour of their argument with that larger utterance which is the soul of true literature. Writers on philosophy sometimes require to be reminded of Landor's warning: "Clear writers like fountains do not seem as deep as they are: the turbid look most profound."

Hindu systems of thought believe in the power of the human mind to lead us to all truth. Our ordinary mind is not the highest possible order of the human mind. It can rise to a level almost inconceivable to us. Each system prescribes a discipline or a practical way of reaching the higher consciousness. Faith in the ultimate values which characterises the philosopher in Plato's Dialogues, as distinct from the pseudo-philosopher or the sceptical sophist, is not a matter of dialectics or sophistry but of spiritual awareness.

The idealist tradition both in the East and the West has asserted the supremacy of spirit in man. Mere physical desire and passion, impulse and instinct, even intellect and will do not exhaust his nature. The spiritual status is the essential dignity of man and the origin of his freedom. It is the state anterior to the divisions between intellect, feeling and will, where consciousness forms a unity which cannot be analysed. It is the presupposition, the limit and the goal of our divided consciousness. When the spirit, which is the mind in its integrity, is at work, man has the immediate intuition of his unity with the eternal, though, in the derived intellectual consciousness, he remains apart and works into the grounds of his own being and discerns his relation to and dependence upon the presence behind the trembling veil of phenomena.

This essential truth is expressed in the language of religion as the indwelling of the Logos. There is the image of God in man, an almost deathless longing for all that is great and divine. The values of the human soul are not earth-bound but belong to the eternal world to which man can rise through discipline and disinterestedness. He can transcend the old law of brute creation which gives the race to the swift and the battle to the strong and accept the principle that he that saves his life shall lose it. When, in response to the imperative voice of conscience, he renounces everything and dies, he touches infinitude, lays hold on the eternal order and shares his kinship with the divine. At the centre of the soul there is a something, a spark "so akin to God that it is one with God, and not merely united to Him" (Eckhart).

Spiritual apprehension or the kind of awareness of real values which are neither objects in space and time nor universals of thought is called intuition. There is the controlling power of reality in intuitive apprehension quite as much as in perceptual acts or reflective thought. The objects of intuition are recognised and not created by us. They are not produced by the act of apprehension itself.

Ours is an age which is justly proud of its rationalism and enlightenment. But any sound rationalism will recognise the need for intuition. St. Thomas observes: "The articles of faith cannot be proved demonstratively. The ultimate truth which is the criterion by which we measure all other relative truths is only to be experienced, not to be demonstrated."[1] Descartes, though a thorough-going rationalist and admirer of the geometrical method, uses the intuitive principle. While he employs the process of doubt to free the mind from error and prejudice and insists that we should accept only what presents itself to the mind so clearly and distinctly as to exclude all grounds of doubt, he finds what is clear and distinct in his knowledge of himself as a thinking being. It alone is beyond all doubt, self-evident, dependent upon nothing else. Descartes distinguishes perception, imagination and syllogistic reasoning from intuition which he defines as "the undoubting conception of an unclouded and attentive mind, and springs from the light of reason alone. It is more certain than deduction itself in that it is simpler." While the truths intuition grasps are self-evident, training, or what Descartes calls method, is necessary to direct our mental vision to the right objects so that our mind can "behold" the objects. In so far as our minds are not creative of reality but only receptive of it, we must get into contact with reality, outward by perception, inward by intuition, and by means of intellect interpret and understand it. Logical proof is not self-complete. Certain *a priori* principles constitute limits to it. We are not referring to the psychological *a priori*. The temporal priority in an individual mind may be traced to social tradition or race memory but there are certain propositions which are presupposed in experience which can neither be proved nor disproved. These unproved first principles are known by intuition. Thus we have a sense of the organic wholeness of things while intellectual knowledge is abstract and symbolic. And again, the higher the reality the less adequate is our knowledge of it. Analytical intellect cannot give us a full understanding of the ecstasy of love or the beauty of holiness.

It is unfortunate that insistence on intuition is often confused with anti-intellectualism. Intuition which ignores intellect is useless. The two are not only not incompatible but vitally united. Plato is the classic on this question. He says in the

[1] *Summa Theol.*, q. 46, n. 2.

Symposium (211) that we know the essence of beauty in a supreme beatific vision, which is, as it were, the consummation of the philosopher's searching enquiry. Similarly in the *Republic* (vii and viii) we are told that the world of forms is apprehended by us through the exercise of reason, though Plato is quite clear that it is not through mere reason.[1] Intuition is beyond reason, though not against reason. As it is the response of the whole man to reality, it involves the activity of reason also. The truths of intuition are led up to by the work of the understanding and can be translated into the language of understanding, though they are clearly intelligible only to those who already in some measure have immediate apprehension of them. Intuition is not independent but emphatically dependent upon thought and is immanent in the very nature of our thinking. It is dynamically continuous with thought and pierces through the conceptual context of knowledge to the living reality under it. It is the result of a long and arduous process of study and analysis and is therefore higher than the discursive process from which it issues and on which it supervenes.

Intuition is not used as an apology for doctrines which either could not or would not be justified on intellectual grounds. It is not shadowy sentiment or pathological fancy fit for cranks and dancing dervishes. It stands to intellect as a whole to a part, as the creative source of thought to the created categories which work more or less automatically. Logical reflection is a special function within the concrete life of mind and is necessarily a fraction of the larger experience. If it sets itself up as constitutive of the whole life of mind, it becomes, in Kant's words, a "faculty of illusion." The different energies of the human soul are not cut off from one another by any impassable barriers. They flow into each other, modify, support and control each other. The Sanskrit expression "saṁyagdarśana" or integral

---

[1] Cp. Burnet: "To anyone who has tried to live in sympathy with the Greek philosophers, the suggestion that they were intellectualists must seem ludicrous. On the contrary, Greek philosophy is based on the faith that reality is divine and that the one thing needful is for the soul, which is akin to the divine, to enter into communion with it."—*Greek Philosophy*, vol. i, *Thales to Plato*, p. 12. This is certainly true of Plato.

insight, brings out how far away it is from occult visions, trance and ecstasy.

Simply because the deliverances of intuition appear incontestable to the seer or happen to be shared by many, it does not follow that they are true. Subjective certitude, whose validity consists in mere inability to doubt, is different from logical certainty. The sense of assurance is present, even when the object is imaginary and even such objects, so long as they are believed to be actual, evoke feelings and attitudes quite as intense and effective as those excited by real ones. While religion may be satisfied with the sense of convincedness, which is enough to foster spiritual life, philosophy is interested in finding out whether the object believed is well grounded or not.

Intuition requires cultivation quite as much as the powers of observation and thought. We can realise the potentialities of spirit only by a process of moral ascesis which gradually shapes the soul into harmony with the invisible realities. Plotinus tells us that the path to the goal is long and arduous, traversing first the field of civic virtues, then the discipline of purification and then the contemplation which leads to illumination. Indian thought requires us to abstract from sense life and discursive thinking in order to surrender to the deepest self where we get into immediate contact with reality. To know better, we must become different, our thoughts and feelings must be deeply harmonised. Intuition is not only perfect knowledge but also perfect living. The consecration of the self and the knowledge of reality grow together. The fully real can be known only by one who is himself fully real.

IV. ART AND MORALITY

What we need to-day in our life is a breath from the spirit of another and a more abiding world. We must recapture the intuitive powers that have been allowed to go astray in the stress of life. Our contemporary civilisation with its specialisms and mechanical triumphs knows a large number of facts but not the mystery of the world in which these facts are. Other disciplines than exact sciences are required—art and literature, philosophy and religion—to quicken the perceptions of wonder and surprise, of strangeness and beauty, of the mystery and miraculousness of the world that surrounds us, if only we could see with eyes which are not dulled by use and wont. Science can dissolve the physical world into electrons and bombard the atom but cannot account for the genius who can do all these things, for the noble human countenance, for the expression of its eyes and the affections that shine through them. Man has the roots of his being struck deep into the nature of reality. On this bedrock are all his creative activities firmly based.

A great writer on aesthetics, Theodor Lipps, regards artistic intuition as an act of Einfühlung, which has been translated as "empathy" on the analogy of sympathy. If sympathy means feeling with, empathy means feeling into. When we contemplate an object, we project ourselves into it, and feel its inward rhythm. All production is an attempt at reproduction, at an approach to things seen and heard and felt. If a work of art fails, it is generally due to its lack of empathy. In a Sanskrit drama *Mālavikāgnimitra* (ii. 2), where the picture fails to bring out the beauty of the original, the failure is attributed to imperfect concentration (*śithilasamādhi*) of the painter. The mind concentrates on the material, becomes thoroughly possessed by it, gets as it were fused into it, absorbs it, and remoulds it according to its own ideals and thus creates a work of art. This act of pure contemplation is possible only for perfectly free minds which look at the objects with utter humility and reverence. This freedom is as rare as that purity of heart which is the condition of seeing God. It is a state in which all our energies are heightened, tautened and sublimated. We draw or paint, not with our brains but with our whole blood and being.

Art is the utterance of life. It is the expression of the soul's vision and is not wholly rational. It oversteps the limits of the rational and has, in Bacon's phrase, something strange in its proportion. The artist's attitude to the universe is more one of acceptance than of understanding. He sees the burden of mystery in all things, though he does not shudder in fear of it. He tries to pluck the mystery out of the thing, and present it to us. This, he is able to do, not by means of his reason, but by a riper reason, his intuitive power, which is the nexus, the connecting link, between the appearance and the reality, the flesh and the spirit. Until we have the inevitable fusion of the divine and the temporal, the subtle interpenetration of the spirit through the whole man, we will not have the quiet fire that burns, the lightning flash of vision that illuminates the darkness of the earth and the virgin apprehensions that take away the sting from the pains of mortality. All great artists, who have the subtle, spiritual appeal, convey a stillness, a remoteness, a sense of the beyond, the far away.

In my Hibbert Lectures on *An Idealist View of Life*, I complained that many of our best writers are too intellectual and did not attain to the heights of real greatness. They touch the mind but do not enter the soul. For great art, what is needed is inspiration and not intellectual power, what the Indian poet Daṇḍin calls natural genius (*naisargikī pratibhā*). Great art is possible only in those rare moments when the artist is transplanted out of himself and does better than his best in obedience to the dictates of a *daimon* such as Socrates used to say whispered wisdom into his ears. In those highest moments, the masters of human expression feel within themselves a spark of the divine fire and seem to think and feel as if God were in them and they were revealing fragments of the secret plan of the universe. Matthew Arnold said that, when Wordsworth and Byron were really inspired, Nature took the pen from their hands and wrote for them. In other words, they are activities of the pure spirit, manifestations of the human consciousness, at its highest, purified by detachment and disinterestedness. Some of our best writers skim the surface, look on it, examine it but do not take the plunge. That is why they do not feed, refresh and renew the spirit. Their works are not works of art but exercises in ingenuity. They have intellectual power, technical skill but not that rare adequacy of mind which engenders strange values from another world, through the perfect arrangement of a few colours on the canvas or a few lines of poetry.

But, let it not be forgotten that the true work of art is charged with thought. It is not the expression of mere emotion. A good deal of system and symmetry, of reflective determinateness is involved in the unfolding of the artist's experience. A Beethoven symphony or a Shakespeare play has one indivisible inspiration but its expression involves elaborate labour on the intellectual plane. This labour is the effort of man to create its embodiment.

As consistent thinking is not creative thinking, as intellectual verse is not inspired poetry, in conduct respectability is not righteousness. Mere correctitude of behaviour is not the last word of morality. It may be conventional good form but it is not creative good life. The moral hero is not content with being merely moral. When Socrates refused to escape from prison, he did not behave like the conventional good man of his age who would have wriggled out at the first chance. Jesus's behaviour before Pilate is not motived by prudential morality. Common sense and worldly wisdom tell us that if a doorway opens for a man who is in prison, he is a fool if he does not make use of it. Holiness is however different from vulgar prudence. It is an inner grace of nature by which the spirit purifies itself of worldly passions and appetites and dwells in patient, confident communion with the universal spirit. Those who have this chastity of mind and spirit which lies at the very heart and is the parent of all other good see at once what is good and hold to that and for its sake humble themselves even unto death. Well-being, comfort, luxury, all these things which mean so much to the common run of men, leave them indifferent, if they are not felt as burdensome hindrances to the heroic life of creative love. This is true not only of the well-known sages of India and Greece, the prophets of Israel and the saints of Christendom, but also of the many obscure heroes of the moral life who go below the precise formulas and get at the social aspirations from which they arise and lead humanity forward.

Most of us are slaves of impulse and emotion, habit and automatism. We are not normally aware of the large influence of automatic thinking, of mental habit and the great hold which

274 CONTEMPORARY INDIAN PHILOSOPHY

our past experience has on our present outlook and decisions. Human nature has in it the tendency to set or harden into fixities of habit. There are habits not only of the body but of the intellect and the feelings. Anything strange or uncommon appears to be immoral, for it is contrary to the routine habits which are settled —what we may call the social conscience. We live or try to live by a code which we have not examined but have accepted without adequate consideration. We eat and drink, play and work, attend to business and adopt hobbies not because we have chosen these activities for ourselves but because the environment in which we grew up indicates them for us. We accord to society what it expects from us, fulfil the duties which our station assigns to us. This is passive acquiescence, not active creation. We do not live our lives but in a sense are lived by our condititions. But this cannot go on for long, unless we surrender our thought and will and reduce ourselves to the level of automata. Our little understood urges from within, our likes and dislikes, our passions of greed and ambition soon produce conflicts. Society makes large demands on our life and adaptation to them is not always easy. Sometimes, we may feel that we are acting as traitors to humanity, by obeying the rules which our narrow group imposes on us. Often, personal relationships happen to be unfulfilled. Life, that sphinx with a human face and the body of a brute, asks us new questions every hour. The backward or those who are still children in the game of life allow their activities to be governed by automatic attractions and repulsions but their activities are by no means free. To hold the balance between instinctive desires and cravings and social obligations is the task of the moral life. Only when man attains unity, when he has discovered his whole nature and ordered it, has he the right to say "I will." His free decisions seem then to come of themselves and develop of their own accord, though they may be contrary to his interests and inclinations. They infringe on the ordinary routine of life and bring into it a new type of power. These creative decisions cannot be foreseen, though they may be accounted for in retrospect. Though they defy anticipation, they are thoroughly rational. There is a wide gulf between mechanical repetition and free creation, between the morality of rules and the life of spirit.

V. RELIGIOUS EXPERIENCE AND ITS IMPLICATIONS

Religion is, in essence, experience of or living contact with ultimate reality. It is not a subjective phenomenon, not mere cultivation of the inner life but the apprehension of something that stands over against the individual. The real is known not as the conclusion of an argument but with the certainty of a thing experienced. We cannot prove the reality of God in the same way in which we prove the existence of a chair or a table. For God is not an object like other objects in nature. God is spirit which is distinct from the knowing subject or the known object. All proofs for the existence of God fail because they conceive of God as an objective reality. Spirit is life, not thing, energy not immobility, something real in itself and by itself, and cannot be compared to any substance subjective or objective. The divine is manifested in spiritual life or experience. It is given to us in life and not established by ratiocination.

Though religious experience is analogous in some respects to the other manifestations of spiritual activity, such as scientific genius, artistic creation or moral heroism, it cannot be identified with any of them. It is unique and autonomous. The spirit is at home with itself in religion and its life satisfies every side of our being. The peace which we obtain through it is not mere emotional satisfaction. In it the mind becomes irradiated with the divine light and obstinate questions of reason find an answer. The will loses its irresoluteness as it becomes one with the divine will. Spiritual geniuses possess the highest that man can possess, constant contact with the creative principle of which life is the manifestation, coincidence with the divine will, serene calm, inward peace which no passion can disturb, no persecution can dismay.

Any philosophic account of the universe must consider all known data, our hopes and fears, our efforts and endeavours. While philosophy cannot take anything for granted, it cannot ignore the testimony of religious experience to the nature of ultimate reality which it also seeks to apprehend. If art initiates us into truth, if the object of poetry is "truth which is its own testimony" (Wordsworth), it may well be that even religious experience makes a real contribution to the understanding of the world, and possesses a profound metaphysical significance. It is our duty as seekers of truth to listen with reverence to the judgments of those seers who have cultivated the religious sense and are specially endowed with a fine discrimination in matters of spirit.

Simply because there are persons to whom religious experience is unknown, we cannot say that it is either unreal or impossible. Our limited experiences are not the standard for all. There are many for whom beauty is a word and music only a noise, but that does not mean that there is no reality in the artist's experience. Again, religious experience is exceptional only in the sense that all genius is exceptional. It does not mean that the experience cannot be verified by those who take the necessary trouble. Even though all of us may not give utterance to the voice of spirit, still it finds an echo in the depths of our soul. To suggest that men who have religious experience are mental invalids is inconsistent with the well-known fact that some of the greatest mystics are men of remarkable intellectual power, shrewd discrimination and practical ability.

The sceptics dismiss the experiences of saints and mystics as due to unsoundness of mind or psychological tricks. They are perhaps justified by the history of religious experience where it has often been confused with emotional thrills and edifying feelings. This fact only reminds us of the need for careful scrutiny and examination of what claims to be religious experience. Simply because religion has often been mistaken for what it is not and got mixed up with fantastic notions and wanton cruelties, we cannot disregard the entire field of religious experience as baseless. We are not willing to dismiss sense perception as illusory simply because we have dreams and hallucinations. Our experiences are liable to misinterpretation and our judgments are not infallible. We are nowadays reverent even to the experience of ghosts: we need not be rude to the experience of God. If we adopt a narrowly rationalist view, not merely religion but all the higher activities of mind become unmeaning and pathological. Such a view narrows the range of vision of the human mind.

Though religious experience has developed into varied doctrines and expressed itself in different intellectual notations, there is a certain kinship of the spirit among the religious geniuses who have made their mark on history, who join hands across the centuries and bid us enter into the kingdom of the spirit. They affirm that the self perceives directly the ultimate reality which is there, existing in its own right, untouched by the imperfections of the world. It is intimately present to and in ourselves. Truth, beauty and goodness are not subjective fancies but objective facts. They are not only ultimate values included in the purpose of the world but supreme realities. Their objectivity and sovereignty are sometimes brought out by calling them attributes of God. We have a consciousness that we belong to that which is ultimately real. Again, we cannot eliminate the element of mystery in religion and attempt to measure the transcendent and the eternal by finite and temporal standards. Any effort to make religion absolutely rational would be to misconceive its essential character. Baron von Hügel has a pregnant observation on this question. To expect clearness with regard to the knowledge of the Supreme, he says, "indicates a thoroughly unreasonable, a self-contradictory habit of mind."[1] When we hear enthusiastic descriptions of ultimate reality, it is well to remember Lao Tse's dictum that he who knows the Tao may be recognised by the fact that he is reluctant to speak of it. Plato in his Seventh Epistle declares his intention of publishing nothing on his *Idea of the Good*: "There is no writing of mine on this subject nor ever shall be. It is not capable of expression like other branches of study but as the result of long intercourse and common life spent upon the thing, a light is suddenly kindled as from a leaping spark, and when it has reached the soul, it thenceforward finds nourishment for itself." The mystics appeal to us to build the ideal society, the universal

[1] *Essays and Addresses on the Philosophy of Religion*, First Series, p. 100.

republic where there is neither Jew nor Gentile, neither Greek nor barbarian, where all men *qua* men are of equal worth. Religious geniuses are devotees of the ideal of universal brotherhood, based on the conception of the sanctity of the human person.

While those who share the experience do not seek for proofs for the existence of spirit, but feel immediately certain of what is experienced, proofs have to be offered for those who do not share the experience. The rationality of the faith requires to be demonstrated. Though the famous arguments for the existence of God may not be logically conclusive, they show the inadequacy of naturalistic explanations. Nature is not its own *raison d'être.* No part of it contains its own explanation. There is in the procession of events we call nature, the emergence of higher qualities whereby, as Browning put it, "out of three sounds we frame not a fourth sound but a star." Life emerged out of the non-living when the cooling earth was able to support life. Physico-chemical explanations are admittedly inadequate for life, and for the rise of mind and personality. The characteristics of the higher level cannot be deduced from those of the lower. While science can describe the precise circumstances under which higher qualities emerge, it cannot say why they do so. Naturalistic evolution which attempts to account for the development of new species by the theory of accidental variations preserved by selection and fixed by heredity assumes a series of miracles. We must grant an intention of nature to account for the co-ordination of complementary variations in a manner beneficial to the organism and its transmissibility to its descendants. Bergson in his *Creative Evolution* suggests that the evolution of the species is not the result of the mechanical action of external causes but is the expression of a vital impetus operating in individuals, carrying them in a given direction towards ever higher complexities. The theory of vital impetus is an admission of the mystery of life and its movement. The more we examine organic evolution, the more do we find that there is very little of the random. Life grows to some end and the end is the growth of spirit. A universe that has produced man cannot be indifferent to his highest good.

Any process is intelligible in view of the end it aims at achieving. The character of the different stages and their qualities are determined by the end. In the cosmic process, we find that life uses matter for its instrument. Similarly mind uses the living organism. The highest order of being called spirit which is mind illumined by the ideals of truth, goodness and beauty is rooted in human intelligence and grows from it. The universe attempts to realise these ideals and cannot be understood except in the light of them. They are not only the goal of the universe in the temporal sense but are the timeless principles in the light of which alone the universe becomes intelligible.

Professor Alexander is prepared to concede that "deity" which is the next higher quality to emerge is the explanation of the world process, though for him it is yet non-existent, though the world is striving for its existence. It is yet an ideal and an existent only in so far as the tendency is operative in the world. It is always to come but never comes. It is the name of the next higher quality which is to emerge but which has not yet emerged. In a sense, Alexander's "deity" is not the creator but the created. It cannot serve as the explanation of the world, if it does not exist and operate in some sense. It does not yet exist in the temporal sense. It must therefore exist in a timeless way. This world has meaning and value only in so far as it realises in time and existence that which transcends time and existence. No explanation of the cosmic process is possible without a transcendental reference.

The cosmic process is sometimes traced to an experimenting life force with which Bergson has made us familiar. The advocates of life force are impressed by the inadequacy of purely naturalistic explanations. They hold that life force will continue to produce higher types of existence. They have sufficient faith in the trustworthiness of life force and its responsiveness to our deepest aspirations. Bergson suggests that it discovers original solutions to the problems set by external conditions and overcomes obstacles in an intelligent way. If we are so certain that the life force will behave in a reasonable and purposive way, it is not fair to think of it as an unconscious agency. If it is the operative principle of the cosmic process and contains, as Bergson suggests, the essential characteristics developed in the different lines of evolution in a state of reciprocal implication, "instinct and intelligence being mere views, taken from two different points, of that simple reality," then it is unmeaning to call it vital impetus or life force. In his latest work on *The Two Sources of Morality and Religion,* Bergson argues that the creative energy, the principle of life in general which inward intuition reveals, is to be defined as love and is God Himself.[1]

God is the timeless spirit attempting to realise timeless values on the plane of time. The ideal of the cosmic process which at the same time is its goal and explanation is real in one sense though wanting to be realised in another. The ideal is the greatest fact in one way and a remote possibility in another. The values which the cosmic process is attempting to achieve are only a few of the possibilities contained in the Absolute. God is the definitisation of the Absolute in reference to the values of the world.

There are aspects in religious experience, such as the sense of rest and fulfilment, of eternity and completeness, which require the conception of a being whose nature is not exhausted by the cosmic process, which possesses an allfulness of reality which our world only faintly shadows. This side of religious experience demands the conception of the supreme as self-existence, infinity, freedom, absolute light and absolute beatitude. On the other hand there are features of our religious experience which require us to look upon God as a self-determining principle manifested in a temporal development, with wisdom, love and goodness as his attributes. From this point of view God is a personal being with whom we can enter into personal relationship. Practical religion presupposes a God who looks into our hearts, knows our tribulations and helps us in our need. The reality of prayer and sacrifice is affirmed by the religious life of mankind. It assumes the reality of a concrete being who influences our life. To leave the Absolute in abstract isolation dwelling in Epicurean felicity is to reduce it to an ornamental figurehead who lends

[1] E.T. (1935), p. 320.

an atmosphere to an essentially agnostic view of the cosmic process. The permanent reality beyond the transient world of struggle and discord is also here and in everything. In religious experience itself there is no conflict. The supreme satisfies both sets of needs. But for philosophy of religion, the central problem is to reconcile the apparently conflicting views of the supreme as eternally complete and of the supreme as the self-determining principle manifesting in the temporal process.

In Greek thought, Plato and Aristotle conceived the Divine being as self-sufficient in His own perfection and undisturbed by any changes of the world. Plato sets up a hierarchy of Ideas with the Idea of Good at its apex. For Aristotle, God is the unmoved mover, a thought thinking itself, self-enclosed, operative only by the appeal of its own perfection. The God of the Hebrews is of a different type. He is personal and active in history and interested in the changes and chances of this developing world. He is a being who holds communication with us. Christianity represents a blend of the Hebrew and the Greek traditions, though it has not yet succeeded in reconciling them.

The Hindu is aware of this fundamental problem and as early as the period of the Upaniṣads we find attempts to reconcile the doctrine of the changeless perfection of the Absolute with the conviction that God is also responsible for this changing world.[1]

The way in which the relation between the Absolute and God is here indicated is not the same as that either of Śaṁkara or of Bradley, though it has apparent similarities to their doctrines. While the Absolute is the transcendent divine, God is the cosmic divine. While the Absolute is the total reality, God is the Absolute from the cosmic end, the consciousness that informs and sustains the world. God is, so to say, the genius of this world, its ground, which as a thought or a possibility of the Absolute lies beyond the world in the universal consciousness of the Absolute. The possibilities or the ideal forms are the mind of the Absolute or

[1] For the views of the Upaniṣads, the Bhagavad Gītā and the great teachers, Śaṁkara, Rāmanuja and Madhva, see the writer's *Indian Philosophy*, vols. i and ii, second edition.

the thoughts of the Absolute. One of the infinite possibilities is being translated into the world of space and time. Even as the world is a definite manifestation of one specific possibility of the Absolute, God with whom the worshipper stands in personal relation is the very Absolute in the world context and is not a mere appearance of the Absolute.

When the Old Testament says, "Before even the earth and the world were made, Thou art God from everlasting, and world without end," it is referring to the Absolute and not to God who is organic with the world process. The Absolute is joy: God is love. Joy is a self-existent reality, an absolute which does not depend on objects but only on itself. The divine power of love spends itself on the objects of its love without expecting any return from its self-expenditure. In the course of the cosmic process, God accepts an element of the given, certain necessities which His will does not approve, though He is struggling to transform them through His creative effort. God appears to be finite in the process though His infinity reveals itself when the world plan reaches its fulfilment.

In a famous passage of the *Microcosmos*, Lotze repudiates the objection to the personality of God, which affirms that the distinction between self and not-self is essential for the existence of personality and as the divine self is infinite and therefore has no other, it cannot be personal. Lotze's answer to this difficulty is that while the contrast between self and not-self is an invariable accompaniment of personality as known to us, it is not an essential quality of it. The contrast is characteristic of human personality but not of the Divine. But if the being of God is a positive activity, this activity has meaning only when it is opposed or limited by conditions which are not created by itself. Whether or not the contrast of self and not-self is essential to personality, human or divine, life of a personal being is not possible except in relation to an environment. If God has no environment on which He acts, He cannot be personal. If God is personal, He cannot be the Absolute which has nothing which is not included in it in every possible sense of the word.

God can only be a creative personality acting on an environment, which, though dependent on God, is not God. Though the acting of God is not forced on Him from without, still it is limited by the activities of human individuals. The personality of God is possible only with reference to a world with its imperfections and capacity for progress. In other words, the being of a personal God is dependent on the existence of a created order. God depends on creation even as creation depends on God. In the sphere of thought, being and non-being are opposites. The being of which we have experience is not absolute being. Whatever falls short in any degree of absolute reality has in it an admixture of non-being. In the world of experience, we have a conflict between being and non-being. In and through their mutual hostility, the world exists. If there were no non-being, there would be no being. Each presupposes the other. The two are not related to each other as the carpenter to the wood or as the potter to the clay.

The world exists in and through an act of self-assertion. The self which asserts itself and which says "I am" is the divine self. Over against this self, this will to be, is the infinitude of non-being, the passive resistance which has to be met and overcome. The spirit of God moves over the waters, the formless matter, the totality of possible existence.[1] Vital impetus and raw matter are, for Bergson, the complementary aspects of creation. We cannot eliminate the dualism between subject and object, between God and the given in the process of the universe.

At the beginning, God is merely the knower with ideas and plans, which are realised at the end when the world becomes the express image of God. The difference between the beginning and the end is analogous to the difference between the "I" and the "me." The "me" become an adequate representation of the "I" at the end. All things move towards the creator. When the creator and the created coincide, God lapses into the Absolute. Being in a sense which both attracts and eludes our thought is the ideal goal of becoming. In attaining this goal, becoming fulfils its destiny and ceases to be.

[1] Cp. Gahanam gambhīram . . . apraketam salilam. *R̥g. Veda*, x. 129.

Creation marks the beginning of this world with time, though not in time. The Newtonian conception of time as a prior framework within which events happen, which is said to flow on at an even pace without cessation and without end, is now given up. Time has no existence apart from events. It is a conceptual construction from the experience of successive events. The universe though unbounded is said to be finite. It has a beginning and an end. If we give up this view we will be committed to the belief in the eternity of this world. A dualism of God and the world where one of them will have a precarious, illusory existence will result. The ideal of the world is not an ever elusive perfectibility, working ineffectively above the world of the actual but what is most real and decisively operative in it and will one undated day be achieved.

Evolution and history belong to the world and are real and not mere appearances or illusions. God is not absolutely timeless, though He is not in time in the sense that His whole being is subject to succession and change. Though God does not consist of a succession of states, succession is real for Him. The future has meaning for God who executes designs in the sphere of the created order. In a sense God Himself is subject to change. There is a stage in which He attempts to realise an ideal and another in which the ideal is realised. The contrast between the ideal aimed at and the actual is real for God.

Again, what appears in subhuman forms as tendency or striving becomes in man conscious will which is guided by the idea of value. Men are active agents, not passive participants in the return of all things to God. They can work with God or turn away from Him. The religious soul who has direct contact with the Divine in an experience where the distance between the subject and the object, the lover and the beloved is overcome identifies itself with the Divine will and participates in the creative work of God. When once the possibility of working out an evolutionary manifestation of values is accepted, God becomes the agent of creation achieving power, light and love through the overcoming of inertia, darkness and death. The self-existent Absolute becomes for this world with its resistance of finite things to the unity of the whole, God, compassionate, consenting, helpful, the soul of truth in all things and the saviour of mankind. He redeems the corrupt and reconciles the hostile, evolves rhythm out of chaos. God's work does not cease until He has fashioned immortal substance out of evanescent nothingness.

The Absolute transcends not merely its finite but also its infinite expressions taken singly or in a finite number. In its range of expression or degree of expressiveness, the Absolute transcends all finite limits. The question of immanence and transcendence does not arise with reference to the Absolute. For immanence implies the existence of an Other in which the Absolute is immanent. But the Absolute represents the totality of being and there is nothing other than it. The Absolute is in this world in the sense that the world is only an actualisation of one possibility of the Absolute and yet there is much in the Absolute beyond this possibility which is in process of realisation.

God is the Absolute with reference to this possibility of which He is the source and creator. Yet at any moment God transcends the cosmic process with its whole contents of space and time. He transcends the order of nature and history until His being is fully manifested. When that moment arises, the word becomes flesh, the whole world is saved and the historical process terminates. Until then, God is partly in *potentia*, partly in act. This view is not pantheistic for the cosmic process is not a complete manifestation of the Absolute.

So far as the Absolute is concerned, the creation of the world makes no difference to it. It cannot add anything to or take away anything from the Absolute. All the sources of its being are found within itself. The world of change does not disturb the perfection of the Absolute. "Though suns and universes would cease to be, Every existence would exist in thee" (Emily Brontë). We cannot say that the world follows from the nature of the Absolute even as the conclusion of the syllogism follows from the premises, as Spinoza would have us believe. The Absolute is the ground of the world only in the sense that a possibility of the Absolute is the logical prius of the world. The world would not be but for this possibility in the Absolute.

As to why this possibility arose and not any other, we have to answer that it is an expression of the freedom of the Absolute. It is not even necessary for the Absolute to express any of its possibilities. If this possibility is expressed, it is a free act of the Absolute. Hindu writers are inclined to look upon the act of creation more as the work of an artist than that of an artisan. It is *līlā* or free play. The world is the work of an artist whose works are worlds. His fertility is endless. Saṁkara says that the world originates from the supreme without effort (*aprayatnenaiva*), on the analogy of sport (*līlānyāyena*), like human breath (*puruṣāniḥśvāsavat*).[1]

VI. CONCLUSION

True religion is born of spirit, not of flesh and blood, not of codes and customs, not of races and nations. The life of spirit consists precisely in being free from these things and in penetrating into true being. Systems of theology and codes of conduct are elaborated for the sake of the large numbers who have no first-hand experience of religion and so require to be directed in the way of religion. So long as there are men who have not reached the spiritual level in which there is immediate contact with the divine reality and are therefore dependent on the experience of others, there is justification for authoritative religion.

Dogmas and codes are not an absolute embodiment of religious truth. They express particular stages in man's spiritual development. What is revealed is distorted and assimilated according to the make-up and spiritual development of the persons receiving them. The intuitive seer understands the variety of theological doctrines and codes. They are but attempts to express the inexpressible, to translate into human words the music of the divine. In the face of the ineffable glory, nothing avails save the renunciation of the artist and the austerity of silence. The creed we adopt, the label we bear is largely accidental. We stay

[1] Saṁkara on *Brahma Sūtra*, i. 1. 3.

in the fold in which we are born simply because we are more at home in it than in any other. The dogmas and rites employed by religion for its expression and diffusion are only means for bringing about that elevation of the soul which can dispense with them all. To bestow a sacred character on racial traditions is to give a false turn to the life of spirit. To submit the infinite spirit to finite forms leads eventually to the enslavement of spirit.

Intellectualism admits the possibility of attaining a perfect system of divine knowledge. It refuses to see the super-being of God and denies the mystery of religion. It confuses the reflection of God in the mind of man with divine nature itself. It gives to the outward forms of the historical process an absolute justification. Intellectual religion pledges us to rigid definitions and obsolete dogmas. It encourages a hardness of belief almost mathematical in its rigidity. It does not believe in any half-tones between white and black, any fine shades between truth and falsehood. In its anxiety to bend all individual wills to the purpose of the group and establish social cohesion, it enforces rites and obligations peculiar to the group and ignores the claims of humanity. It declares that what it affirms is the truth, the whole truth and nothing but the truth. Different systems of theology acquire a sacred significance which is absolute and unchangeable and this leads to a quenching of the spirit.

The spirit in us is life and it resists death in all its forms, blind instinct, unthinking custom, dull obedience, intellectual inertia and spiritual dryness. A man's religion must be his own and not simply accepted on trust or imposed by authority. While trust and authority may put him on the way, it is his own independent search that will take him to the goal.

Religion is a manner of life dependent on the discipline of one's being, body and mind. It is to make oneself of a certain quality, to fashion one's being to a certain temper to reshape the stubborn world, to so change one's life as to enter the vital movement of the universe. Creative power of the spirit has not yet been seen in its widest scope. It has not yet achieved its full stature. Civilisation is in its infancy, and religion yet in the making. Human progress is to be defined as the process by which society is transformed increasingly in a spiritual way. The world is unfinished and it is the task of religion to go forward with the task of refining it.

On this view, religion is not quiescent but combative, exposing the hostility and hollowness of the irreligious principle. It means a profound dissatisfaction with the existing state of humanity and an active preparation for a new life, whether it be the kingdom of heaven on earth or beyond. Religion is an eternal revolutionary because no order of life can ever satisfy it. It demands the most radical transformation of man and society. It will not be content until a new social order with basic economic justice, racial brotherhood and equality, free intellectual and spiritual co-operation and true friendship among the nations is established. So long as man has to earn his bread by the sweat of his brow, he will spend his energies in the pursuit of food, but if society is organised with courage and vision so as to secure for all its members food, clothing and shelter, the individuals will be freed for the pursuit of the higher things of the mind and spirit. If a radical change in what may be called the mechanics of living is brought about, the art of living will receive a fresh impetus and the destiny of humanity will be achieved.

It is not enough to change outward forms and institutions. We must transform the feelings and passions of men. We require not a revolution in opinion but a revolution in behaviour. False intellectualism has led us to prefer in artistic life the supremacy of form to content; in politics, organisation to liberty; in morals, authority to personal experience; and in religion, orthodox systems to spiritual life. A discipline of our whole being including the emotions which are the springs of action is essential for restoring to the world the inspiration which it has lost.

PRINCIPAL PUBLICATIONS

The Reign of Religion in Contemporary Philosophy. Macmillan & Co.
Indian Philosophy, 2 vols. Second Edition. George Allen & Unwin.
The Hindu View of Life. Third Impression. George Allen & Unwin.
An Idealist View of Life. Second Edition. George Allen & Unwin.
East and West in Religion. George Allen & Unwin.
Kalki, or the Future of Civilisation. Second Edition. Kegan Paul.
The Religion We Need. Benn.
The Heart of Hindusthan. Third Edition. Natesan & Co. (Madras).

THE EVOLUTION OF MY OWN THOUGHT

by R. D. RANADE, M.A.

Born July 3, 1886; Professor of Philosophy, University of
Allahabad

THE EVOLUTION OF MY OWN
THOUGHT

I. INTRODUCTORY

WE cannot prize too highly the endeavours which Professors Muirhead and Radhakrishnan have been making to give Indian Philosophy its proper place in the World's Thought by arranging for a volume dedicated to Contemporary Indian Philosophy in the Series in which have already appeared the volumes on British and American thought. India glories in her philosophic past, but on account of her new relationship with Western Philosophy and Western Science, she has to incorporate many new ideas into her old scheme in order to make it workable in the modern world. Various methods have been hitherto followed by the writers in the Series above referred to; some have had a perfected system of their own, which they only summarise in their essays; others cull out a chapter from their general contribution to thought; others give mainly biographical details with an interspersing of reflection. Not having published hitherto any completed system of my own, I am obliged to seek another method. In the small contributions that I have hitherto made to Indian and European Philosophy, I have followed the method of construction through critical exposition, and even though a perfected system of my own has not been in print, I thought it might not be irrelevant to take certain portions from my writings in order to show what line a completely systematised philosophy would take for me. This method may not exclude altogether some little biographical detail, in order that it may give to my philosophic thought a certain background on which might be seen the rough outlines of the picture I wish to draw.

As I have been looking at the evolution of my own thought from my early years, I cannot but wonder how the pendulum has swung exactly to the other extreme. I definitely remember the day, when, as an Undergraduate, in the year 1905, who had as yet hardly passed his teens, I was inducing my nephew not to offer Philosophy as one of his optional subjects at the B.A. I was myself going to offer Mathematics, and why any Science which was not as precise as Mathematics was entitled to any serious study was to me beyond comprehension. On a deeper consideration, however, of the reasons which might have led me to take such a hostile attitude towards Philosophy, I have now found that this dislike of Philosophy was not due to the subject itself, but to the books which were prescribed in the University in those days, as well as to the method of teaching of the subject adopted in my college. The only books which students were asked to study in the Bombay University in those days were Mill's *Lògic*, Aristotle's *Nicomachean Ethics*, Wallace's *Kant*, and Martineau's *Types of Ethical Theory*, and this was to me no very tempting intellectual fare. Nor had the teacher, who had been teaching the subject for about thirty years, any relieving feature in his method of exposition which could attract and inspire a young ambitious student. Dislike for the books and for the method of teaching, therefore, it seems, was transferred, in modern psychological terminology, to the subject itself, and the result was that if small things could be compared to great, I hated Philosophy, as Saul did Jesus before the enlightenment came.

II. AN EARLY SPIRITUAL MONADISM

Unconsciously, however, the impulse of Philosophy was strong within me, and even though I took my B.A. in Mathematics, even while I was a Fellow at the Deccan College, Poona, and when, as yet, I had made no systematic study of Philosophy at all, and had not even heard that Leibniz was the founder of Monadism, while I was once observing a cricket match for about six hours on the college grounds, the thought came to me powerfully that the whole Universe might be regarded as full of Spirit; and as soon as I went to my room I began to put down on paper the thoughts which had struck me in that great day-reverie. It was inevitable for me, however, to start with a Pluralistic conception of Spiritual Reality, because that was

the conception which was likely to give satisfaction to the enquir-
ing mind in its earlier stages; and the result was my unconscious
philosophising in a monadistic-spiritualistic vein. I take the
liberty of quoting the following excerpt from one of my earliest
writings on "The Centre of the Universe" (1908), because it
gives in an autobiographical manner the starting-point from
which my thought was to proceed in succeeding years. It will
be evident to any scrutinising reader that I was at that time
under the spiritual influence of Carlyle, and was philosophising
after the manner of Teufelsdroeck:

"Our Professor was generally supposed to be an eccentric man.
Careless in his dress, unmindful of the manners which the fashion of
his time imposed on him, indifferent to his equals, and heedless of
those who posed as his superiors, he nevertheless manifested his
precious soul to those fortunate few who, after a long apprentice-
ship, had come to win his confidence. To those who judged him from
what he seemed to be, he appeared more or less a lunatic; and they
were encouraged in this belief by the doctrine of our Professor that
'all Greatness is Lunacy.' Our Professor steadily maintained that
all great men must be lunatics, and that it was these lunatics who
were the salt of the earth. Our Professor was thus known by the
humorous title of the 'Apostle of Lunacy.'

"The present writer was one of the fortunate few who had won
his confidence, though it must be admitted that he only brought up
the rear among them. Long would he listen, and with ever-increasing
interest, to what his master would impart to him. He has seen him
pouring out his soul in those fits of fantasy when, like a lunatic, he
seemed to be 'of imagination all compact.' His lectures were never
given regularly; for regularity was not a word to be found in his
dictionary. If he was regular in anything, it was only in his irregu-
larity. 'Why bind ourselves by the fetters of Time and Space,' he
used to exclaim, 'let us succumb to their power if they at all force
us, but what is the use of courting voluntary imprisonment?' Rolling
in a fine frenzy, the eye of our Professor glanced from Heaven to
Earth, from Earth to Heaven. In the searchlight of his criticism, not
the smallest or the darkest cranny of the Universe remained
unilluminated.

"The present writer has been fortunate enough to hear him on
several topics, and his great wish has been that what was in his
thought should not die out. He must make apology to his master
for having published his thoughts against his will; for it must be

remembered that the Professor, following the bent of his eccentricity, is very averse to having his thoughts published. If, in doing so, the present writer has disobeyed the Professor, it is only because the consideration of the spread of Truth has weighed with him more than that of disobedience. And it is in the animation of this thought that he strings in the following pages his master's reflections on the Centre of the Universe.

"One day while he was in a pensive mood, with his mind focussed on a transcendental thought, I happened to sit at his feet, expecting every moment that his long and deep meditation might bring forth something worth hearing, when he suddenly began to think aloud in the following strain: 'The Centre of the Universe! Will not a discussion of this Centre lead to important truths? Is not the Centre of anything supposed to have peculiar properties? And are not people tempted to find out the Centre of anything, even when there is none? The fact is that people want to find unity in diversity, and order in chaos. Are they not hopelessly tempted by their "idol" of regularity? As in geometry, they know that a circle has got a centre, as in geography they assume that there is a centre of the Earth, as in astronomy they look upon the Sun as the centre of the planetary system, so do they try to find the Centre of the Universe. As in the former cases, they give the centre a definite position in space, even so do they consider that the Centre of the *Universe* is restricted by space. And herein they are mistaken. The Centre of the Universe is either Nowhere or Everywhere.'

"You will now ask me what is my own philosophy of the Centre of the Universe. The old Archimedes said that if he could get a fulcrum for the Earth, he could lift its whole weight with the least effort. I say, in a similar style, that if we can come to know the Centre of the Universe, we shall have solved the Problem of Problems! The questions that can be asked about this centre are the 'where' and the 'what'; and the 'where' determines the 'what.' *Where* is the Centre of the Universe?

"I summarily answer Everywhere. Man is but a speck when compared to the Earth, the Earth is but a speck when compared to the Solar system, and the Solar system vanishes before the Universe! How ridiculous would it then be to suppose that the centre of this infinite Universe is restricted to any place! Men had rather die with shame than entertain such a foolish idea! Where then is the centre of the Universe? Everywhere! Every particle of this infinite universe is its centre! Every particle of water, every particle of wind, every particle of matter is its centre, or, we had better say, hides its centre. The centre is rather *in* the particles than the particles themselves! The particles may perish, but the centre does not! It is indestructible, imperishable;

without end, and without beginning! Weapons cannot pierce it, fire cannot burn it! In Geometry, they speak of the centre of a circle as the *one* single point from which the distances to the circumference are all *equal*. And is this not true of the centre of the Universe, namely, its Presiding Element, that it is only *one*, and equally near to all? Again, they endow the centre of the Earth with the power of attracting everything on its surface—with the power of Gravitation. How far, then, would this be true of the centre of the *Universe*! How powerful would the Gravitation of *this* centre be! Conception fails to make an estimate of the Force with which all creation gravitates towards the Presiding Element! The Presiding Element is Everywhere! The Universe is but an Infinite Circle, with its Centre Everywhere, and Circumference Nowhere! "

This excerpt will suffice to show how I was already full of a spiritual idea even though I did not know how to philosophise about it. The early hatred of Philosophy had now given place to a new search, and I was thus brought to think that I must study my own Indian Philosophy, especially as I had been taking an acute interest in the Sanskrit language, and was full of respect for one of its greatest philosophers—Śaṁkarāchārya. I also feel myself bound to mention at this place that when I happened to pay a visit to Benares from Poona in October 1908, I had been to see the remnant of the Mutt of Śaṁkarāchārya at Benares, when on a cool evening I happened to hear the devotional songs of Śaṁkarāchārya recited in the Mutt, which made me pause and think how a so-called Advaita Philosopher could at the same time make room for devotional songs in his philosophical teaching. That to me was a crux, which impelled me to study Indian Philosophy all the more. Just at this time I suffered a physical breakdown in my health which took some time to disappear, during which my mind turned definitely spirit-ward. As a consequence, the problem became all the more insistent for me how to justify spiritual experience in terms of philosophic thought. I definitely recollect that after that date I began a serious study of European Philosophy, with the intent of finding in Eastern and Western philosophic thought a justification for the spiritual life.

K*

III. BRADLEY AND ŚAṀKARA; WARD AND RĀMĀNUJA; MCTAGGART
AND SĀMKHYA

One of the first things I noticed in the course of a few years
of my study was that in Philosophic thought the East was East,
and the West was West. This was not a thing which I supposed
was desirable. The problem of philosophy to me was one and
identical all the world over, and there was no distinction of
country or race in the world of thought. I felt it, therefore,
necessary to say that Indians should not remain content with
the study of Indian Thought, but should study European
Thought also; and that the Europeans should not remain content
with the study of their European Thought, but should study
Indian Thought as well. In fact, I advocated a definite correlative
study of Indian and European Philosophy. It was thus that
I wrote an article "On the Study of Indian and European Philosophy" in 1914, in which, among other things, I said:

"It is with the view of showing that Indian Philosophy is as rich
and varied as European Philosophy that we wish to enter here on a
brief correlation of different types of philosophy in India and
Europe. It is not until we have shown that Indian Philosophy has
such great similarities with European Philosophy that we can understand the importance of our own Philosophy: it is not until then
that we can understand the significance of Deussen's words 'Indians,
keep to your philosophy.' The correlation must necessarily be brief,
and in order that this brevity may be attained, we shall devote
more attention to the similarities than to the differences.

"To begin with, we might note the great resemblance between the
ancient metaphysical systems of India and the present metaphysical
systems of the West. The Absolutism of Bradley has numerous points
of contact with the Advaitism of Śaṁkarāchārya. Both suppose that
the Absolute is the only ultimate real. With both, God is different
from the Absolute. With both, God is unreal as compared to the
Absolute. Both consider that our souls, our bodies, the worldly
objects that we see, are ultimately appearances. And both hold
that Space and Time are only phenomenal, and are transcended in
the Absolute. Such a dictum involves that the Absolute be super-
moral, beyond good and bad. And we find that with Śaṁkara and
Bradley, the Absolute transcends moral relations. Moreover, with
regard to the content of the Absolute, both Śaṁkara and Bradley

hold that it is of the nature of intuitive experience. It is usual to speak of Śaṁkara's Absolute as being of the nature of the unconscious, but those who will think deeper will find that Śaṁkara's Absolute is Sat, Chit and Ānanda, that is Being, Thought and Bliss. Royce points out that though Bradley talks of a personal Absolute as being an intellectually dishonest conception, still Bradley's Absolute 'despite all Mr. Bradley's objections to the self, escapes from self-hood only by remaining to the end a self' (*The World and the Individual*, i, p. 552). And if this interpretation be correct, Śaṁkara's Absolute Consciousness, Bradley's Absolute Experience and Royce's Absolute Person differ, if at all, only in names. . . . Nor is Śaṁkara a determinist, as is ordinarily supposed. He does allow freedom to souls in the sense that they are free so far as they express the eternal purposes of the Absolute, and in this he is on a par with the other Idealists. The great difference between Royce and Śaṁkara is that while the former says that the soul comes into existence in time, Śaṁkara says that, seen from one point of view it is eternal, while seen from another and higher, it is merely an appearance as compared with the absoluteness of the Absolute, which is Bradley's position. This, as the reader will see, is not determinism in the ordinary sense. What we have tried to represent is that Śaṁkara's Philosophy may be best described as an Absolutism, or a Spiritual Monism, but not as a mechanistic, deterministic Pantheism.

"Other philosphers we must treat more briefly. Rāmānuja's system, which is a numerically pluralistic but a qualitatively monistic system, has its best parallel in the theism of Professor James Ward, and in Personal Idealism generally, represented by such writers as Rashdall. Rāmānuja's Absolute is God and the world, the world including souls. Such is also the Theism of James Ward (*The Realm of Ends*, p. 242), and of Protestant Christianity generally. William James has a clever remark in his *Pragmatism*, where he talks of the 'pantheism' of the Anglo-Hegelian school 'having influenced the more studious members of our protestant ministry, and having already blunted the edge of the traditional theism in protestantism at large' (*Pragmatism*, p. 17).

"Coming to other systems, we find a great resemblance between the plural souls of the Sāmkhya without a ruling God, and the 'system of selves or spirits, uncreated and eternal, forming together a unity but not a conscious unity' of the non-theistic Idealist, McTaggart. Both of these differ from the theistic monadism of Leibniz, who postulates a God, as pre-establishing the harmony between one monad and another, and between microcosm and macrocosm. And it is curious to find that while McTaggart's philosophy is non-theistic, Sāmkhya is also *nirīśvara* (God-less).

"There are many other correlations between Indian and European Philosophy, into which we do not here enter for want of space. Not only is metaphysical correlation possible, but also epistemological, logical and ethical. We can easily find parallels in European Philosophy for the nihilism of the Mādhyamikas, the subjectivism of the Yogāchāras, the Representationism of the Sautrāntikas, and the Presentationism of the Vaibhāshikas (Cowell and Gough: *Translation of Sarvadarśanasamgraha*, p. 15). The resemblances between the Aristotelian Logic and the Logic of Gautama are written in such 'text and capital letters that he who runs may read them.' The Hedonism of the Chārvākas may be paralleled by that of the Epicureans; the rigorism of the Bauddhas by that of the Stoics; and the threefold ethical ideal of the Bhagavad Gītā, namely, its activism, its ideal of duty, and its self-realisation by those of Eucken, Kant and Green respectively."

IV. RELATIVISM AND TRUTH

After these early essays the first definite period in my work on philosophic subjects was connected with Greek Philosophy. One of the great Greek Philosophers who was the first to catch my attention was Herakleitos. It was well known how he propounded the law of Relativism. He said there was no absolute distinction between night and day, between life and death, between good and bad. The sea, he said, was both purest and foulest water. It was purest for fish, but foulest for men, thus pointing to the conclusion that there was no absolute nature of sea-water. In my discussion of Herakleitos' philosophy (1916), however, I saw that there was a point at which my Relativism broke, namely, at God, a fact which was acknowledged by Herakleitos himself:

"If we ask Herakleitos whether his law of Relativism holds good in the case of God, he gives two different answers at two different places. Once he says that the law of Relativism holds good even about God: the First Principle, he says, is willing to be called Zeus, and unwilling to be called Zeus: λέγεσθαι οὐκ ἐθέλει καὶ ἐθέλει Ζηνὸς οὔνομα. But he says elsewhere that the law of Relativism stops at God, even though it holds good about men: to God, he says, all things are fair and good and just, but men hold some things unjust and some just: τῷ μὲν θεῷ καλὰ πάντα καὶ ἀγαθὰ καὶ δίκαια, ἄνθρωποι δὲ ἅ μὲν ἄδικα ὑπειλήφασιν, ἅ δὲ δίκαια. The conclusion at which Herakleitos arrives is that 'God is both day and night, war and peace, surfeit and hunger; but He takes various shapes, just as fire, when it is mingled with spices, is named according to the savour of each.' In short, says Herakleitos, every one gives Him the name he pleases: ὀνομάζεται καθ' ἡδονὴν ἑκάστου."

The upshot of such a doctrine is that Relativism has no application to Divine Life, while its proper sphere of application is only to the phenomenal and ephemeral sphere. In this, I heartily concurred with Herakleitos.

Protagoras failed to see this inapplicability of the law of Relativism to God. He applied it to the phenomenal and ephemeral sphere, and he supposed that Herakleitos' philosophy gave him sufficient justification for this. Aristotle, who saw this point cleverly, in his criticism of Protagoreanism first tried to take away the Herakleitean bottom from Protagorean relativism. It is well known how he tells us that the nemesis of the Herakleitean doctrine of flux was reached in the extreme doctrine of Cratylus, who did not think it right to say anything, but only moved his finger, and who rebuked his master for having said that it was impossible to step twice into the same river, for he thought that this could not be done even once, for, he said, "in the very process of your stepping into the river, the waters have run off" (*Metaphysica*, 1010. a. 10–15). Then again, Aristotle said, exactly like Kant, that it was only the permanent that could change, and that it was only from a pre-existing thing that change or motion could take place; and in addition that the process of change could not go on *ad infinitum*, and that therefore there is no meaning in the idea of incessant change: "If a thing is coming to be, there must be something *from* which it comes to be and something *by* which it is generated, and this process cannot be *ad infinitum*" (*Metaphysica*, 1010. a. 20–22). The last criticism that Aristotle passed on the Herakleitean doctrine of flux was that its author had unduly extended the sphere of application of the idea of change from his immediate surroundings to the whole universe. Granted that what immediately surrounds us is always in process of destruction and generation —this is, be it remembered, not even a fraction of the whole—

it would thus be juster to acquit this part of the world because
of the other part than to condemn the other because of this.
So that, says Aristotle, it is evident that there is something
whose nature is changeless, and if we were given the only
alternative between "rest" and "change" as predicates of the
Cosmos, we had rather decide for "rest" than for "change"
(*Metaphysica*, 1010. a. 28–36). Protagorean Relativism was
attacked by Aristotle also for other reasons than its Herakleitean
origin. Percipients, according to him, were not all on the same
level. The judgments of different people were not equally valid;
e.g. the judgment of the physician and the judgment of the
ignorant quack were not equally decisive in regard to a disease
(*Metaphysica*, 1010. b. 12–14). Finally, the most important
criticism that Aristotle passed upon Relativism was that it did
not take any account of "Differences of Value" and that it had
no adequate theory of "Truth." I heartily concurred with
Aristotle in his view of Absolute Truth, when he said that so
far from there being any question of Degrees of Truth and
Error, there were only Degrees of Error. Truth is one, absolute,
and immutable, and that is in God. To quote from my essay on
Aristotle's Critique of Protagoreanism (1916):

"The most important criticism, however, which Aristotle passes
on the relativistic sceptic is where he says that the sceptic does not
recognise differences of worth among things. If opposite courses
are equally welcome to our opponent, asks Aristotle, 'why does he
not walk early some morning into a well or over a precipice, if one
happens to be in his way? Why do we observe him guarding against
this, evidently not thinking that falling in is alike good and not
good? Evidently he judges one thing to be better and another worse.'
It is in this last remarkable sentence δῆλον ἄρα ὅτι τὸ μὲν βέλτιον
ὑπολαμβάνει τὸ δ' οὐ βέλτιον (*Metaphysica*, 1008. b. 18–19), that
Aristotle shows an insight that is wonderful. It is the argument
from differences of value among things which is the final answer
to the relativistic sceptic who would say that to be or not to be is
to him equally welcome. Aristotle does definitely say that there is
a more or less in the nature of things: τό γε μᾶλλον καὶ ἧττον
ἔνεστιν ἐν τῇ φύσει τῶν ὄντων (*Metaphysica*, 1008. b. 32–33). He
who thinks that two and two make five is, according to Aristotle,
less wrong than he who thinks that they make a thousand (*ibid.*,

1008. b. 34–35). The absolute truth in such a case is that two and two make four. The nearer a thing is to the norm, the less of an error it would be. Thus it follows that while there is an Absolute Truth, there are various degrees of error. It would be wrong according to Aristotle to say that there are degrees of Truth. In his very original theory of Truth, Aristotle would say that Truth is one, but error infinite. This would in fact be necessitated by the metaphysical consideration that while, according to him, all the sublunary things are capable of motion and so are emblems of infinite error, the First Mover is himself unmoved and so is the emblem of Absolute Truth."

V. IDENTITY OF THOUGHT AND BEING

In pursuing my studies on Greek Philosophers, I was once greatly astonished to see how Parmenides, the great Greek Ontological philosopher, and Śaṁkarāchārya, the great Indian Vedāntist, had made exactly similar attacks on the conception of the Idea or the Universal. The question, which both had raised, was—Is the Idea or the Universal fully immanent in the Particulars, or not? If it is fully immanent, it is distributed in so many Particulars. If it is partly present in the Particulars, then it is divisible. It is, therefore, either many or divisible, and hence is not entitled to the name of "Universal." This was the criticism which Parmenides and Śaṁkarāchārya alike passed on the conception of the Universal; and this led me on to the closer study of Parmenides himself. His identification of Thought and Being seemed to me to be quite analogous to the Indian identification of "Sat" and "Chit." Zeller and Burnet had interpreted Parmenides in a materialistic fashion, and I could not sympathise with their interpretation. I went, therefore, to study Parmenides from the Sources, and I found there was a fallacy lurking in the materialistic interpretation, which I criticised as follows in my Essay on *Aristotle's Criticism of the Eleatics* (1919):

"The merging together of substantival and adjectival existence has, for Parmenides, not merely a logical significance, but a metaphysical significance as well. As, from the logical point of view, Parmenides asserted the unity of subject and predicate, so, from the metaphysical point of view, he asserts the unity of thought and being. τὸ γὰρ αὐτὸ νοεῖν ἐστίν τε καὶ εἶναι, said Parmenides. This very thought he reiterates in his *Poem* once more when he asserts, ταὐτὸν δ' ἐστὶ νοεῖν τε καὶ οὕνεκέν ἐστι νόημα: 'thinking and that by reason of which thought exists are one and the same things' (Fairbanks, *First Philosophers of Greece*, p. 90, 1. 40, and p. 96, 1. 94). Plato and Aristotle understood these expressions quite correctly as implying an identification of the real and the rational. Some modern critics, however, have rejected this interpretation, and have found in Parmenides' philosophy a crass materialism. Burnet thinks it a mistake to call Parmenides the father of Idealism; on the contrary, he says that all materialism depends on his view of reality (*Early Greek Philosophy*, p. 208). He asserts that it would be a Platonic anachronism to regard Parmenides as having made a distinction between appearance and reality (*ibid.*, p. 209, n. 2). We find Zeller also crediting Parmenides with the idea of a mere globular form of ultimate being, 'a fixed and homogeneous mass, symmetrically extended from its centre on all sides' (1. 589). Zeller, however, admits a little further on that we would be justified in rejecting this description as metaphorical, only if we could otherwise find any indication that Parmenides conceived Being as incorporeal (*ibid.*).

"The fundamental mistake of Burnet and Zeller and other similar interpreters of Parmenides consists, in the present writer's opinion, in their fallacious identification of analogy with fact. Shutting their eyes deliberately to the general tenor of Parmenides' *Poem*, which is unmistakably ontological, these critics have pinned their hope on a single passage which is as follows:—αὐτὰρ ἐπεὶ πεῖρας πύματον, τετελεσμένον ἐστὶ πάντοθεν, εὐκύκλου σφαίρης ἐναλίγκιον ὄγκῳ μεσσόθεν ἰσοπαλὲς πάντῃ.

"Now anybody who will take the trouble of interpreting this passage will see immediately that Being is here 'compared' to a sphere, and not 'identified' with it. It must be remembered that Parmenides here uses the word ἐναλίγκιον which implies that he regards being as 'resembling' a sphere. It is gross injustice to the spirit of Parmenides to pin one's interpretation of him on a single passage without looking to the tenor of the whole, and then to distort it in such a way as to make him self-contradictory. Once the foundations of a materialistic interpretation are laid, Burnet has no difficulty in raising an equally materialistic edifice on it: the Being of Parmenides is 'a finite, a spherical, motionless, corporeal plenum' (*Early Greek Philosophy*, p. 208), and later he adds the word 'continuous' (*Thales to Plato*, p. 68). If Parmenides regarded Being as *finite* it was partly because he had not yet risen to the sublimer conception of Melissos who regarded Being as infinite, and partly because he was yet under the thraldom of the Pythagorean identification of finitude and goodness. As a matter of fact, all the epithets which Burnet interprets materialistically could also be interpreted in an idealistic sense. To crown all, the following excerpts from Parmenides' *Poem* should be eloquent enough to support our interpretation: 'Being is without beginning, and is indestructible. It is universal, existing alone, immovable, and without end. Nor was it, nor will it be, since it now is. . . . Powerful necessity holds it in confining bonds. . . . Therefore Divine Right does not permit Being to have any end. It is lacking in nothing; for if it lacked anything it would lack everything' (Parmenides' *Poem*, ii, 59–89)."

Other commentators on Parmenides were not affected by this materialistic jaundice. Adamson understood Parmenides to have at least risen to the conception of the Non-corporeal, if not to that of the In-corporeal, that is, mental or psychical existence. Gomperz interpreted Parmenides' philosophy in a Spinozistic fashion. The Material Being of Parmenides was incontestably a Spiritual Being as well: it was universal Matter and universal Spirit at once. This was at least not an unfair interpretation. A Spinozism is much more of an Ontologism than a crass Materialism could be. It is unfortunate that Burnet did not see that the identical meaning which he later found in the two questions "Is it, or is it not?", and "Can it be thought, or not?" (*Thales to Plato*, p. 67), laid the axe at the root of his early materialistic interpretation.

VI. THE STATIC PHILOSOPHY AND THE PHILOSOPHY OF THE INFINITESIMALS

Even though, therefore, Parmenides and his school carried my full sympathy, I could not explain how Zeno's plausible arguments could hold the field for so long a time, and no adequate answer be given to them. Zeno had proved by a sleight-of-hand that motion was inconceivable; but experience forbade such a false view of the universe. Equally false was the explanation of motion which Plato and Aristotle had themselves to offer as due to the initiation of the Soul: it was no less mythological

CONTEMPORARY INDIAN PHILOSOPHY

and crude. Plato and Aristotle had played out their cards; Zeno
had remained unbeaten; the problem was what trump-card
could modern Mathematics and Science show?

"The fact is that Zeno could not be finally answered until it comes
to be definitely realised that motion is a spatio-temporal relation.
It is neither a purely spatial, nor a purely temporal, function. It
consists of a correlation between places and times. As a modern
mathematician has cleverly put it, 'there is motion when different
times . . . are correlated with different places; there is rest when
different times . . . are correlated with the same place. . . . Motion
consists broadly in the correlation of different terms of t with different terms of s.'[1] In his arguments against motion Zeno with his
right hand shows the card s and then withdrawing his right hand,
with his left shows the card t; we must compel him to show the
cards simultaneously. All the Sophisms of Zeno against motion,
the flying arrow, the Achilles and the rest, depend upon a promiscuous
huddling up of s and t and the clever passing off of one for the other.
To put the whole thing mathematically, motion must be understood
as defined by the differential coefficient ds/dt; it is neither mere $\delta\sigma$
nor mere $\delta\tau$; it is a correlation of the two, different from either,
and qualitatively new. It is this fact which has been urged upon us
by the Neo-Herakleitean French philosopher, Monsieur Bergson.
Time and again in his books he has urged that movement is indivisible: 'Motionless in each point of its course, says Zeno, the arrow
is motionless during all the time that it is moving! Yes, if we suppose
that the arrow can never *be* in a point of its course. . . . To suppose
that the moving body *is* at a point of its course is to cut the course
in two by a snip of the scissors at this point, and to substitute two
trajectories for the single trajectory which we were first considering.
. . . The other three arguments all consist in supposing that what
is true of the line is true of the movement . . . which is regarded
as decomposable and recomposable at will' (Bergson, *Creative
Evolution*, pp. 325–8. Also *Time and Free-will*, p. 113, and *Matter
and Memory*, p. 250). It may be easily shown that Zeno's arguments
could be disposed of by giving to motion the things which are
motion's.

"We must not forget, however, to take account of certain Neo-
Zenoist tendencies of modern thought. As we have a rehabilitation
of Herakleitos in Bergson, so we have a rehabilitation of Zeno in
Mr. Bertrand Russell. He preaches a philosophy of what he is
pleased to call 'static change' (*Principles of Mathematics*, p. 350).

[1] Russell, *Principles of Mathematics*, p. 473.

With an eloquence which comes out of intense appreciation, he expatiates on the capriciousness of posthumous fame: 'One of the most notable victims of posterity's lack of judgment is the Eleatic Zeno. Having invented four arguments, all immeasurably subtle and profound, the grossness of subsequent philosophers pronounced him to be a mere ingenious juggler, and his arguments to be one and all sophisms. After two thousand years of continual refutation, these sophisms were reinstated, and made the foundation of a mathematical renaissance, by a German professor, who probably never dreamed of any connection between himself and Zeno. Weierstrass, by strictly banishing all infinitesimals, has at last shown that we live in an unchanging world, and that the arrow at every moment of its flight, is truly at rest' (*ibid.*, p. 347). At rest, indeed, and with a vengeance! For does not Mr. Russell say that all such conceptions as velocity, acceleration and force, which may to the slightest extent imply the existence of a changing, moving world, are mere fruitful fictions (*ibid.*, pp. 473, 482) of the scientific imagination? Is not Mr. Russell a fit associate of Weierstrass in banishing the conception of the infinitesimal, and in urging that there exist 'no infinitesimal differences at all'? For are not infinitesimals 'an attempt to extend to the *values* of a variable, the variability which belongs to it alone'? And finally, does not Mr. Russell justify the sophism that the flying arrow is always at rest, as being merely an illustration of a very widely applicable platitude that 'every possible value of a variable is constant'? (*ibid.*, p. 351). But the Nemesis of a static philosophy soon overtakes Mr. Russell. He bethinks himself that Zeno may probably have erred: he may have erred 'in inferring (if he did infer) that, because there is no change, therefore the world must be in the same state at one time as at another' (*ibid.*, p. 347). And, to crown all, he is in the end compelled to reject the Achilles argument (*ibid.*, p. 359) and favour the Tristram Shandy even though both are equally ridiculous, forgetting all the while that the rejection of the Achilles takes the bottom off the philosophy of rest!

"The fact is that the Infinitesimal Calculus cannot be so slightingly treated, as has been done by Weierstrass and Russell. The Infinitesimal Calculus has come to stay, and mathematicians can ill afford to despise its rules. If the notions of infinity and continuity are to any extent valid—and that they are valid must be recognised by every thinker—the Infinitesimal Calculus must hold its own in spite of the Casca-like thrusts of Herr Weiestrass. Well might we say to Mr. Russell '*Et tu, Brute?*' His attack on the Infinitesimals is the unkindest cut of all. The Infinitesimal Calculus supplies us with the only possible answer to Zeno's sophisms."

When we have once understood how Zeno's arguments can be disproved by the help of the Infinitesimal Calculus, we may know how Reality may no longer be regarded as a mere block universe, but that it may conceivably make room for motion and change.

VII. THE EPISTEMOLOGY OF SELF-CONSCIOUSNESS

After my studies in Greek Philosophy, I gave myself to a consideration of Indian thought. In one of the volumes hitherto published on the subject, *Constructive Survey of Upaniṣadic Philosophy* (1925), I discussed certain problems which might have a bearing on several subjects discussed in Contemporary Thought. One of the important questions which the Upaniṣads discuss is the epistemological significance of "Self-consciousness." The consideration which I gave to this question in *Upaniṣadic Philosophy* may be set down as follows:

"Epistemologically, we are told in various passages of the Upaniṣads, it would not be possible for us to know the Self in the technical meaning of the word 'knowledge.' Our readers might bring to mind the fact that Kant equally regarded Reality, as consisting of God and the Self, as technically unknowable. These were, he said, merely matters of faith. The Upaniṣadic answer is that it is true that God and the Self are unknowable, but they are not merely objects of faith, they are objects of mystical realisation. Then, again, the Upaniṣads do not regard the Self as unknowable in the agnostic sense of the word, for example, in the sense in which Spencer understands it. Rather, it is 'unknowable' from the standpoint of philosophic humility.

"(i) The Ātman, say the Upaniṣadic philosophers, is unknowable in his essential nature. 'That, from which our speech turns back along with mind, being unable to comprehend its fulness, is the ultimate reality,' says the Taittirīya Upaniṣad. 'Of that, to which the eye is unable to go, which neither speech nor mind is able to reach—what conception can we have, except that it is beyond all that is known, and beyond all that is unknown?' asks the Keno-paniṣad. The philosopher of that Upaniṣad says in an Augustinian mood that he who thinks he knows does not know, while he who thinks he does not know does really know. *Cognoscendo ignorari, et ignorando cognosci.* The Kaṭhopaniṣad in a similar vein says that 'the Self is not in the first instance open to the hearing of men, and that even having heard him, many are unable to know him. Wonderful is the man, if found, who is able to speak about him; wonderful, indeed, is he who is able to comprehend him in accordance with the instruction of a Teacher' (v, sec. 13a). We see in all these passages how the Ātman is to be regarded as unknowable in his essential nature.

"(ii) There is, however, another side to the subject of the unknowability of Ātman. The Ātman is unknowable, because he is the Eternal Subject who knows. How could the Eternal Knower, ask the Upaniṣads in various places, be an object of knowledge? 'The Ātman is the Great Being,' says the Śvetāśvatara Upaniṣad, 'who knows all that is knowable; who can know him, who himself knows?' In the Bṛihadāraṇyakopaniṣad in various passages, we are put in possession of the bold speculations of the philosopher Yājñavalkya. 'That by whom everything is known, how could he himself be known? It is impossible to know the knower.' 'It would not be possible for us to see the seer, to hear the hearer, to think the thinker, and to apprehend him by whom everything is apprehended.' 'He is the eternal seer without himself being seen; he is the eternal hearer without himself being heard; he is the only thinker without himself being thought; he is the only comprehender without anyone to comprehend him; beyond him there is no seer, beyond him there is no hearer, beyond him there is no thinker, beyond him there is no being who comprehends' (v, sec. 13b). We thus see that the question of the unknowability of Ātman has another aspect also, namely, that he is unknowable because he is the Eternal Subject of knowledge, and cannot be an object of knowledge to another beside him.

"(iii) But this raises another fundamental question. Granted that the Self is the eternal knower of objects, granted also there is no other knower of him, would it be possible for the knower to know himself? This very subtle question was asked of Yājñavalkya in another passage of the Bṛihadāraṇyakopaniṣad, and here again we see the brilliant light which the sage Yājñavalkya throws on the problem. It *is* possible, he says, for the knower to know himself. In fact, Self-knowledge or Self-consciousness is the ultimate category of existence. The Self can become an object of knowledge to himself. According to the philosophy of Yājñavalkya, nothing is possible if self-consciousness is not possible. Self-consciousness is the ultimate fact of experience. We see here how boldly Yājñavalkya regards both introspection and self-consciousness as the verities of experience. We also see the nudity of the doctrines of Kant and Comte when they try to deny the fact of introspection. Introspection is a psycho-

logical process corresponding to Self-consciousness as a metaphysical
reality. Self-consciousness is possible only through the process of
introspection. The Self is endowed with the supreme power of
dichotomising himself. The empirical conditions of knowledge are
inapplicable to the Self. The Self can divide himself into the knower
and the known. It is wonderful how Kant should have posited the
'I am I' as the supreme metaphysical category, which he called the
transcendental, original and synthetic unity of apperception, and
yet should have denied the reality of the corresponding psychological
process of introspection. The answer of Yājñavalkya is that Self-
consciousness is possible, and is not only possible, but alone real.
King Janaka asked Yājñavalkya what was the light of man?
Yājñavalkya first said that the light of man was the sun. It is on
account of the sun that man is able to sit and move about, to go
forth for work, and to return. 'When the sun has set, O Yājñavalkya,'
asked King Janaka, 'what is the light of man?' Yājñavalkya said
that then the moon was the light of man. For, having the moon
for light, man could sit, and move about, and do his work, and
return. 'When both the sun and the moon have set,' asked King
Janaka, 'what is the light of man?' 'Fire indeed,' said Yājñavalkya,
'is man's light. For having fire for his light, man can sit and move
about, do his work, and return.' 'When the sun has set, when the
moon has set, and when the fire is extinguished, what is the light
of man?' asked Janaka. 'Now, verily,' says Yājñavalkya, 'you are
pressing me to the deepest question. When the sun has set, when the
moon has set, and when the fire is extinguished, the Self alone is
his light' (v, sec. 13c). Yājñavalkya is here cleverly positing what
Aristotle called 'νόησις,' the act of pure self-contemplation in which
the Self is most mysteriously both the subject and the object of
νοήσεως, knowledge."

VIII. SELF-REALISATION: ITS ETHICAL AND MYSTICAL ASPECTS

Closely allied to the metaphysical problem of Self-consciousness,
we have the ethical and mystical sides of what may be called
Self-realisation. The question is not merely of the perfection of
the various faculties of man, but of the realisation of the Self
within. The Upaniṣadic seers understand that what is meant
by Self-realisation is the unfoldment and realisation of the Ātman
within us, instead of the insipid and soul-less realisation of the
various "faculties" of man, such as the intellectual, the emotional and the moral, in which sense Contemporary Moralists

understand it. Self-realisation, according to the Upaniṣads, is invariably connected with the enjoyment of bliss. This bliss cannot be measured in terms of pleasure and happiness. It is an experience of its own kind:

"Indeed, there cannot be any physical scale for the measurement of spiritual values. The bliss of Self-realisation is entirely of its own kind, absolutely *sui generis*. To cavil at the theory of Self-realisa-tion by saying that the Self 'is realised' already, and that therefore there is no necessity of 'realising' the Self seems to us to be merely a listless evasion of the true significance of Self-realisation. When Canon Rashdall says that the Self is realised already, he is speaking about a metaphysical fact. On the other hand, when it is said that the Self is to be realised, we are asked to take into account the whole ethical and mystical process by which the human being is gradually weaned from the allurements of the not-Self, and the Self to be realised in its native purity and grandeur. It is in the doctrine of Self-realisation that the ethical and mystical processes meet, a fact to which we shall have to allude presently. It need hardly be said that by Self-realisation, as the Upaniṣadic seers understand that expression, is meant the unfoldment and the visualisation of the Ātman within us, instead of the insipid and soul-less realisation of the various 'faculties' of man, namely, the intellectual, the emotional and the moral, in which sense Bradley and other European moralists have understood that expression. The Bṛihadāraṇyakopaniṣad tells us that the Ātman, who constitutes the Reality within us as without us, is and ought to be the highest object of our desire, higher than any phenomenal object of love, such as progeny, or wealth, or the like, because, the Upaniṣad tells us, the Ātman, being the very kernel of our existence, is nearmost to us. 'If a man may say there is another object of love dearer to him than the Ātman, and if another replies that if there be God overhead he shall destroy his object of love, verily it shall so happen as this man says. Hence it is that we ought to meditate on the Ātman as the only object of desire. For him who worships the Ātman in this way, nothing dear shall ever perish' (vi, sec. 12*a*).

"The ethical and mystical sides of Self-realisation are fused together nowhere better than in that celebrated passage from the Chāndogya Upaniṣad, where having started an enquiry as to what it is that induces a man to perform actions, and having answered that it is the consideration of happiness which impels him to do so— for, we are told, had he experienced unhappiness in his pursuit, he would not have taken any action at all—the author of the Chāndogya Upaniṣad comes to tell us that real happiness is the happiness which one enjoys in the vision of the Infinite, and that every other kind of happiness is only so-called, and of really no value whatsoever as contrasted with it. It thus comes about that, according to the author of that Upanishad, there are two radically different kinds of happiness, namely, what he calls the Great and the Small. Great happiness consists in seeing, hearing and meditating upon the Ātman. Little happiness consists in seeing, hearing, and meditating upon other things besides the Ātman. Great happiness is immortal; little happiness is perishable. If the question be asked, in what this Great happiness consists, the answer may be given, in Herakleitean fashion, that it consists in its own greatness and possibly not in its own greatness! People say that cows and horses, elephants and gold, servants and wives, lands and houses— these constitute greatness. No, says the author, these rest in something else, but the Infinite rests in itself. Great happiness is experienced when the Infinite is seen above and below, before and behind, to the right and to the left, and is regarded as identical with everything that exists; when the Being, that calls itself the 'I' within us, is realised above and below, before and behind, to the right and to the left, and is regarded as identical with everything that exists; when the Ātman is seen above and below, before and behind, to the right and to the left and is regarded as identical with everything that exists. He who thus realises the triune unity of the Infinite, the I and the Ātman, and experiences the truth of the Upaniṣadic dictum *So'ham Ātmā*, is alone entitled to enjoy the highest happiness. One who comes to see this, and think about this, and meditate on this, really attains Swarajya; he loves his Self, plays with his Self, enjoys the company of his Self and revels in his Self (vi, sec. 14). In this way, according to the Chāndogya Upaniṣad, the ethical *Sommum Bonum* consists in the mystical realisation of the triune unity as the goal of the aspirant's one-pointed endeavour."

IX. INTUITION, THE MYSTICAL FACULTY

The question may be raised as to whether there is any faculty in man by which this realisation of the Self is to be attained. Indian Seers have always said that there is such a faculty, and that it is the faculty of Intuition. It is not merely an artistic or poetical faculty. It is not the mere sense of life, as some modern philosophers have understood it. It is the faculty of Mystical realisation. It lies at the back of all the faculties in man which ordinary psychology recognises. Instead of contradicting Intelligence, Feeling or Will, it lies at the back of them all. I have discussed this question in my recently published work on *Indian Mysticism* (1932):

"Mysticism denotes that attitude of mind which involves a direct, immediate, first-hand, intuitive apprehension of God. When Mysticism is understood in this sense, there is no reason why it should be taken to signify any occult or mysterious phenomena as is occasionally done. It is an irony of fate that a word which deserves to signify the highest attitude of which man is capable, namely, a restful and loving contemplation of God, should be taken to signify things which are incomparably lower in the scale of being. Mysticism implies a silent enjoyment of God. It is in this sense that mystical experience has often been regarded as ineffable. It is not without reason that Plato, in his 7th Epistle, which is now regarded as his own genuine composition, says: 'There is no writing of mine on this subject, nor ever shall be. It is not capable of expression like other branches of study. . . . If I thought these things could be adequately written down and stated to the world, what finer occupation could I have had in life than to write what would be of great service to mankind' (341 *c–e*; *vide* Burnet, *Thales to Plato*, p. 221).

"The ineffable character of mystical experience is closely linked with its intuitional character. It has been very often supposed that for mystical experience no separate faculty like Intuition need be requisitioned, but that Intellect, Feeling and Will might suffice to enable us to have a full experience of God. Now it is a matter of common knowledge that even for heights to be reached in artistic, scientific or poetic activity, a certain amount of direct and immediate contact with Reality is required. Far more is this the case in the matter of mystical realisation. It is thus wonderful to see how people like Dean Inge contradict themselves when once they declare that 'the process of divine knowledge consists in calling into activity a faculty which all possess but few use, what we may call the seed of the Deiform nature in the human soul' (quoted by Selbie: *Psychology of Religion*, p. 257); and yet again that 'there is no special organ for the reception of Divine or spiritual Truth' (*Philosophy of Plotinus*, i. 5). People who would otherwise openly side with Intuition, yet declare that Intellect alone is sufficient for the reception of Divine knowledge; but their real heart-beat tells us that they believe that not mere Intellect is sufficient, but that a higher faculty is necessary. Intuition, so far from contradicting Intelligence, Feeling or Will, does penetrate and lie at the back of them all. Intuition would not deny to Mysticism a title to Philosophy if

Intellect requires it. As it connotes a determinative Effort towards the acquisition of Reality, it implies a definite, prolonged and continuous exercise of the Will. Mysticism, *pace* Dr. Inge, necessarily makes a place for Emotion in a truly mystical life. It is strange that Dean Inge should fight shy of emotions, and deny to them a place in mystical life, when he says that Mysticism consists only in 'seeing God face to face' (*Philosophy of Plotinus*, i. 3). We may venture to suggest to him that unless the emotions are purified, and are turned towards the service of God, no 'seeing of Him face to face,' of which he speaks so enthusiastically, is ever possible. Thus it seems that Intelligence, Will and Feeling are all necessary in the case of the Mystical endeavour: only Intuition must back them all. It is this combined character of mystical experience, namely, its ineffable and intuitive character, which has served to make all God-aspiring humanity a common and hidden Society, the laws of which are known to themselves if at all. We may even say that they are known only to God, and not even to them!"

X. THE MORAL CRITERION OF MYSTICAL EXPERIENCE

It has, however, been a debated question as to how far Mystical experience is linked with Morality. In my opinion the answer is absolutely definite (*Indian Mysticism*, Preface, pp. 27–9). There would be no mystical experience and no development in it, unless there is a corresponding heightening of the moral sense. To try to achieve Mystical experience without a corresponding development of Morality is to enact the drama of *Hamlet* without the Prince of Denmark:

"The chief criterion of the reality of mystical experience is its capacity for the definite moral development of the individual and the society. It has been urged by critics of Mysticism that it tends on the one hand to a life of amoralism, and on the other, to a life of passivism. Dean Inge has said that those schools of Philosophy which are most in sympathy with Mysticism have been, on the whole, ethically weak; and he instances as a case in point what he calls Oriental Pantheism—as if it stands in a category apart— which regards all things as equally divine, and obliterates the distinction between right and wrong (*Studies of English Mystics*, p. 31). It is to be remembered that he also points out that there are two dangers to which such a mysticism is liable—Antinomianism and Quietism. Antinomianism teaches that he who is led by the

spirit can do no wrong, and that the sins of the body cannot stain
the soul; while Quietism teaches a life of contentment with anything
whatsoever by sitting with folded arms (*ibid.*, pp. 30–1). Now
it is to be remembered that this criticism of Mysticism comes from
Dean Inge, who is more of a mystic than anything else; and a Mystic,
saying that Mysticism starves the moral sense, is only attempting
to throw stones at a glass-house in which he is himself living. On
the other hand, we find that a true life of Mysticism teaches a full-
fledged morality in the individual, and a life of absolute good to
the society. We can scarcely find in the world's ethical literature
anything that would come up to the very clever and accurate
analysis of the different virtues which Jñāneśvara makes in his
Jñāneśvarī (*M. M.*, pp. 71–107) in point of excellence of analysis,
boldness of imagination or accuracy of portrayal. A Mystic like
Jñāneśvara who insists on these virtues can scarcely be regarded
as teaching the 'effacement of all distinctions between right and
wrong.' If we go to Plotinus, we find the same perfection of moral
virtues in mystical life insisted on. 'The vision,' he tells us, 'is not
to be regarded as unfruitful. In this state the perfect soul begets
—like God himself—beautiful thoughts and beautiful virtues'
(*Enneads*, 6. 9. 9). St. Teresa also speaks of the peace, calm and
good fruits in the soul attained by contemplation on God, and
particularly of three graces: 'The first is a perception of the greatness of God, which becomes clearer to us as we witness more of it.
Secondly, we gain self-knowledge and humility as we see how
creatures so base as ourselves in comparison with the Creator of
such wonders, have dared to offend Him in the past, or venture to
gaze on Him now. The third grace is a contempt of all earthly
things unless they are consecrated to the service of so great a God'
(*The Interior Castle*, 6. 5. 12). St. John of the Cross teaches that 'in
a truly mystical life, a knowledge of God and His attributes overflows into the understanding from the contact with Him, and the
soul is admitted to a knowledge of the wisdom, graces, gifts and
powers of God, whereby it is made so beautiful and rich' (*Cant.*
14. 16. 24. 2). Rāmadāsa also tells us the same story when he speaks
of the moral results produced in a mystic by contemplation on
God (*M. M.*, pp. 394–5). Then, again, so far as the utility of the
mystic to Society is concerned, we may almost regard it as a truism
of Mysticism that a Mystic who is not of supreme service to Society
is not a Mystic at all. It is true that here again there are temperamental differences among mystics. One mystic may choose more or
less to be of a quietistic, and another more or less of an activistic
type. But the fact remains that in either case he is of supreme
value to mankind by calling their attention from moment to

moment to the vision and greatness of God. Thus Dean Inge's
denial of the title of a Mystic to Thomas à Kempis, because the
latter teaches Quietism, can hardly be justified. There have been
mystics who, like Aristotle's God, have moved the world by their
divine contemplation. They might be called, what a psychologist
calls them, men of a world-shaking type. St. Ignatius is a case in
point, and James speaks of him assuredly as 'one of the most
powerfully practical human engines that ever lived. Where, in
literature,' he asks, 'is there a more evidently veracious account,
than in St. Teresa, of the formation of a new centre of spiritual
energy?' (*Varieties of Religious Experience*, pp. 413, 414). Plotinus
also tells us that 'Those who are inspired, those who are possessed,
know this much, that within them they have something greater
than themselves, even if they do not know what. From what they
feel, from what they speak, they have some conception of that
which moves them as of something higher than themselves' (*Enneads*,
5. 3. 14). Rufus Jones narrates how mystics have their consciousness
invaded by the in-rush of a larger life: 'Sometimes they have seemed
to push a door into a larger range of being with vastly heightened
energy. Their experience has been always one of joy and rapture.
In fact, it is probably the highest joy a mortal ever feels. Energy
to live by actually does come to them from somewhere. The universe
backs the experience' (*Studies in Mystical Religion*, p. xxx)."

XI. CONCLUSION

One can see from what has been said hitherto what my opinions
are in regard to some of the main subjects which are on the
anvil of Contemporary Thought. It is clear that I have given
only a rough outline of my views through a critical exposition
of some of the problems attempted in Ancient and Modern
European and Indian thought, and that I have not stated them
deliberately, and on my own behalf. To have given a full account
of my opinions on various philosophical subjects within a short
compass would have been impossible; to have given only an
aspect of my thought would have been like doing injustice to
the whole. I hope, however, that my readers may forgive me
for this. One can see, nevertheless, how I was inclined from
early days to spiritual life; how I thought that a correlation
between Indian and European Philosophy was not only possible

but necessary in the interest of the development of Philosophy in general; how I sympathised with the doctrine that Relativism failed at God; how I regarded "Truth" to be One, and its existence to be only in God, while all other things were full of error; how the ontological strain of thought interested me; how I thought that a place must be made for motion and change even within a static philosophy; how Self-consciousness was not only possible, but alone real; how there were ethical and mystical sides to the problem of Self-realisation; how Intuition was the only faculty by which this Self-realisation could be attained; and how, finally, mystical experience had no meaning apart from moral development. These were the problems which affected my thought until I took up my position in the Allahabad University in 1928. I am much indebted to the opportunities which I have had at the Allahabad University to widen my philosophical horizon during the last few years of my stay there. These years have opened out a new intellectual vista before me, enabling me to define more accurately to myself my own position in philosophy from the side of contemporary developments in Metaphysics, Ethics, Psychology and Religion. I only hope it may please Providence to enable me to place my views on these matters before the philosophical world in course of time. Spiritual life has been my aim from the beginning of my philosophic career; let me hope that it would be its culmination also.

MAN'S INTEREST IN PHILOSOPHY
AN INDIAN VIEW

by V. SUBRAHMANYA IYER

Born 1869; President, Board of Sanskrit Studies
and Examinations, Mysore
and
Reader in Philosophy to His Highness
the Maharaja of Mysore

BIOGRAPHICAL

EIGHT of my direct ancestors devoted their lives *entirely* to philosophy. While at the Madras Christian College, as a youth, I commenced my studies under Dr. Charles Cooper, Professor of Logic and Philosophy, who kindled in me a passionate love for metaphysics. Then, after a course in Physiology under Dr. J. R. Henderson, Professor of Biology, in the same college, I felt a deep interest in Thomas Huxley and Herbert Spencer, which made me turn to Physical Science and Mathematics, under Dr. John Cook, at the Bangalore Central College. I next privately pursued a course in Natural and Social Sciences. Subsequently I spent a number of years in learning *Vedānta* under the *late* Swāmi, the Jagadguru, of Sringeri, who was held in the highest esteem as a most learned and genuine philosopher. As Registrar of the University and as President of the Board of Sanskrit Studies and Examinations, in Mysore, I have had occasion to come into close contact with many distinguished Pandits and Professors of Eastern and Western thought, which was an education in itself. Among modern interpreters of Indian Philosophy or Life, no one can ignore the most outstanding figure of Sir S. Radhakrishnan, whose striking originality has often called up new vistas of thought in me. My knowledge has been considerably widened by my association with those who have studied and are still studying philosophy under my guidance, some of whom are among the leading members of the famous religio-philosophical body, the Sri Ramakrishna Order. Far greater is my indebtedness to an eminent royal personage, whose exceptional interest in philosophy reminds one of Marcus Aurelius. During the past fourteen years I have had the valuable privilege of being a Reader in Philosophy to His Highness Sri Krishnaraja Wodiyar Bahadur IV, Maharaja of Mysore, a ruler of remarkable metaphysical insight and attainments, who has been referred to, in contemporary literature, as a modern "example of Plato's conception of the Philosopher-King."

MAN'S INTEREST IN PHILOSOPHY
AN INDIAN VIEW

I. WHAT IS PHILOSOPHY?

As is well known in India and as was acknowledged by many a scholar and thinker of the West, one of India's distinguished philosophers of our own times was the late Sri Sacchidānanda Sivābhinava Narasimha Bhārati Swami of Sringeri, in Mysore. It was while sitting at his feet as a pupil that I learnt some of the most valuable lessons in this subject. One of them is that Philosophy is Knowledge that rises above creed and scripture, vision and ecstasy, art and science, its sole object being a complete realisation of all that life implies. He used to say: whoever has wants physical or mental, and fears present or prospective, is impelled to satisfy the former and overcome the latter. Various are the attempts made to attain these objects, and various are the degrees of success attending them, all of which are comprehended under one or more of the heads: religion, art, science and their numerous developments. The endeavours of most men cease when they are satisfied with whatever they achieve. But to some men, remedies incomplete or tentative, or applicable only to individuals and groups of men, or of an ascetic character, or lastly of the nature of promises to be fulfilled after death, fail to appeal sufficiently. They ask whether all wants (including the craving for knowledge), and all fears, wherever found, cannot be perfectly satisfied or eradicated, *in this life*. They evidently aspire to an absolute or universal and verifiable solution to their question. For this purpose they seek a knowledge of all that exists. Exceedingly unpractical or unattainable as the quest may appear, those who pursue it nevertheless are known in India as philosophical enquirers.

But before the solution is finally reached and tested in life, doubts arise as to whether the enquiries are proceeding on right lines. And the disappointments in them, which imply error or ignorance, further stimulate the urge to get at truth, which seems

L

to recede farther as men seek to approach it. The necessity, therefore, for a clear knowledge of it, is felt at every stage of the enquiries. So the Swami often said that the student of philosophy must first be able to distinguish between "*Tattvam*" and "*Matam*," i.e. between Philosophy on the one hand and Religion, Theology, Scholasticism, Mysticism, Art, Aesthetic experience and Science on the other, especially because the latter have often been mistaken for Philosophy. Philosophy is what seeks, as the *end* of all thinking, the truth that admits of no difference of views and of no doubts whatever. Or, as the Hindu thinker would put it, Philosophy seeks a complete eradication of ignorance, the cause of all error. And as two plus two are equal to four is true for all, so must the truth sought by Philosophy, as its aim implies, be universal and necessary. Contrariwise, in all matters of knowledge other than this, in so far as they are communicable, there always exists some actual or possible difference of view. Hence, the disagreeing views are known as *Matam* which is private or individual; whereas *Tattvam* is public or common.

Enquirers in general being eager to find satisfaction as quickly as possible, take satisfaction to be truth itself or the final test of truth. But experience shows that satisfaction often fails to reveal truth, which has therefore to be sought independently, though satisfaction invariably *follows* truth. For satisfaction is often found in error also. Hence its unreliability. Even the earliest Indian philosophers held that the highest satisfaction (*Anandam*) is but a cover (*Kosa*) that should be dropped before reaching *differenceless* truth. Those who seek truth by making satisfaction the test, like those who make satisfaction itself the ultimate goal, as do the mystics and others, belong to the world of *Matam*.

Philosophic enquiry naturally proceeds by steps which are by some termed "degrees" or "kinds" of truth, the goal—being denominated the "highest" or "ultimate" truth. Religions, revelations, ecstatic experiences, intuitions, visions, opinions, hypotheses are all not merely valuable, but indispensable, as steps. What characterises the steps are various degrees of difference of view, actual or possible, in respect of truth. Among them truths of science rank highest, science being the nearest gateway to philosophy. For science, to a greater degree than all others, aims at differencelessness in its conception of truth, though *not absolutely*, as does philosophy. Even in the past, they who tried to reach the heights of Philosophy, through religious paths, had subsequently to pass through the gates of *Scientific method*, though they did not call it "Science."

Progress in philosophy does not mean in India the attainment of new concepts of ultimate truth, but the starting, as knowledge advances, at higher levels and the finding of less difficult approaches, if possible, to the *same* peak of *Tattvam*.

Lastly, in India the philosopher seeks "That knowledge which, if attained, makes everything known." Philosophy is, therefore, not only the "Science of Sciences" and the "Art of Arts," but also, as the Indian philosopher holds, the "Truth of truth," the "End of all knowledge." But this end means also the fulfilment of the purpose of life; for, to him nothing remains unknown, and nothing remains unattained in life.

Philosophy in India, therefore, does not subscribe to Fichte's view that "The kind of philosophy that a man chooses depends upon the kind of man that he is." This idea of philosophy is *matam*; for it is *matam* that so varies, not *tattvam*.

A FUNDAMENTAL ISSUE

To some philosophy is only "speculation" and *Ultimate* truth a chimera. It is argued by many, that if the highest knowledge of philosophy cannot remove wants and fears, its pursuit could be no better than an exercise—or a diversion in solving a problem in chess or geometry. Some say that philosophy yields only conceptual knowledge, whereas religion and mysticism lead to actual felt *experience*, and that therefore they naturally appeal to the largest number. They even declare that "truth" value with which philosophy is concerned is not of so much consequence as other values. They start with the belief that whatever idea or object they are most attached to must be ultimate and point to the absolute reality. But the fact that others do differ or may differ is proof that such values cannot be *ultimate*. Europe has felt the need for taking a higher step towards what it calls a "Transvaluation of Values."

A most marked tendency among the great scientists and philosophers of our day, when they attempt to deal with ultimate facts, is to lose themselves in mysticism of some kind. That is due, as the Indian philosophers long ago observed, to a lack of the strength and courage needed to pursue truth to the end. To the Western speculative philosopher, his Eastern brother who avers the possibility of attaining ultimate truth and eradicating pain and want, is either a mystic, a religious fanatic, or a primitive, self-deluded being. But what constitutes philosophy, in India, is the *rational* knowledge, that directly results in the removal of wants and fears. It is *verified* only by appeal to life, *as a whole*. That knowledge and life are intimately connected is known to everyone. But what *complete* knowledge might reveal as regards their relation is not known to all. A fundamental issue, therefore, is whether knowledge is a means or an end or both in life. If knowledge be only a means to the attainment of some reality other than knowledge itself, is there any means of ascertaining whether knowledge reveals this reality *beyond all possibility of doubt* ?

This is somewhat akin to the question of the relation between what are known in the West as "Thought" knowledge and "Sense" knowledge.

KNOWLEDGE

To many knowledge seems to signify something different from what it means to the Indian philosopher. To the former it is what is "known" of the external or the internal world (matter and mind). To the latter, however, it implies something more, which can never be included in the "known." For the "known" cannot comprehend the knowing agent or factor, i.e. "awareness," which is something entirely different in character from everything known or knowable. Awareness is always the knower, which is distinguished from knowledge and the known. When we try to know or think of awareness, we only betake ourselves to a thought, which is only something known. We never get at awareness itself as the knower. Again, if there be more awarenesses than one, how is one to be distinguished from another? Nor is awareness known to have any limits like those of a body or an external object. Nothing can be outside of it. The West does not treat awareness as something distinct from the mental contents of which it is aware. Even the "I," the ego, the self[1] as generally understood, is only something thought of or "known." The latter changes, while the former perceives the change. It is therefore unique. The knower or awareness is not the same as the self, which is used in several senses.

Again, it is generally held that by knowledge is meant what is known or thought about in the waking state. The West, though it has specially studied dream and deep-sleep psychologically and physiologically, has not enquired into them metaphysically. Their reflections from the metaphysical standpoint are confined to the waking state alone. Whereas the Indian philosopher's metaphysics covers the whole field of the *three* states. The others consider all experiences, *assuming* the waking experience to be the standard of reality, the rest being treated as less than real. The fact, however, is that all the *three* states are on the *same* level, they being the known. And the objects of the waking state are as much ideal or real as those of the dream. The common distinction between what is internal (mental) or ideal[2] and what is external (material) or real, is of comparatively less philosophic consequence; for, "externality" and "internality" obtain with equal force in the mental world of dreams also. The argument that in the waking state others witness the same objects and contribute to our common knowledge has no special

---

[1] In Indian Philosophy "Self" means the *common* factor or feature of all individual cognisers. To avoid ambiguity the word "awareness" is used here. "Contentless consciousness" is used by some writers.

[2] "Ideal" or "mental" comprehends *all* that is *known* as existing in the mind: thoughts, feelings, volitions, visions or intuitions.

force, because this holds true of the experience in dreams also. As it is with objects, so it is with space in which they exist, or with time and cause by which they are bound. So long as the dream lasts, it is as real as the waking state. The distinction of real and ideal has value only so far as the waking state or, as it is called, the *practical* world, goes. But from the philosophical standpoint it is of less importance. When one starts with the assumption that the waking world is real, he is a realist. When one realises that the waking world is like the dream, an idea, he is an idealist. The idealist's view, or "mentalism" as some prefer to call it, is being reached by the modern scientific thinker also.

But the Indian philosopher does not stop with the dream. When he proceeds to a consideration of deep-sleep he finds that all objects, external (material) and internal (mental) of both dream and waking states, disappear then. They being all *ideas* are refunded into or are absorbed by the mind. Even the body and the "I" to which one is so strongly attached, being but ideas, cease to exist as such. The "I" is a something of which "awareness" becomes cognisant, and which, therefore, belongs to the world of the "Known" or object (mental). Next, it does not signify the same thing every time it presents itself to consciousness or awareness. The import of the notion "I" when one is doing business as a shopkeeper or a banker is not the same as he himself understands by it when he thinks himself a father or a brother. These different connotations change endlessly in life. The "I," therefore, instead of being a factor of the "greatest certainty," as some philosophers hold, is a most unreliable, nay an *unreal*, something.

This may appear ridiculous. For, it will be said that the universe does not consist of one man alone. Others see the material objects while one is asleep. But this is to forget that the entire universe is "idea." Unless one abjures one's love of truth and science, one cannot help recognising this fact. As for the "I" (personality or self) in particular, the phenomena of double and multiple personalities will bear out in the waking state itself what has been just said. All the states disappear into and reappear from that which in the waking state is called "mind," but which is really, by itself, indescribable. This is sometimes pointed to as the Fourth, inasmuch as it is that which is aware of the appearance and the disappearance of the other three states. *Here is no solipsism as will be evident from the sequel.*

At this stage the standpoint is neither that of the realist nor that of the idealist. The known is unreal or illusory. But though there is nothing of the known in deep-sleep, this does not imply absolute non-existence; for, non-existence is not known as such then. Here one must guard against the mistake of thinking that if this beautiful material world and the more beautiful world of thought or mind, which though called ideal or unreal, disappear every day in deep-sleep, one must be the greatest loser. But the truth is, *"Nothing is ever lost."* The appearance and the disappearance of the universe only proves that it is made of the same "stuff" or "essence" as that into which it disappears. As such essence, the entire universe is ever indestructible. If one chooses to call this essence of the all X or Y or reality, the all would be X or Y or real. But truly it is beyond the reach of word and thought.

The *rationale* of the three states is that in the world of the known, totality of data gives us the whole truth, part of the data gives only fractional truth. The waking or the dream state or even both lead only to fractional truth. The three states which yield fulness of data are what philosophy is concerned with. If to this totality of the known be added the factor of the knower or awareness, then this added totality, or what is more than totality, is what reason is concerned with. It may be noted that the term totality or whole implies parts which are found in the known only. What knowledge implies in addition, is awareness which has no parts.

That there is variety (many) in the waking state is universally admitted. But the West appears not to note that there is non-variety in deep-sleep.

REASON, INTELLECT AND INTUITION

Once again, it has to be pointed out that many in Europe and America seem to confine reason to a part of what is really such. It is confounded with intellect which is Reason *limited* to the experience of waking and dream states. Reason is the highest court of appeal in the world of thought. That intellect is Reason working in a limited sphere is evident from the fact that logic, the science of intellectual processes, invariably *assumes* universality and uniformity, which the mind derives only from Reason. Without this assumption, logical process can have little value. Further, Reason reveals the limitations and contradictions of not only intellectual processes but all knowledge based upon the fractional data of single or double states. And the intellect, whenever it rises to its original level as Reason, frankly admits its inherent defects; nay, even points to a something unknown, beyond itself.

Many a thinker when he becomes alive to this feature of the intellect, jumps to intuition which vainly seeks exemption from the criticism of intellect or Reason. Reason points out the vagaries and contradictions of intuition also. And knowledge based on it disappears like that based on intellect, in deep-sleep. Intuition being something "known," has validity only in the single state of either waking or dream. But those that know that "intellect" is only Reason cribbed or cabined, seek to free the intellect, instead of appealing to intuition. This freeing process is what is known in India as "purifying" the intellect, "sharpening" it, or making it "one-pointed." As this process brings the intellect nearer its original, Reason, it sees more of the ultimate truth, based on the oneness of life than either of the former. In India, therefore, philosophy is based finally upon *Reason*—not authority, tradition, revelation, intellect or intuition and the like, though all these with their data are needed for enabling one to rise from intellect or intuition to "Reason." The sole function of Reason is to detect and eliminate the cause of error whether of intellect or of intuition.

What is instinct at a lower level is intuition at a higher.

Intuition is the natural or raw knowledge yet untested by intellect as to its truth-value. Intellect tests it by comparing intuitive experience with the experiences of the waking and the dream states. Intuition implies a something known and therefore implies a *duality* which is the field of *intellectual* criticism. Whereas Reason, which comprehends deep-sleep also, rises above duality and compares intuition with deep-sleep experience as well. Reason declares intuition to belong to the sphere below the Ultimate Truth, i.e. to the world of *duality*. Reason negates all duality, in seeking the Ultimate Truth or Truth *beyond all doubt*.

OBJECTIONS TO THE DOCTRINE OF TOTALITY

1. The modern psychologist will tell us that it is only primitive, infantile or insane minds that mistake dream objects for the real ones of the waking state. But what the Indian philosopher does is to label both "dream" and "waking" objects alike. If the dream world be not real, the waking is not real either. If the latter be real, the former also would be the same. Or again, both could be called ideal. Some of the sanest minds of the world have felt the waking world to be no more than a dream. The Indian philosopher does not consider dream objects real and waking unreal.

2. Some critics think that idealism, when pressed too far, lands one in *solipsism* which, though not a logical fallacy, is opposed to all common sense. Indian philosophy fully recognises the weakness of solipsism, and does not find it in its view of idealism. It is only in half-baked idealism that solipsism is met with. Once again it has to be pointed out that by idealism the West seems to understand only a part of what it means. Idealism fully understood points to the "Ideal" character or unreality of the "*I*" (ego) on the assumed reality of which solipsism depends. Solipsism is a warning against halting half-way in idealism. The "three-states" comprehend evidently more than one, the waking. In the waking, we take full account of *all* the experiences and thoughts of other men. To this are added our experiences

L*

of dream and deep-sleep. Indian philosophy does not omit anything so as to be liable to the charge of solipsism, which has a meaning in waking experience only. For in it alone it is possible to think of others and of ignoring others' knowledge.

3. The critic may say that what proves the reality of external objects of the waking world is the irrepressible sense of reality. But the same sense is equally forcibly felt in dreams while they last. In fact, the dream while it lasts is felt to be waking. There also exists the sense of "givenness" on which the realist so firmly relies. When the two states are compared, "givenness" is found to be no distinguishing mark of the reality of external objects of the waking. Should it be argued that the "givenness" of the waking world does not depend upon the mind's own creative power, whereas that of the dream is so dependent, the reply is, first, that the "givenness" of external objects in dreams is also felt to be non-dependent. Next, the "given" of the waking as well as the dream disappears alike in deep-sleep. The sense of reality, untested by reason, is no criterion of reality.

4. If the standpoint of the "three-states" proves the futility of the feeling or sense of reality, what does this feeling or sense signify? This taking the unreal to be the real is perhaps the greatest problem of life. There are two stages in understanding it. First, we ask what this material universe is. And we learn that it is a mental construct (Idea or thought), like a dream, a conclusion confirmed by the latest scientific investigations also. Next we ask what an "idea" or "thought" is. And, as the Indian philosopher says, we learn that it is a non-entity inasmuch as it disappears or dissolves into the mind every moment, and beyond all doubt during deep sleep. Lastly, we find that both the material and the mental universes are in themselves non-entities, illusions, therefore unreal. How then are we to account for the feeling or sense of reality? Since all ideas or thoughts are of the same stuff as the mind essence, the only reality existing, they are, as such stuff, real, and that always. The unreal therefore *appears* as real. When the states are analysed it is seen that the entire factor, the "known," is unreal, which is no theory, but fact.

5. If in deep-sleep all the "known" should disappear, including

my own self, my own body and my intuitions of the highest realities, can there be any basis for ethical life? Is there any use in living? It has already been said that deep-sleep does not mean a blank (non-existence): it is that into which the universe, the *known*, is refunded. As the universe reappears, entity cannot come out of non-entity. So long as the existence of other men and beings is admitted, as it is, in the waking state, ethical life is indispensable and its value is fully recognised. Its significance will be further considered under Ethics.

6. If the entire universe (mental and material) be only ideas, and if they completely disappear in deep-sleep, what becomes of the eternal God and visions of Him, which are among men's dearest possessions? The ideas called God and Visions of Him are absorbed into that which is called "mind" in which no distinctions exist as in deep-sleep. If this is the truth and if even God Himself disappears, is truth higher than God? In answering, we have three alternatives before us: God is higher truth is higher, or both are on the same level or non-different. That God is higher than truth and that truth itself cannot reach God but can only point to Him, is the view of religion. And it logically relies upon faith. That truth is higher than God is held by many a thinker who makes the Absolute, the Unconditioned, the Unknowable or the Supreme Existence, the truth. But there are other philosophers who say that Ultimate Truth is itself God, the two being non-different. Now, if God be something "known" He does disappear in deep-sleep. If He be not "known," He must be the knower; or, He does not exist at all.

TRUTH

We have proceeded till now assuming that we know what is meant by truth. For truth as commonly understood is one's knowledge of some item of experience, internal or external. In respect of truth also, as in that of knowledge, many thinkers seem to confine it to a part of it. They ignore the knower as something different from the "I" or other contents of the mind. The whole mind including its contents, such as the "I" and its acts, is the "knower" for them. Owing to this defect, though truth is admitted to be knowledge, whether all knowledge is truth is still a controversial matter. Further, so far as the Western conception goes, whatever meaning be given to truth, "copy," "correspondence," "coexistence," "coherence," "harmony," "pragmatic import" or any other, in all cases two factors are implied. The two are not the knower (awareness) and the known, but mind (as a whole) and matter. And if matter (the object) be considered mental, both the factors are mental. Whatever the nature of the factors their relation is still a subject of doubt, to remove which the Indian philosopher proceeds to his "Truth of truth" which takes him to awareness itself. The relation between awareness and the known, i.e. mind and matter, is also one of non-difference in their essence; for as "ideas" both mind and matter disappear into the distinctionlessness of deep-sleep and then reappear.

According to an Indian analysis all knowledge is not truth. Knowledge may be true or erroneous. And there are two stages in the interpretation of truth: first, the ordinary (empirical) in which the knower and the known are un-analysed, and secondly, the critical, in which the two are fully enquired into. In both, truth is a bridge sought to be thrown across the two factors to bring them together: the closer they come the less is the room for doubt or error.

Truth, as has been already indicated, like two plus two are equal to four, admits of no difference of view. Man therefore at every stage of making sure that his knowledge is true seeks agreement either by quoting authorities, ancient and modern, or by repeating his observations, or, as in religious proselytisation, by compelling others to hold his own view, so that he may have the satisfaction derived from non-difference, which is the essential characteristic of truth. But as it is not possible to find out what all men—past, present and future—think of any item of experience, the first necessary condition to be fulfilled in this quest is that the item of experience, knowledge of which is sought, in itself excludes all possibility of difference. This condition can be fulfilled only in "Non-duality."

Next, ordinarily (in the waking state) we find two sources of doubt or error: (a) the knowing mind and (b) the object sought to be known. The knowing mind has various capacities at different times. And there are many minds. The matter to be known appears to present various aspects and that at different times. Each mind sees some one aspect at a time. Hence arise doubts. *To be free from all possibility of doubt,* one's mind should comprehend at a given moment all minds and all their capacities, and the matter to be known should likewise comprehend all its aspects of all times and should present them at once. The existence of two such factors, the one knowing the other absolutely, is impossible, unless they be non-different.

Again, even when there are only two minds, one cannot know the other truly (beyond all doubt), unless the two be non-different. Similarly, no one can say that one knows God (who is not a material being) truly, unless one be non-different from Him. Similar is the difficulty of comprehending totality, whether the knowing mind be included in the total or excluded from it. Non-difference is a necessity in attaining truth beyond doubt. Absolute non-difference in thought or knowledge is the same as non-duality in existence or being. It must be absolute, for there may be two entities, non-different in all respects, excepting in regard to their location in time and space.

It is sometimes said that if the ultimate truth be non-duality, what is there to prevent the knower from undergoing change and knowing it himself? But how can change have a meaning, unless distinguished from changelessness, and unless change be known to something unchanging? The impossible feat of conceiving an entity remaining unchanged and at the same time undergoing change is attempted by some. But the problem disappears on deeper enquiry, which leads one to the second stage in which the knower is unchanging awareness only. The final problem, therefore, is how can the unchanging and indivisible awareness know the changing as non-different, so that truth may be attained. The appeal is made to life. All changes disappear in deep-sleep which is non-duality. Change, therefore, is unreal, being an idea appearing and disappearing. Change appears with the waking and ceases with it. And what constitutes the essence of ideas is non-duality, which is beyond change and changelessness. In non-duality all distinctions of knowledge (thought) and existence (being) cease to exist. There is no proof that the *known*—which is idea—exists or can exist apart from awareness. It is needless to consider the unprovable hypothesis that a third unknown entity produces all ideas.

Some philosophers make no distinction between "Monism" and "Non-dualism," but say that "Unity" is what they also seek in philosophy. But Monism and Non-dualism are poles asunder. They do not see this because they ignore the uniqueness of the knower. When one is conscious of the idea (concept) of Unity, the knower is one and the *known* (concept) is another: there are two. Unity here really implies duality. Non-duality only means that what is beyond duality cannot be characterised either as "Unity" or as "Non-existence." For unity has no meaning unless distinguished from multiplicity; nor can non-existence have a meaning apart from the notion of existence. They refer, therefore, to the world of duality, where no term can have a meaning without reference to any other. The Ultimate Truth negates all duality. But truth is no truth unless verified.

VERIFICATION

Is non-duality a mere word or sound, like the "Barren woman's son," or a mere concept? No; it is actually realised in life. In deep-sleep there is no known, no second, no duality. Nor is it absolute non-existence. But this is only an instance of non-duality in *one* state, which is enough to prove its possibility in actual life. What philosophy seeks is the Non-duality in all the three states. Now, into the distinctionless non-duality of deep-sleep disappears the entire known (universe). Then nothing else is known to exist to which could be traced the origin of the universe of ideas—the known, of the waking and dream states, in which (states) the universe reappears. It may be likened to the *water* of the sea, which remains the same whether the sea be waveless or full of waves. The waves, when they arise, cannot be said to be different from water in their substance. Whatever that non-dual distinctionless entity of deep-sleep be, that is what constitutes the substance of the waking and the dream states. Again, the existence of the waking or the dream worlds is unthinkable unless distinguished from their non-existence, which is deep-sleep. Further, there is no memory either in deep-sleep; for memory implies something known, which is then absent. When, therefore, non-duality is said to be known, it only means that in it there is no distinction of knowing and being. There, *to know is to be.* When some men think that they grasp non-duality, they only form a concept, a sort of dummy, and delude themselves by mistaking the imaginary dummy for what they vainly attempt to grasp. Similarly, when others say that non-duality is something attained in mystic ecstasy or vision, they only think of it from the standpoint of *intellect*, not from that of "*Reason.*" For we have non-duality for instance in deep-sleep, which is common to all men and even to lower animals (and plants) which no one takes to be mystic realisation or intuition. For attaining the truth, i.e. the non-duality verified in the three states, which philosophy seeks, Reason is needed—not intellect. To one confined to intellect, Reason appears mystical.

Were Non-duality not the truth beyond doubt, philosophy would be, as it is to so many men, mere chaff, mere words. It is so to those who talk the grandest conceptual philosophy, living at the same time the most unethical lives. With the absolute non-difference reached in knowledge, perfection is reached in life. They are non-different. In philosophy Non-duality is not only the Ultimate truth but also the Ultimate reality.

CAUSALITY

The importance of this subject to the philosopher in India may be measured by the fact that there it is the knowledge of its meaning that marks the qualification needed for one to enter the gates of philosophy.

The notion of cause and effect is found associated with all

that is known, i.e. with the waking and dream states. Nothing
in the world of science, religion, and even art in some aspects,
has meaning apart from the idea of "cause." But as the entire
universe is only an idea or mental phenomenon, cause also is of
this nature. That stories of creation found in all the scriptures
are but fairy tales or myths meant for children, and have a
value only as such, was known thousands of years ago in India.
Even the modern scientific theory of evolution is no more than
a concept, useful for scientific or practical purposes. Nevertheless,
causal relation even in the waking state itself is an enigma.
Everyone knows that what at one stage is a seed, is a shoot
at another, and a plant or tree with fruits, flowers and foliage
at a third stage. But who knows how a seed transforms itself,
or other materials, into all these? What kind of continuity or
connection is there? Various explanations have been attempted
in the West. But in India three are offered to suit different
stages of thinkers. (1) The effect fully exists in the cause, though
it manifests itself as effect subsequently, both being in essence
the same. (2) The effect has new forms which did not exist
in the cause but which spring out of nothing. (3) The effect
is only an idea or concept superimposed on the cause, which
remains unaffected by the effect. All these fail to satisfy Reason
because of the contradictions in them and because the phenomena
of the world of "cause and effect" disappear in deep-sleep.
"Cause and effect" in the world of duality convey sense. But
to talk of them with reference to what is beyond duality is
meaningless. That God (the Absolute, Unmanifest, Unconditioned or Infinite) created, produced, manifested or in any
manner became the universe, is from the standpoint of truth
meaningless. From the waking standpoint, that is, of duality,
mind cannot but think in terms of cause and effect. The mind
when it posits a cause for this world, *imagines* it to be antecedent
to the world as effect. Causal relation is only characteristic of
the thinking process, which enables the mind to know the world
of experience. This is well known to Europe also. The urge to
seek a cause for the world is an urge to transcend the effect,
because the known universe is unreal, or as it is sometimes said,

"not self-subsistent." Considered from the standpoint of "substance," cause cannot be different from the effect, even in the waking state. But what appears significant now is that even modern science in its quantum theory is approaching the same truth. Seeing that all Ideas and concepts are wiped out in deep-sleep, they are, as such, unreal. This universe, when viewed as unassociated with the concept of causal relation, is neither produced nor destroyed.

Space and time which causality implies, share the same fate. Modern science has seen the old truth that the former two are inseparable. It will also see in the future that even "cause" is inseparable. It is not "space-time" but "space-time-cause" that really forms the fourth dimension of matter. Perhaps the meaning of cause will then be extended.

MEANING OF EXPLANATION

The greatest value of "causal relation" lies in the fact that it gives a meaning to the term "explanation." When an explanation of any fact is sought, it is the cause that is usually sought. But the need for the "cause" arises because the "effect" by itself is meaningless without its correlative. The two form a whole. In other words, it is the whole and its relation to the part, that "explains." The true explanation of life or existence, therefore, lies in the knowledge of the relation of awareness to the three states, that is the whole of life to each of them.

SCIENCE, RELIGION, ETHICS AND ART

There being no field of experience that science does not study or attempt to study, even Religion and Art cannot be beyond its reach. As already indicated, all these do, but only in certain degrees, contribute to the attainment of ultimate truth. They also satisfy wants and remove fears in a measure. In indicating their trend or outlook, nothing more than a bird's-eye view, and that from the standpoint of philosophy alone, is attempted under this head.

Science, as knowledge, is concerned with the known only, not the knower (simple awareness), which can never be an "object" and cannot, as such, be studied. Psychology, physical and natural science, social and sociological sciences, which deal with "objects," mental or material, are all of unquestionable value in the waking state. But philosophy deals with the totality of the data of the three states. What interests the philosopher ultimately is not so much the conclusions or the applications of science, as its method and outlook. The conclusions of the scientists of to-day may be scrapped to-morrow, but their method and outlook continue.

The features of science that philosophy values are:

First, science aims at generalisation, which is a measure of differencelessness. Next, science has the great virtue of not accepting anything as truth till that is verified as far as possible, though the test be confined to the waking state alone. It makes the meaning of the term "explanation" clearer. Turning next to its conclusions, physical and natural sciences have now reached the stage in which it is recognised that all phenomena of the material world or the mental world imply not merely change but also exchange. It is a truism to say that the constituents of one form of existence become in part, or in entirety, the constituents of another and vice versa. Loss in or of one is gain to another, elsewhere. There is no absolute destruction of anything. This is the meaning of what are known as growth, decay and death, or transformation and whatever constitutes life. The food I now eat formed part of something different from me, and has now, after my eating it, become my body. Even so, what I give up from my body forms part of the world outside. This goes on continuously. No line can be drawn between my body and the rest of the world so far as the constituents go. The lesson of philosophical significance learnt here is that ultimately non-difference characterises the highest truths of the sciences of the world of matter and energy. What the world considers the most wonderful achievements of practical scientists is based upon the transmutability of one kind of matter or energy into another, which in turn points to Non-duality.

The case is not different with the objects or contents of the mental world with which psychology deals. As already indicated, all the contents of the mind, namely thoughts, volitions, feelings, including visions, intuitions and ecstasies, are only transformations of the stuff (if the word may be used) of the mind. No line can be drawn between the stuff of the mind and the stuff of the volitions or feelings and other phenomena. So psychology also points in the same direction.

Thirdly, the latest science is the most emphatic on the inference that mind and matter are not two different entities in their stuff. The entire universe is resolvable into mind or a third common entity. Non-duality again meets us here.

Fourthly, science doubts the existence of causal relation as it does in its theory of indeterminacy and approaches philosophy in holding this relation to be a concept only.

Next, we turn to the science that answers the question: of what practical use is science to the growth of society or mankind as a whole? Men die, but man or society lives. What promotes its growth and life? This is what sociology is concerned with. The whole urge in the world of sociology is towards the gradual realisation of the *unity of interests, negating differences*, so that society may live. To take only a few instances. In politics, whatever the form of government, the struggle is to overcome the painful consequences of the failure to realise one's self as the *all*. . . . The elimination of difference so as to lead to unity in interests is the goal, but not merely the changing of forms such as monarchy into democracy and so forth. Any political organisation or institution can give satisfaction only to the extent to which this truth is recognised. Political disturbances arise when difference is accentuated in any form. They are least where the feeling of difference is least. It is even so with all other sociological concerns. Social progress and stability are promoted to the extent to which the negation of differences is achieved.

It is the same with forms of Religion, whose number is legion. It is ever multiplying, and developing differences and distinctions. But this urge to seek spiritual satisfaction does not cease till in the mystic the individual is merged in the Absolute or God. In the lower stages he seeks to approach God or realise God in his thoughts and acts. But merging into Him is the goal. Even then the urge might continue for knowing or realising the *whole* of God. All doubts can cease only when man identifies himself with God. Though the science of religion teaches that religion in general seeks an Ultimate Unity called God, yet this Unity cannot be reached except by negating differences. Man comes nearer God by eliminating differences and realising that both are of the same stuff called "spirit" whatever significance that term may have. But so long as something known as satisfaction, hitherto unattained, is sought and for this purpose one has to depend upon another, *absolute* non-difference cannot be said to be contemplated in religion or mysticism.

The conception of God as a perfectly good Being is contradicted by the presence of evil in the world created by Him. He is saved from this inconsistency by the Hindus with the help of their doctrine of *Karma*. Philosophy indicates that one's body and personality (self) are, like the universe, only ideas or creations of the mind. Man is, therefore, said to be the architect of his misfortunes also. And the continuity characterising that into which all ideas are refunded, gives to the Hindu the closely allied doctrine of *re-incarnation*. These two are of great value, not only in religion, but also in ethics. They serve to check the impulse towards hatred, the curse of life, which only means the accentuation of difference. And what is more valuable still, is that they are powerful stimulants in making men seek an ethical life, which grows in strength as differences disappear.

In ethics the first rule of right conduct starts from the urge in the mother to identify herself with her child in pain or pleasure and to seek common good. It proceeds in ever-widening circles of such identification, till it includes the whole of humanity. The various ethical ideals find their final explanation in the Hindu doctrine that another is non-different from one. The goal is to see one's self as all and all as one's self. The all here comprehends even animals and plants. Hindu ethics enjoins not only the seeking of the common good but also the scrupulous avoidance of injury to anyone because by inflicting injury one not only ignores non-difference but also perpetuates the error of the conception that one's self or ego is a reality and that separate from the self the injured. The ideal in ethical conduct is to realise not merely the "non-difference" of ego and non-ego, but the fact that the ego or the individual self, as "idea," is unreal. The more one represses the ego till it is effaced as a separate entity the greater the virtue. This is not done by suicide or chloroform. For, beginning with self-restraint, ethics leads one up to self-sacrifice in life, which means the dissolution of the ego in others or in the all. And this is the same as saying that the realisation of the all as the ego is the ideal or goal.

In Art and Aesthetics, which deal with the urge to derive pleasure from what is considered beautiful, two facts are noticeable. Art consists first in conceiving ideas and then in projecting them into the world of the senses. The artist finds in the world of ideas whatever pleasure the layman or he himself would find in the world of the senses. The artist often forgets his body and the material surroundings when he is engrossed in the ideas, which for him constitute everything. And when he expresses himself in sounds, words, stone, wood, on the canvas and so forth, he seeks only the realisation of his ideas there, emphasising the non-difference of mind and sense world. The other aspects of art which point to the realisation of time, space and cause as ideas cannot be discussed here.

Aesthetic enjoyment comes from what is considered beautiful, in the material or the mental world. The externally beautiful first produces in the enjoyer ideas, which have truth enough to give pleasure, and enable him to enter into the substance or life of the sense world and to realise the common mental character, indicating his essential non-difference from it. This is most evident from the feelings of sympathy evoked at the sight of forests, mountains, rivers, sky and the like; and especially when men feel impelled to address them as living beings.

When the artist seeks expression in the sense world, so that it may evoke similar mental states in other men, he realises himself in others. In all the processes of conceiving, expressing

342 CONTEMPORARY INDIAN PHILOSOPHY

and communing there is a forgetting of one's self. This forgetting gives pleasure because the truth is then realised that individuality is unreal. The source of pleasure, the beautiful, is found everywhere to the extent to which one is able to look beyond the unreal limitations of appearances or to negate the sense of difference and duality.

Those whose feeling of reality is based most on external objects derive pleasure most from the *sense* world. Those whose real interest is greater in the mental world derive it most from conceptual or intellectual constructions. Those whose notion of the real rests on neither of these two, find satisfaction in ignoring them both as some mystics do. Those, however, who seek to rest on that which is the stuff of all existence find delight in feeling themselves to be one with the all. But they have first to know the meaning of the all, which is the philosopher's aim.

In religion, ethics and aesthetics, not to say sociology in particular, the highest significance is attached to what is known as "LOVE," which only means the realisation, though in different degrees, of "NON-DIFFERENCE."

ULTIMATE TRUTH: HOW ATTAINED

A bird's-eye view of religion, art and science points to the fact that while they imply truth-values they do not aim at *Ultimate* truth. They stop at the stages where they find the satisfactions they seek, which are no criteria of philosophic truth.

The very fact that philosophy seeks the truth *common* to *all*, is proof that it can be no construction of any human mind or minds. Truth is there already and it has only to be "discovered" or as the Indian thinker says "uncovered." Philosophic effort only aims at removing the cover of ignorance, the cause of error and doubt.

Some men reach it quickly and others slowly, often with considerable effort. This labour is needed only to remove mental or material obstacles, such as are implied in personal predilections, temperaments and limitations of the power of observation or of intellectual capacity. When the mind is not strong enough

to remove all obstructions, it seeks satisfaction by imagining the
ultimate truth (as in Religion), or the immediately next higher
degree of truth (as in Science). But philosophy does not stop
till the end is actually attained and therefore it strictly pursues
the path of science to the end in freeing the mind of all its errors.
In it, as in science, only verified facts count. For eliminating
error, Indian philosophy lays down certain conditions as indicated below, which, excepting the last, are common to both
philosophy and science.

1. To know that there is something more than appearances
for one to seek.

2. To eliminate all personal predilections or preconceptions
regarding the object of enquiry.

3. To possess calmness, self-restraint and patience, concentration, and an absence of religious bias.

4. To possess the supreme determination to eradicate all
doubts and their possibilities and all causes of error and all
ignorance.

The scientist does not admit the last (No. 4); for, he does not
seek ultimate truth, which he presumes to be unattainable.

The most important of the conditions common to both
philosophers and scientists is "Depersonalisation" or "Self-
elimination" leading to the detachment of awareness, which is
a *sine qua non*. But scientists admit it only to a limited extent.
This item and a few others, however, show to what extent
moral discipline is needed for removing the cause of error and
for sharpening the mind. Philosophy insists upon an unqualified
fulfilment of the moral condition. Egoism within limits does not
seriously obstruct the pursuit of truth in the intellectual field;
but attachment to the ego, which is unreal, is a positive hindrance
of the greatest magnitude in the world of Reason. Religion lays
emphasis on moral discipline, and Science on intellectual, but
Philosophy upon both, in the highest degree.

Doubt and possibilities of error can never cease so long as
one confines oneself to waking experience. And there can be no
end to philosophies springing up so long as men build solely
upon waking experience ignoring the rest. Reason alone leads

to truth beyond all doubts. Philosophy based on Reason, therefore, is, and can be, only one.

Theology, Scholasticism and the like do make use of logical or intellectual arguments in interpreting authorities, scriptures and so forth. They are no doubt valuable as disciplines. But as they do not appeal to Reason in its universal character, they can never lead directly to truth beyond all possibility of doubt. Nor can authority and scripture or their interpretation constitute philosophy.

LIFE

The touchstone of philosophy is life. As shown above, all life's activities comprehended under science, religion and art tend towards the realisation that not only the universe is an idea, but that there ultimately exists no difference between thought and being, knowledge and existence or life. The past years that one has lived enjoying or suffering, achieving or failing, waking or sleeping and the past world of one's childhood and youth, all so real then, are now no more than ideas or knowledge. Such is also the past history of man and his past world, so real while they lasted. Everything known resolves itself into knowledge or idea. The man of knowledge, feeling, thought or intellect, be he scientist, artist, theologian or whatever else, to the extent to which he rises above the gross world of the senses, is, and is held, superior to others. Every man, whether he likes it or not, converts according to his capacity all experience or life into knowledge, something known in the mind, that he may value it.

Philosophy rises above distinctions of creed, caste, colour, race, calling, age or school of thought. Its most distinguishing feature is that the philosopher seeks the supreme realisation of himself as the all and the all as himself. This perfection is either for all or for none; for to the philosopher individually there is no perfection inasmuch as the universe as an idea is in him and of him. Till one realises this existence by eradicating ignorance one thinks life, world or God to be different from "knowledge." And one will not have realised "Non-duality."

But for the man who has not attained perfection, who has not realised himself as the all, the many with differences exist; and for him, no one has attained the truth of non-difference. Absolute non-difference or non-duality has no meaning when the thinker excludes or differentiates himself from another or the rest. To the imperfect, therefore, the so-called perfect man is imperfect or at less imperfect than others. Perfection looks most like mysticism to the man of mere intellect. But to the man of perfect reason nothing is more real, more universal.

Philosophers do not seek to distinguish themselves from the rest of mankind in any manner, for all distinctions are but ideas and therefore unreal. Philosophers discharge, like their fellow-men, all duties, pleasant or unpleasant, and all functions in society as well as they can. Whatever the circumstances in which they are placed, prosperity or adversity, on the battlefield or in the parlour, with a crown of diamonds or of thorns, in the mountain caves or in market places, whether praised or condemned, they remain ever balanced, resting on the Ultimate Truth. They only strive to help others to reach the goal that they have themselves reached. Their sole object in life is to make others reach this perfection. The philosopher is he who in various ways seeks to realise himself in the all and the all in himself, their joy being his joy and their sorrow his sorrow. When all ignorance is dispelled, when everything is found to be of the same stuff as that which is labelled knowledge, when there is no second or other, and when there remains nothing unattained, then there can be no room for "want" or "fear" of any change or even of death which is unmasked by truth.

Why do men not reach this goal easily? The failure is due to the inability to see that the external world including the body and individuality are mental, that the body and the universe are not outside the mind but all is idea.[1] The inherited and almost ineffaceable prejudice or preconception that these are what they appear, in spite of the everyday experience of

[1] This difficulty increases when the question is raised as to the relation of mind to its contents (ideas, thoughts, etc.). But that is beyond the scope of this essay.

deep-sleep, is erroneous knowledge which mankind is most reluctant to give up. Even the thought of death fails to teach this lesson. Men with preconceptions cannot hope to attain, as Indian philosophers say, even scientific truth, much less philosophical truth. Divesting the mind of its preconceptions is a gradual process, which takes the mind through the disciplines of religion, art and science.

The supreme test of Philosophy or supreme verification of Ultimate Truth lies in life, i.e. life of the three-states, but not in any intellectual solution of the problems, nor in weaving conceptual webs called "systems" of thought, which must be interminable. Philosophical enquiry based on Reason, therefore, leads one beyond vision, intuition—however unique—intellect and concept. Reason, which with a view to removing the *intellectual* misgiving that such a goal may be non-existent or unattainable, names it Non-duality. It is nothing but awareness together with the three-states, in which, like the water of the sea, with the waves (as in waking and the dream states) or without them (as in deep-sleep), the distinctionless Non-duality is never non-existent, to which has been given the name *Atman*.

In India, Philosophy is sought for the sake of the one and only lesson it teaches man: How to attain and live the life in which is realised the all as himself and himself as the all. It is sought only by him who pursues the truth that admits of no doubt or possibility of doubt, which reveals the absolute non-difference of complete knowledge and perfect life. Such a man (*dhira*) will not stop, come what may, till he reaches the end, in which Reason makes absolutely sure that there exists nothing unknown and unattained.

To what extent mankind attains to this truth, to that extent does it approach perfection, known as *Brahman*, and to that extent is it philosophic. When perfection is reached, there is none imperfect, no imperfection anywhere. When perfect knowledge is attained, perfection of life in all its aspects is attained, which is "the highest good comprising all possible good in itself."

PRINCIPAL PUBLICATIONS

Avastātraya: the three States (Mysore and Leipzig, 1931).
The Final Test of Truth (Calcutta, 1927).
Modern Vedānta (Leipzig, 1928).
Anubhava: The Criterion of Truth (Baroda, 1920).
Śaṁkara and His Modern Critics (Madras, 1932).
Reason or Revelation (Poona, 1915).
Introductions to *Dṛg Dṛśya Viveka* and *Māndūkya Upaniṣad*
(Mysore, 1931–6).

PRAGMATIC IDEALISM

by A. R. WADIA

Born 1888; Educated at Wilson College, Bombay, Oxford
and Cambridge
Professor of Philosophy, University of Mysore

BIOGRAPHICAL

POETRY is fundamentally imaginative, and philosophy fundamentally logical. But I have always believed that in the last resort both are born of intimate personal experience. A man's thought can be appreciated in its true perspective only in the concrete setting in which it takes its birth. If my thought has any interest for anybody, a brief account of its genesis will not be out of place.

The Wadia family is an old Parsee family that has played since 1735 a great part in the civic life of Bombay. It has been very wealthy, but I was born at a time when the fortunes of our branch of it were at their lowest ebb, and perhaps it was not altogether a disadvantage that I was not brought up in any luxury. I had to live rather on the tradition of wealth than actual wealth, and stories of past luxuries merely whetted my imagination, and in course of time made me deeply introspective as I heard of old friends of the family and rich relations gradually turning their backs on us. The sense of injustice was burning into my soul, and even as a boy I became thoughtful and found it difficult to believe that a just God could exist with so much misery and evil in this world. I should have assuredly drifted into atheism but for the Hindu belief in Karma. This belief does not find any sanction in Zoroastrianism, but centuries of contact with the Hindus have made it a part and parcel of the Parsee faith. The experiences of my childhood have left me the legacy of an odd mixture of shyness and pride, which persists till the present day. Temperamental aristocratic feeling has gradually yielded place to a reasoned-out democratic sympathy. I have not failed, however, to notice within myself a conflict due to the fact that though an aristocrat by temperament I have grown to be a democrat by conviction.

Bred up in more or less orthodox traditions I early imbibed a great reverence for all the old forms and rituals and prayers, but more than anything else I imbibed a passionate sense of duty, a firm belief in morality as the highest good in life. My mother never tired of impressing on us that she did not care whether we learned or not, whether we earned much or not, but that she wanted us to be good. Ever since those days nothing appeals to me except in so far as it can stand the test of morality. My main philosophic interest has been predominantly ethical.

As I grew up and took to English I became a voracious reader, a tendency accentuated by the fact that under medical advice at the age of twelve I was prevented from taking any part in sports. My reading comprised all branches of literature, history and religions.

There were leanings towards philosophy, though I read no distinctively philosophical books till 1908, when I took up philosophy
as my optional in the B.A. Class. Till that year all my high-school
and intermediate education had been in Jesuit institutions: St.
Xavier's High School and College. I learned method and discipline
from them, and for the late Father Devine, an Englishman, I shall
always cherish a deep affection. The college authorities were against
teaching philosophy, but for more reasons than one I was bent
upon taking up the subject, and so I preferred to leave my old
college for Wilson College, where the Professor of Philosophy
was the Rev. J. R. Cuthbert, a very earnest and clear-headed
teacher.

In 1910 I left for England. For a year I studied in London and
attended lectures of Professor Carveth Read, perhaps the most
interesting teacher I have ever come across, and Dr. William Brown.
In 1911 I joined Oxford University. My plans were somewhat
uncertain. I was not sure if I could continue long enough at Oxford
to take any degree. So I studied for the Diploma in Economics and
Political Science and secured it with distinction. Along with it I
continued to study philosophy without any reference to examination
requirements. This was an advantage, as it made my study more
spontaneous and untrammelled. I was able to read books an average
Oxonian, burdened with the examination curriculum, would not
worry about. I attended the lectures of Professor J. A. Smith,
Mr. C. C. J. Webb, Mr. A. L. Smith, Dr. A. D. Lindsay and Professor
A. G. Adams. I particularly came into contact with my tutor, Mr.
C. C. J. Webb, who later became the First Oriel Professor of the
Philosophy of the Christian Religion. My weekly meetings with
him were a most valuable experience and made me appreciate the
tutorial traditions which have made Oxford great. My contact with
Professor Webb still continues to be a living one, as even to-day
I can count upon him for sympathy in my difficulties.

At Oxford, oddly enough, more than anywhere else I began to
feel an Indian as I had never done in my life before. The traditions
of my family had been almost ultra-loyalist, and I had been
far more interested in Queen Victoria and in Gladstone than in
Dadabhoy Naoroji or Tilak. It was my inordinate admiration for
Gladstone that had made me hanker after Oxford. When this ambition came to be satisfied, I found the centre of gravity of my interests
shifting slowly but surely from England to India. At Oxford I had
the good fortune of coming into contact with some of the choicest
spirits, both Hindu and Muslim, among my fellow-Indian students.
In their company I felt more and more proud to be an Indian. A
wanton attack on India in the pages of *The Varsity*, run by under-

graduates, put the coping-stone on my nascent patriotism, the most priceless legacy of my Oxford days.

Circumstances made it possible for me to stay a year longer in England so that I could take a degree, but Oxford in those days had no degree in Philosophy except as a part of the Literae Humaniores course, and I found it necessary to migrate to Cambridge in 1912. There I graduated in 1913 in the Moral Science Tripos.

Cambridge represents the traditions of British empirical philosophy, and for that reason the philosophic teaching of my learned teachers did not touch my soul. I became conscious there of a tendency to reduce philosophy to mere logic or to mere science. In the former case one always appears to be hovering about the portico, never entering the main building itself. In the latter case one tends to deny the genuine philosophical categories. Even the Cambridge Idealists like Ward and McTaggart and Professor Sorley did not go far enough in their Idealism to satisfy me. But I dare not deny the intellectual value of Cambridge training. If Oxford tends to soar too high, Cambridge tends to make us cling more closely to the hard soil of facts. Without Cambridge English philosophy would be too dreamy; without Oxford it would be too soulless. Real thought should be a mixture of both: true to facts, but steeped in ideals, for only ideals make life worth living.

In 1913 I was called to the Bar. I had no particular taste for practising as a lawyer, but I enjoyed the study of Roman Law and Constitutional Law and developed a taste for Jurisprudence.

My stay in England was of a peculiar type. I was for a year at each of the three great centres of learning. It brought me into contact with a large number of men and introduced me to varying standpoints in philosophy. But I was not long enough at any one place to strike root there. On the whole I must admit that the teachers whose lectures I attended did not influence my thinking as much as might have been expected. I did learn a lot from them, but in developing my own thought I have been influenced far more by the books I have read and digested than by the lectures I attended.

My reading has always been of a very varied and heterodox kind. Among European philosophers I have learned most from Plato, Kant and Hegel, and even more fundamentally from T. H. Green's Ethics and Politics. Fichte was perfectly right in his idea that "The kind of philosophy that a man chooses depends upon the kind of man that he is." I could never be anything but an Idealist, but the Absolute Idealism of Bradley-Bosanquet type I could not accept. Their static Absolute left me cold. My fundamental philosophical problem, the problem of evil, was not satisfactorily solved. My thought drifted in a direction which gained great impetus from Bergson and Croce.

I have learned from many, but I have never been able to give a whole-hearted allegiance to any one thinker so as to justify my being labelled as a follower of this or that particular thinker.

My approach to philosophy has been from the side of literature and religion with Ethics as the fulcrum. Science did not have any direct appeal for me till comparatively late. I fully appreciate its value for life, but science can never be a substitute for philosophy. In this conviction I am confirmed by scientists and mathematicians like Einstein and Sir James Jeans, Whitehead and Eddington. Metaphysics is not an end in itself with me. I value it as giving a background to our life. My main aim in thought is the life of man. This has led me on to a study of politics and in recent years my best endeavours have been making for a study of Sociology with particular reference to Indian social institutions. My interest in Indian Sociology has driven me to a more intensive study of Indian metaphysics and Indian Dharma Sastras. What my thought has come to be I have given expression to in my scattered writings and lectures, many of which I have not had time to reduce to writing. Conditions of work in Indian universities—except where only postgraduate classes are taken—unfortunately do not give one as much time to write as one would wish.

I shall now proceed to give a brief résumé of what I believe to be the essence of philosophy, and I can but trust that this brief biographical note will make it more intelligible to all who may happen to be interested in what I think.

M

PRAGMATIC IDEALISM

"WHY this injustice?" This was the question that very early
in life thrust itself on me and it started the train of thought
which has culminated in a view which I can best speak of as
Pragmatic Idealism. Why should evil exist? Can it be justified?
Can it be transcended? These questions revolved through my
mind and clamoured for a solution. The traditional reply that
a pious Zoroastrian could give is that evil is all the work of
Angra Mainyush, the conceptual ancestor of Satan in Judaism
and Christianity and of Iblis in Islam. But a rival to God who
could nullify his work appeared to me highly unsatisfactory.
Even assuming that Angra Mainyush could spoil the work of
God, God should have ultimately the power of undoing the work
of his rival, and traditional Zoroastrianism seeks to solve this
problem in terms of heaven and hell. But how can a just God
abandon even a wicked man to the tortures of hell till the day
of Resurrection? What parity can there be between the wickedness of a man in the short span of a life, which does not cover
even a hundred years, and his punishment for centuries and
millennia? The whole thing appeared to me mythical, at best
merely symbolical, having a certain moral value, but no truth.

Why should one person be so different from another in his
looks, in his abilities, in his circumstances, in his character?
To these questions I got a satisfactory answer only from the
Karma theory of the Hindus. If one man is born a king and
another a beggar, it must be due to their past Karma: actions
in a previous birth. All my subsequent reading and thought
have not dislodged this principle from my thought. In European
philosophy I do not find any serious or successful attempt to
grapple with the problem. The story of the Fall is only a myth
and no just God can be expected to visit the sins of the fathers
on the heads of their innocent children millennia after millennia.
It has always been a puzzle to me why European thinkers—
apart from the old Pythagoreans or the modern Theosophists—
have not been attracted by the Karma theory. The main reason

assigned against it—that it breeds fatalism—is not entirely
justifiable. For Karma has not merely a retrospective aspect, it
has also a forward look. It is not merely effect, but it is also
cause. I cannot deny that fatalism has taken a grip of most
Hindus, but that is because of their petrified caste system,
which is repugnant to the highest thought of all world religions,
and I believe even to Vedānta. Our past Karma determines the
kṣetra, the field of our life. It is our duty to make what we can
of it, and that will determine our future life. Suffering may be
the effect of our past, but *doing* is our most precious privilege.
This is not a mere dogma, nor a mere matter of faith. The whole
history attests its truth. Success does not necessarily attend the
palaces of kings or the mansions of the rich. It comes as often
to the cottage of the poorest, and men who make history are
often those who have no distinguished pedigree behind them.
Their genius is their success. The world is open to him who
dares.

The problem of evil raises two questions: why does it exist?
and what is the way out of it? Neither of these questions receives
adequate treatment at the hands of the great European thinkers,
while theologians are apt to lapse into mythological dogmas.
The Hindu doctrine of Karma has answered the first question
quite convincingly. The second has occupied the highest thought
of India since the day, nearly 3,000 years ago, when the Upaniṣadic
seers produced the highest metaphysical wisdom that the world
has ever seen. But the doctrine of mokṣa has been variously
presented by the different schools of Hindu thought, and therefore
no cut-and-dried solution is ready to hand, and each thinker
has to pursue his own path of thought.

Armed with the theory of Karma I came to look upon morality
with fresh interest. Here I have all along been a sincere follower
of Zoroaster, and I believe that there can be nothing higher
in life than morality. If a man finds that he can grow only in
society, it follows that the means of maintaining and developing
society is the paramount concern of man, and that can be
nothing but morality. Truth and purity are fundamental personal
virtues; justice and benevolence, fundamental social virtues.

The ethics of Zoroaster has passed into all later religions and it stands firm to-day as much as it did in the age of Zoroaster himself. To a Zoroastrian evil is not merely a negative possibility, it is something which has to be continually overcome. Evil negates the best in man and it has to be fought and vanquished. By evil is meant what harms mankind or wantonly injures other living creatures. Merely different modes of **thought** and worship are not necessarily evil and hence were not persecuted. That is why Isaiah was in raptures over the Persian Cyrus and even Hegel was constrained to admire the tolerant spirit of the ancient Persians. Persian symbolism has centred round fire from times immemorial, and it represents the purifying spirit of knowledge. The Persian spirit has always encouraged the conquest of *Druj* or Lie and the Behistun inscriptions of Darius the Great have borne witness to it through the ages.

The spirit of justice, of benevolence, of independence, of the will to do has always appealed to me and that explains my interest in history and heroic literature. It also explains my deep and abiding interest in social reform. Caste with its pride, its repression of women, its outcasts, its rigidity, its spirit of exclusiveness has always repelled me, and that is why till my stay in England political movements had no interest for me. I used to feel that there were other questions, predominantly social in character, which were far more vital and urgent.

Morality is the greatest thing in life. What are its foundations? This is the question that has engaged my thought for a number of years. Three alternatives suggested themselves: religious, metaphysical and psychological. The last explains the growth of morality as conscience, as the result of the conflict between our egoistic and gregarious impulses and motives. Recent Psychology has certainly deepened our knowledge of moral conflicts. It has made for a humane treatment of criminals and wrong-doers generally. But it has not carried us very far. Psychologically morality remains a subjective phenomenon, and ethics as a science cannot emerge out of mere subjectivity. The ultimate significance of morality Psychology is not thus competent to explain.

Ethics raises certain ultimate questions which can be either dogmatically answered by religion or rationally answered by metaphysics. If God is perfect in Himself, why did He create the world? If He created it, why could He not have created it better? If He could not have created it better, what becomes of His omnipotence, His justice, His mercy? These are difficulties which Kant's God does not answer. The theism of Lotze has appeared to me to be a bold attempt to give a rational account of God and I have naturally admired the theistic philosophy of my own guru, Professor Webb of Oxford. But doubt has always waylaid the theistic emphasis on a personal God. Books on mysticism apparently ally themselves with religion, but in fact they are usually double-edged. For theistic mysticism may appeal to all who have faith, but to others it merely points to the purely subjective psychological origin of all such phenomena.

The merely religious foundations of morality appeared to be crumbling before my very eyes and recourse to metaphysics became inevitable. The process of thought has been easier in this matter, as I have always been an idealist by temperament. Never for a day have I been attracted by Realism as understood in contemporary European philosophy. To set up mind against matter, to look upon mind as merely emergent out of matter, to look upon philosophy as a mere appendix of science, crossing the t's and dotting the i's of scientific categories, or to soothe one's metaphysical conscience by erecting the Unknowable as the highest metaphysical entity—all these have engaged my attention only to be discarded as unsatisfying both logically and ethically. Idealism as emphasising the supremacy of mind or spirit has been my philosophy from the earliest years. On the metaphysical side of Idealism I have learned most from Plato and Hegel, on the ethical side most from Kant and T. H. Green. The concept of the Absolute is the logical culmination of the inter-relatedness of things and I have been most impressed by the close interdependence of all things in the universe. Consciousness of this has made me believe in the doctrine of Internal Relations and no system of pluralism has appeared to me to be logically consistent or even true to our normal experience.

The Absolute as the unconditioned or the self-conditioned is the logical presupposition of all our experience. Within it we have our being and within it we grow. But for me the Absolute itself is also growing, and if the past associations of the term preclude its use in the sense of growing, I would much rather sacrifice the term than the facts which make me believe that it is not a closed system.

My study of Hegel makes me think that the Absolute in his philosophy is not a closed concept. In his Logic that interpretation is possible, but a philosopher's thought is to be gauged in terms of his whole thought and not only in sections. His Logic represents pure philosophy as an attempt to study the movement of thought in abstract and the Absolute becomes the culminating point epistemologically. Metaphysically too it becomes the prius of all existence. The core of his philosophy, however, comes out in his Philosophy of Spirit, which I look upon as his Applied Philosophy. In this we find an emphasis on growth and evolution, and the reality of time is implicit in it. The growth of the parts cannot but affect the whole—the Absolute—if there is a real organic relationship between the whole and its parts. It is from this standpoint that what is usually known as Absolutism, as developed in the writings of Bradley and Bosanquet, is logically defective. For there the Absolute is above all change and is the same from age to age. This would be possible, if we could look upon the Absolute as a huge box within which all sorts of things may be churning in endless forms of different permutations and combinations without in any way affecting the size or the nature of the box. But this reduces the worth of human effort to nothingness. Genuine Absolutism implies an organic relationship between the Absolute and its parts. It is inconceivable that any change in any part of an organism within our experience, say a human body, should not affect the organism as a whole. The Absolute as Spirit *par excellence* cannot be indifferent to the efforts of finite spirits like human beings to express themselves in higher and higher forms of beauty, truth and goodness. From the orthodox religious standpoint a God that is not interested in the salvation of a human soul, however high and omnipotent he may theoretically be, is not worthy of human homage and worship. Similarly, the Absolute which does not gain in worth through the increased worth of finite spirits forfeits its right to be called spirit at all; it can only be fit to be called matter—dead and inert.

This position is repudiated by orthodox Absolutists, as they repudiate change as an ultimate category and consequently also the reality of time. Bradley does at times make admissions which go to show that the Absolute is real only in the experiences and feelings of concrete beings, but on the whole his emphasis falls on the changeless Absolute and the reconciliation of these two ideas is brought about, if at all, by recourse to his notorious mystic term "somehow." His metaphysical genius is undoubtedly great, yet in recent years he has been partly responsible for the contempt into which metaphysics has fallen. The unsatisfactory character of his metaphysical thought is to be found in the unreconciled dual tendency of his thought: a helpless scepticism seeking solace in the arms of religion. These tendencies we see corroding the work of several orthodox idealists. The latter-day Absolutism marks the decay of the great Idealistic philosophy initiated by Kant and Hegel. Bradley's greatest service to philosophy was that he provoked thoughtful reactions and facilitated by contrast the vogue of new philosophers: Bergson and William James, Croce and Gentile, and even the Realists. If they have done any service to philosophy in our times it is that they have raised a note of warning against a metaphysics too much in the sky and too little on terra firma. I have learned a good deal from Bergson and the Pragmatists and the great Italian Idealists, but I differ too radically from many of their fundamental teachings to describe myself as a follower of any one of them.

If the Absolute is the ultimate category of thought, can it be identified with the concept of God? If not, has religion any place in the realm of truth? These are vital questions for me, for I have always had a great interest in religion, especially in view of the fact that while metaphysics is the possession of but a few, religion has found its home in the hearts of millions of men and women. Orthodox theism with its emphasis on the omnipotence, omniscience and perfection of God can rest secure on dogma, but not on a critical examination. Lotze's attempt to found theism on rational grounds has been most noteworthy, but even he does not succeed in solving all the difficulties latent in the theistic position. Personal Idealists have succeeded in giving a new lease to Theism only by sacrificing the omnipotence of God to His goodness, but to the ordinary religious consciousness a limited God sounds like a contradiction in terms.

I have felt that the problem of evil is the rock on which theism flounders. Evil cannot be the expression of a righteous God. Therefore either evil is real and falls outside God, or it is unreal, a mere illusion, and therefore needs no explanation. In the former case we lapse into some type of dualism and God can only be one of the ultimate concepts and not the only one as genuine theism demands. In the latter case we get a very ostrichy metaphysics: an attempt to solve a problem by denying its existence. I can admire Spinoza for his denial of evil as unreal *sub specie aeternitatis*, but I cannot bring myself to deny the existence of evil. Nothing is more real in human experience. All religions have flourished because they point out paths of redemption to achieve freedom from evil. Evil exists as the counterpart of good. Good is real only because of the potentiality of evil, because it is shadowed by evil. Failure to do what we ought to do is evil and may bring us face to face with physical evil, the evil of the body, or moral evil, the evil of the soul. Evil can not be ultimate for then the world would be fundamentally irrational. It is just a stage to be transcended on our onward march. In the very finiteness of our nature evil is inherent, but it has to be overcome. That it has a place in the scheme of existence and that it can be overcome is the presupposition of all Ethics, as it is the presupposition of all knowledge that the world is intelligible. The presupposition of Ethics has to be justified by metaphysics. Theism with its emphasis on a personal God does not do it. Can Idealism in any form do it?

It is at this stage that I have found Indian philosophy much more helpful than European philosophy. Indian seers do not deny evil. In fact they have often been charged by Western scholars of Indian philosophy and religion with being so very conscious of it as to become "pessimists." But no Indian seer, not even Buddha, has allowed himself to be overpowered by the sense of evil. One and all of them teach that it can be overcome in the life of each individual, that *nirvana* or *moksa* is the right of everyone, if not in one birth at least through birth after birth, when a soul purges itself of evil bit by bit and ultimately shines in the full glory of freedom from birth and death. This is accepted by the Jain and the Buddhist as much as the Vedāntin, whether he be an Advaitin, Visistādvaitin or Dvaitin. Karma and the transmigration of soul are the common inheritance of almost every Indian. Even when he changes his religion, in some form or another these beliefs linger in him and consciously or unconsciously mould his life. The spirit in man must be the ultimate victor, and the Indian is not daunted even if the prospect of victory is to come to him in ages beyond computation.

My agreement with Indian thought ceases as soon as the question has to be faced: how is this evil in us to be overcome so as to attain *nirvāna* or *moksa*? The orthodox Indian answer to this question invariably takes the form of some type of ascetic ethics. It aims at an increasing simplicity of life so that the man who has neared or attained the goal should have nothing to call his own. That is why the extreme Jaina Digambar rejects even clothing and the Jain muni insists on moving about naked, unmindful of the presence of men and women alike. This extreme attitude is not taken up by all the sadhus in India, but they all aim at having nothing of their own so that ultimately they have to be dependent on public charity even for their barest needs of life. The notorious beggar problem in India has its roots in this application of Indian thought, and making allowance for a few genuinely advanced souls, the majority cannot escape the charge of being social parasites on one of the poorest communities on earth. Sometimes this asceticism even takes the form of a claim that a liberated soul rises above all social ties. He is said to have no moral duties—a doctrine extremely dangerous in itself. Sometimes it is even claimed that such a soul can do no wrong and that is made an excuse for doing every wrong. Luckily such cases are exceptions, but they essentially point to the perversions that are likely to arise when any school of thought imagines that a man under any circumstances can possibly be above morality.

As I have noted previously, I have never felt it necessary to give up my ethical Zoroastrian inheritance. The spirit of Zoroaster's teaching is anything but ascetic. It has been noted even by non-Zoroastrian students of the old Persian faith that it is the only religion which eschews asceticism in every form. It does not advocate fasts or celibacy. It does not look upon life with sickly eyes. It has faith in a righteous God and believes that in order to succeed man has but to try courageously to rise above all evil temptations. From my own metaphysical standpoint too I see no justification for asceticism. Like the ancient Greek and the Persian I believe that man is most natural when he is most developed and he is most developed in the life of civilisation where arts and literature, science and industry flourish. If the Absolute Spirit lives in all its parts there is nothing which it need repudiate as alien to itself except the evil which hinders its life of harmony. What is needed is the recognition of the oneness of Spirit and therefore the real life of the Spirit is to be found in the interplay of individuals rather than in a studied exclusion from the life around us. Such exclusiveness is justifiable only as a stage of preparation for a fuller manifestation of the life of the Spirit, never as an end in itself.

If Theism breaks on the rock of evil, a very perplexing question arises: what becomes of the great religious teachers, who spoke in the name of God and who have undoubtedly taken mankind to a great ethical height, whatever mess their followers may have been responsible for? This question has certainly caused me a good deal of heart-searching, for as noted before I approached philosophy through literature and religion and the highest literature in the last resort is also religious and ethical. The first suggestion of a possible solution of this problem came from Stewart's *Plato's Doctrine of Ideas*. An original distinction is sought to be made here between Plato the philosopher and

Plato the artist and man of religion. While the former is led
to the impersonal Idea of the Good, the latter is led to personify
it for artistic and religious purposes. It was a case of psychological necessity in the case of Plato. May not the same need
exist in the case of every man? I have never got over the conviction that man in his heart of hearts is profoundly religious.
The animist as much as the monotheist responds to the same
needs of his nature, though their beliefs take different forms
according to the varying standards of their culture. The case
of Comte has struck me as a pathetic example of an intellectual
who would fain deny God, but is driven to raise a new God:
Humanity, in order to give vent to the rich emotional cravings for
worship harboured in his heart. Soviet Russia is another instance
of how the worship of Lenin may take the place of the worship
of Christ, if not with the same paraphernalia, at least with as
great intensity of feeling.

Śaṁkara's famous distinction between Nirguṇa Brahman and
Saguṇa Brahman has also contributed its quota to the development of my own thought in this respect. The orthodox interpretation of Śaṁkara's philosophy generally takes the form of
characterising it as abstract monism as contrasted with the
concrete monism of Rāmānuja or Hegel. *Nirguṇa* literally means
without qualities. If taken literally, it would amount to Hegel's
pure being, which is as good as nothing. I find it difficult to believe
that such a meaning could have been intended by so keen a
thinker as Śaṁkara. The single legitimate meaning of *nirguṇa*
can only be that no quality we human beings can possibly
conceive of can be an adequate description of Brahman,
which in its infinity must necessarily transcend all human categories. I am also driven to agree with him as with European
Absolutism that the highest category cannot be a person without
sharing in all the limitations of personality. *Saguṇa Brahman*
is *Īśvara* or God, who has qualities, but even he is a part of the
world of Māyā, which is usually translated as illusion, but may
more appropriately be translated as appearance. So *Īśvara* is
not ultimately real. He may be worshipped by the masses, but
for the *Jñāni*—the sage—he does not exist in the sense in which

the highest religious consciousness conceives him. No wonder if the orthodox Brahmin of the rival schools looks upon an Advaitin as a *nāstika*, an atheist.

In this connection I may also refer to the phenomena of mysticism. Mystic poetry has had a great appeal for me. But the study of the psychology of mysticism has modified my old naïve enthusiasm and forced me into a fresh interpretation of mystic phenomena. William James's Gifford Lectures on the *Varieties of Religious Experience* I found very suggestive, but Leuba's writings have produced on the whole a more destructive effect. One cannot be blind to the fact that the trances and other paraphernalia of mysticism are found as much in the lowest types of shamanism as in the highest monotheisms. Even in the highest religions mystic experience would have an ultimate value if it not merely speaks of the ONE, but conceives the ONE in an identical manner. In actual fact we find that Christian mysticism centres round Christ, Vaishnavite mysticism round Vishnu, Saivite round Śiva and Kāli. This clearly shows the purely personal origin of many of these mystic experiences. Faith is strong indeed, but its strength is the strength of the human will behind it, as shown abundantly by Couéism and other similar phenomena. No wonder if a real devotee who has the name of Christ or Rām continually on his lips sometimes sees visions. As psychical phenomena they have worth, but whether they have any ontological value is certainly open to question. Mysticism at its highest can lay claim only to one great uniformity: the sense of oneness that the mystic feels with the whole universe and this is philosophically consistent with pantheism as much as with theism. There is a type of mysticism, not perhaps logically deduced, but intuitively felt and intellectually understandable, which we find in the Upaniṣads and in Sufism, in the Stoics and the Neo-Platonists, in Spinoza and in Kabir. Leuba's crusade, so thorough in its onslaught on theistic mysticism, does not touch the deeper form of intellectual mysticism.

What then is the value of religion? *Consolatio religionis* implies a personal God to whom we can pray and ask for boons, on whose justice and mercy we can rely in our darkest moments. But if the ultimate reality is conceived as an It, what possibility is there for an intimate communion between God the Father and ourselves as His children? This has proved a very perplexing question, for my old theistic faith in its orthodox garb does not square with the logic of my thought. A God that could respond to the innermost wishes of my heart is indeed a God that my heart, anybody's heart, can eagerly yearn for. But Kant was devastating when he said that the idea of a hundred dollars is not the same as a hundred dollars actually jingling in one's pocket, and that the idea of God does not necessarily imply the reality of God. A wish of my heart, however intense, cannot be mistaken for an objective reality. Is religion then nothing but an idea, an emotional craving of a lonely and oppressed heart?

Religion has been too priceless a possession of mankind to be so lightly discarded as the atheists of the Bolshevik type seek to do. In what form can it be harmonised with the Idealistic metaphysics? and that is the only metaphysics stamped with truth so far as I am concerned. Religion involves a way of living, essentially practical, but if it is not to dissolve into waves of mere emotions, it must be based on truth, which is fundamentally an intellectual or philosophical category. Religion must in the last resort be Applied Philosophy. Even a fetichist has a philosophy, but a philosophy so crude as to be mere mythology. This applies as much to polytheisms, whether found in India or Babylonia, in Greece or in Egypt. The monotheistic prophets from the days of Zoroaster down to the last of the prophets, Abdul Baha, have brought mankind at least to a consciousness of the unity underlying the whole universe, a consciousness of the brotherhood of men and lastly to a con- sciousness of the moral government of the world. I regard these as the most important contributions of the great religious geniuses to human civilisation, and none of them can be denied without loss to the spiritual worth of men. The insistence on prayer and worship is only of secondary importance as aids to spiritual development. The subjective or psychological need for prayer and worship may give rise to the necessity of personifying the ultimate unity of the world as God, anthropomorphical and very human in His passion for being worshipped and appeased and propitiated. But I feel that the great prophets who have been really responsible for the moral uplift of mankind have not cared for this God, in whose name countless human beings have been sacrificed. Not human sacrifices, not animal sacrifices, not vestal virgins, not even fruits and flowers, not fasts, not mere prayers are in the last resort pleasing to God. He only demands that men shall be righteous and the only offering that He will accept is a pure and contrite heart. This is the gist of the teaching of Zoroaster, of Isaiah, of Christ, of Mahomed, of Kabir. Love and service embody the most precious legacy of the prophets. Idealism by its very emphasis on the fundamental unity of nature in general and mankind in particular links itself with moralism and that is why the particular brand of Idealism that I accept I speak of as Pragmatic Idealism. I do not find the traditional Pragmatism of James or Humanism of Schiller to be intellectually satisfactory, but I do believe with them that a metaphysic which does not ultimately bear on life and make our life better is not worth worrying about.

Religion is fundamentally an attitude, an attitude of reverence reacting to Reality as Truth, in every fibre of which there breathes the fire of Life. This may be called God, not a person one among many, but a living presence that unites each to all. God is the personified aspect of the Absolute, the mind in which everything lives and moves. Prayer and worship are but mere instruments to put us into a *rapport* with this all-pervading presence. God is within us as He is all around us. Kabir gave a lofty expression to this idea when he said: "There is musk within the deer and yet it imagines that the fragrance comes from without and hunts and hunts for it in the forest. So too God is within us, but we mortals pass him by."

Similarly the man was a true mystic who when blamed for sitting with his feet towards an idol said: "In all directions there is God. Where am I not to stretch my legs?" Religion therefore properly viewed is an attitude of reverence and an emotional realisation of what thought discovers as truth in the field of philosophy. The practical realisation of the harmony of life is morality. In the man who transcends his narrow self and merges it in the life of the whole, philosophy as truth, religion as devotion, and morality as goodness meet. Religion in short is the emotional aspect of philosophy. In this sense it is not opposed to philosophy, rather is it the complement of philosophy. For philosophy without religion would be barren, and religion without philosophy would be blind. In short, for me the ultimate reality is Spirit. It does not live in a transcendent world, but within everything that is. It is the life and soul of everything. It is essentially living and growing. Religion as applied philosophy is life in harmony with the purpose of Spirit. And what is the ultimate end of man? To live in the life of the Spirit till life's work be done in a birth or a series of births, and the individual soul finally merges in the Spirit that pervades all.

It is from the practical standpoint that the attitude of the average educated Hindu of to-day leaves me cold, even dissatisfied. The high metaphysics of the Upaniṣads and the ethics of the Gītā have been reduced to mere words by the tyranny of the caste. Emphasising the unity of the whole world animate and inanimate, India has yet fostered a social system which has divided her children into water-tight compartments, divided from one another from generation to generation for endless centuries. It has exposed her to foreign conquests which have left her poor and weak, and worst of all she has become the home of untouchability and unapproachability, which have branded her with the curse of Cain. I am not unaware that with many educated Indians philosophy has come to be looked upon as a subject to be eschewed and treated with contempt. Much against my grain I often think that if metaphysics is merely a matter of intellectual jugglery and religious pride, as it has come to be in India, it would be good for India to take a metaphysical holiday. But it would be far better for India if her sons did not take their social institutions as divinely ordained, which no man dare touch. Rather the great need for India to-day is a new Social Philosophy. It was with this purpose that I attempted a new departure in my presidential address to the All-India Philosophical Congress in 1930. I was prepared for criticism, but I got it much less than I expected, and this only from a few metaphysical highbrows.

Having secured a certain metaphysical standpoint, for the last seven years my main interest has drifted into sociological channels. This has led me to make a more intensive study of Indian sociological problems. If philosophy is not to end merely in talk and endless bandying about of quotations from the Upaniṣads and the Gītā, and still more endless quotations from the numerous commentaries on them, we in India must break loose from the shackles of the past, retain all the good that we can and mercilessly discard the rest. The garden of Indian life and thought has been choked with weeds, in the midst of which a few beautiful flowers may grow and give us the illusion of life, but as a matter of fact there is a certain deadness of outlook in the millions of Indians, hardly redeemed by the political activity of the educated classes. We have yet to learn that political democracy cannot grow on the basis of an antiquated system of a rigid social hierarchy with its twain attendant satellites: a superstitious womanhood and an ignorant priesthood.

Philosophers in the West have always shown great vitality. They have allowed themselves to be influenced by the great currents of thought around them whether in the political field, as e.g. in the days of the Reformation, the French Revolution or the Russian Revolution, or in the scientific field, as e.g. the Copernican Revolution, Darwinian Evolution or Einsteinian Relativity. Sufferings of people have produced in them new vital rejuvenating ethical reactions. In India the dogma of a changeless Brahman has produced lethargy and elevated philosophy above the cares of life only to make it a game for the learned and a butt of ridicule for the irreverent. Philosophy will grow when we think and write and do in the spirit of the poet:

> If nobody listens to thy call,
> Then march thou, all alone.

Consistency may not be a virtue in a politician, but it is an imperative necessity in a thinker. The demand for consistency is the sole justification of a "system" of philosophy. Some thinkers in the West tend to display a suspicion of what they call "system-mongers" and pride themselves on resisting the temptation to produce systems of philosophy. But philosophy is nothing if it is not systematic in the sense that its various parts hang together in some sort of logical cohesion. Absence of this implies loose thinking and vitiates the worth of a man's thought. It is from this standpoint that I distrust a philosophy, Eastern or Western, that teaches universalism in metaphysics and particularism in ethics. I have been anxious to see that the unity or system of a man's thought also permeates his life. It is from this standpoint that the question of the relation of philosophy and religion looms large in my thought. Among the Hindus there has been a tendency to take it for granted that there is a unity of thought in their philosophy and religion, which has not been present in the history of European thought since the days of Xenophanes and Socrates. But I believe that in India too there has been more a juxtaposition of religion and philosophy than a real unity, for while Vedānta as the philosophic contribution of India to the thought of the world is marked by a high universalism, Brahminism as a religion has hardly risen above the level of a national religion, as admitted by so con- scientious a thinker as Professor Hiriyanna. Popular Hinduism revolves round caste, which in its exclusiveness is a denial of the catholicism of Vedānta. India needs to-day a reorientation of thought, realising in practice what has only been taken for granted in thought: the unity of life, the all-pervasiveness of Brahman.

"Philosophy as a human pursuit ought to be no barren speculation but an illuminating vision of truth which inevitably prompts to self-culture and social service. 'An unexamined life is worth nothing' and 'nothing human can be alien to man' are perhaps the two aspects of your teaching which have been the spur to self-development and the awakener of the social con- science in us." On a certain occasion these words were used by an old pupil of mine, now a colleague, to summarise my thought.

They so truthfully express my aim that I cannot better them and that is the only excuse for reproducing them at the end of a statement, which is expected to be an account, in the words of the editor, stating my "convictions on the ultimate problems of philosophy and the processes of thought" by which I arrived at them.

INDEX